MW01687989

Clifford

Copyright © 2007 by Cliff Clarke. All rights reserved. No part of this publication may be reproduced, stored in a retrieval system, or transmitted, in any form or by any means, without prior permission of the authors or, in case of photocopying or other reprographic copying, a licence from Access Copyright, the Canadian Copyright Licensing Agency, 1 Yonge Street, Suite 800, Toronto, Ontario M5E 1E5, www. accesscopyright.ca, 1-800-893-5777, info@accesscopyright.ca. Printed in Canada.

Library and Archives Canada Cataloguing in Publication

Cliff Clarke, 1933
CLIFFORD
An autobiography
Author: Cliff Clarke

Design and layout: Frank Neumann
Printing: Friesens
printed in canada
ISBN 978-0-9784503-0-4

Contents

FOREWORD

Clifford Clarke is a well-known Victoria businessman, restaurateur, and thespian. In 1964 he was responsible for starting the Coach and Four Restaurant, the first business to begin the revitalization of Bastion Square. He went on to establish other major restaurants in the city, the McPherson Seafood and Steakhouse, along side the McPherson Theatre, the Carlton Club, the King's Den Restaurant and the Black Prince Catering in the Queen Victoria Inn on Douglas Street. In the 1970's he changed to a new line of business. He established the Red Barn Antiques in Royal Oak, and later in 1993, the Cobble Hill Country Furniture store.

Paralleling his career as a businessman Clifford followed his love of the stage. He was a devoted actor and singer appearing in and directing many plays at Langham Court and McPherson Theatre. Cliff directed major productions in venues throughout the city including Smockey Night for the Mothers March of Dimes, Black Face Minstrel shows for the Junior Solarium League of Victoria, musicals for the Victoria Operatic Society, and went on to begin the Mill Bay Country Music Festival..

Although Clifford was born in the depression of 1933 and grew up in the turmoil of a divided family, his perseverance and will carried him to the top.

Later in life, he and his wife Barbara bought acreage in Mill Bay. He homesteaded a farm out of the woods and built a large and stately pine house, named Pine Lodge Farm. The house was featured in Country Living magazine and became home for the young stars Clair Danes and Kirsten Dunce during the filming of Little Woman.

In 1998 everything changed when a drunk driver mowed down Clifford and his wife Barbara leaving her dead and him a paraplegic. Clifford, finding new strength in a personal faith in God pulled himself up through the mire and went on to live a productive life.

Clifford now lives in his Mill Bay home beside a garden he built and dedicated to the memory of Barbara. He hosts weddings there in the serene beauty, assured that God watches over the celebrations, and each wedding is blessed.

He carried on his love for the stage and served on the Board of Directors of the Chemainus Theatre, and also established his own theatre, Toad Hall, in the Pine Lodge Farm horse barn. He produces, hosts, and performs in professional musical, storytelling and drama productions.

One of the first Toad Hall productions was The Best Christmas Pageant Ever. Later, he wrote a new version of A Christmas Carol and played Scrooge himself. The latest production was a night of Christmas music with Clifford telling the story of The Fourth Wiseman.

Lymphoma is Clifford's most recent challenge. He is standing in faith through the battle. He wants to leave this book as a legacy to his children, family and friends. Have faith. Never give up.

Gail Neuman

Dedication.

This book is lovingly dedicated to my dear Barbara, my devoted children, my cherished siblings, and my supportive and loving friends, with special thanks to my dear friends Gail and Frank Neuman, David Holmes and Eleanor Fuller who spent an enormous amount of time and effort assembling, correcting, and improving this book for me.

CLIFFORD

Humble Beginnings

On March 6, 1933 I, Clifford C. Clarke was born to Harold and Agnes Clarke in Victoria, British Columbia. For several years the world had been suffering a terrible depression, and my arrival during this time likely added a strain to my parents' finances. Although Dad held a steady job with the motor vehicle branch of the government, he probably felt that his pay was not sufficient to cover all the expenses it took to support a large family, and so my arrival did present some challenges to my parents' economic survival.

My Mom was less than five feet tall, and this was with her shoes on. But, pound for pound, she was a dynamo. She had more energy, charm, and love than anyone I have ever known, and she was very loyal to her family; But! She also had a temper, and woe-betide anyone who riled her. My father managed to do that on a regular basis, and I followed closely in my Father's footsteps. Between the two of us, we managed to keep her on her toes.

I remember thinking that, on the one hand, it would be nice to live in a quiet household but, on the other hand, I appreciated the constant excitement of life with an excitable mother, three brothers and three sisters. Every day some momentous event involved every one of us, and filled our life with both drama and entertainment.

My brothers and sisters and I seldom wasted time in warfare, we made the most of our time together, having fun, telling stories, going to movies, and terrorizing the neighborhood. I must confess that it was probably me that achieved the most notoriety during those years, for there was not a soul in my neighbourhood who had not heard of my shenanigans. Those neighbours probably fostered the idea that my parents would be well advised to send me to some relative, who hopefully lived in a far off land.

I always suspected that one of those individuals got his own back. One summer, when I was five years old, and the fruit trees full of plums, several people were knocking plums out of the trees by hurling things at them. One, it seemed, waited until I was directly under the tree, and then threw a large block of wood into the branches, ostensibly to get the plums; however, I believe it was a determined effort to eliminate me before I could become a direct threat to the world.

When you are five years old the world is a wondrous place, and you do not suspect that standing under a plum tree would be a dangerous place. However, the awakening that takes place when a large block of wood descends and hits you on the head is instant and undeniable. I believe that it was at that precise moment that I developed my propensity for the F word. Up till that time I had no idea what the word meant but, in that instant when the block connected

Cliff with sister Marjorie

with my head, the meaning of the word was fully revealed to me. After that day, whenever I heard that word, I would stop and imagine the terrible pain that person must be suffering. Thereafter, I only used the word in times of great stress, like that time when I hit my thumb with a hammer.

When I was two I had a narrow escape while attempting a getaway from my crib. I slipped and I fell, landing on my head. My sister Marie, who was looking after me at the time, became frightened and, thinking that I might not live, ran to the nearby home of a nurse. The nurse came as quickly as she could, only to find that I was fully recovered and upright, and was endeavoring to put my shoes on, in a bid to attempt the second stage of my escape. Marie, overjoyed at finding her little brother alive and well, showered me with sweets and affection. This display of kindness and affection gave rise to the general opinion that I was an individual who could fall into a barrel of manure and come up smelling of roses.

Apart from that near disaster, which forged a permanent and unbreakable bond between brother and sister, my first three years were largely uneventful. There was, however, some concern that I may have sustained an injury from that particular episode, or the many times that I banged my head on tables, while learning to take my first, faltering steps. However, my mother later told me that all the blows to my head must have hardened it to the point that it was impervious to any assault. Certainly it served me well, for instance, when I was seven years of age.

Mom and I were engaged in a lively disagreement, when my head came in contact with a Pyrex mixing bowl that she was holding in both hands. Now, I don't know if mom dropped the bowl or if I stood up too quickly, but somehow the bowl broke. My mother showed great concern when she saw that her bowl was broken, and warned me not to make her mad, else she would not be responsible for what might happen. Over the years she did lose her temper with me on occasion, but by and large we got along very well.

Later in life I joined a boxing club, winning several bouts. If my adversary hit me on the head I was okay, but unfortunately most of them found my most vulnerable spot, my nose. It did not take me long to conclude that getting whacked on the nose while in the ring was not necessarily my kind of fun. Of course I still managed to engage in a certain amount of fisticuffs over the years and somehow managed to avoid serious injury, sometimes even coming out on top.

Growing up in Victoria during the depression of the 1930's we lived in a house at 633 Cornwall Street, in the Fairfield district. This house was probably the oldest farmhouse in the area, and it belonged to my mother's uncle, Dr. Bavis, a cantankerous old doctor who was married to my Grandfather's sister, Agnes, whom my mother was named after. Agnes Bavis was a nurse and ran a private nursing home at the corner of Richardson and Cornwall Street.

Each month Dr. Bavis arrived on our doorstep to collect his $20 monthly rent. If the rent was not paid on time the old doctor would raise Cain. During his rent day visits, I often tried to engage old Uncle Bavis in conversation, but he never seemed particularly interested in my opinions or my observations and I eventually gave up trying to be nice to him and finally told him what I thought of him. As far as I can recollect, that was the first time that I called anyone an old fart.

My mother had very little sense of humour, I tried to tell her that I was trying to be funny when I called old uncle Bavis an F word, but she was hard to convince. She spent quite some time explaining to me the right and the wrong way to address people, particularly old people. I never forgot that lesson, and to this day I never use any of the F words with old people, aside from the odd exception.

My mother's father had a brother named Charlie who was severely injured during the First World War. After he left the army he settled on 200 acres of land, part of a land grant given to War Veterans. The land was between Ucluelet and Tofino, on a stretch now known as Long Beach. Eventually the Government reclaimed all the land on the beach side of the Highway, for a park, leaving him with about 160 acres on the other side of the road.

At that time, the area was extremely isolated and Uncle Charlie became a virtual recluse, seldom venturing out to civilization. He built his house deep in the bush, carrying everything he required, on his shoulders. Over the years, the strain of that back breaking labour crippled him to the point that he was no longer able to stand upright, and eventually he moved in with one of my uncles, on mother's side, to live with him in Victoria.

My recollections of Old Uncle Charlie are vivid. Like most of my mother's family, he was fairly short, and he walked stooped over to the point that it was difficult for him to see beyond a few feet. But to me he was a giant. He would sit for hours, telling us kids about his life growing up in England, telling us all about our mother and what she was like as a girl. He described her family home in Cheltenham, England, and that the home in Cheltenham was situated on Nob Hill overlooking the countryside. He described how he would chase mom up the hill, but she would run like the wind, beating him every time.

Later on in life, my wife and my daughter Marlene and I visited England and drove to Cheltenham to see if we could find mom's old home. Remembering Uncle Charlie's vivid description, we searched until we found an ancient house that matched his description, and then drove up the long drive to the house and knocked on the door. An elderly lady answered the door, and we explained who we were, and that we thought that my mother had grown up in the house, and could we look around. The dear old soul said, "Yes, but watch out for the cats"

The house had about fifteen rooms, and as we walked the long hallways looking into empty room after empty room, we were overwhelmed by an incredible smell of cats. There was no furniture but there were cat droppings everywhere, and the unbelievable stench of cats permeated our every pore.

My wife and daughter were practically overcome by the odors, and begged me to leave at once; however, having waited so many years to see the old house, I insisted on staying until we had inspected every room.

When we finally took leave of that wonderful, but pungent mansion, we decided that a long walk in the open air was probably the best thing we could do under the circumstances, so we strolled the streets of Cheltenham, much richer for the discovery of my mother's childhood home. Old Uncle Charlie would have been pleased that we found our mother's childhood home, even though it was now inhabited with many, many cats.

When Uncle Charlie died we were devastated. I remember feeling that life would never be the same again, for I had always looked forward to his visits as one might look forward to visiting Royalty.

Uncle Charlie left his acreage to my mother and her three brothers. I was fifteen, and I dreamed that one day I might own the land. But soon after his death the three brothers quickly decided to sell the estate, ignoring my pleas to sell it to me, and allow me to make monthly payments for as long as it would take to pay it off. When I suggested the arrangement, they laughed, probably assuming that a boy of fifteen would never be able to carry it off. Well, I thought I could handle it; after all I did have a paper route and a steady income.

When I was three I can recall living on Cornwall Street. I was inquisitive, always getting into trouble. I always believed that I was not merely a small child, but a person on his way to being fully grown. Whenever anyone asked me my age I would try to imagine what they thought my age should be, and then act accordingly.

When I was twelve my sister Marie was in St. Joseph's Hospital with her first child. I went to visit her, and there was a sign stating the visiting hours, and underneath it said *No One Under Eighteen Allowed*. Well, I slipped by the front desk and went to a nursing station and asked the nurse where I might find my sister Marie McRae.

She looked at me, and said," How old are you."

I said," Eighteen."

Of course, she turned me away, and then went and told my sister. Heck, I thought that I looked eighteen, what was it with adults anyway.

On my third birthday I was given a tricycle. I wondered just how far that bike would take me and I set out on a scouting expedition. I passed the Five Point Confectionery at the corner of Moss and Fairfield, a block away from home; I didn't have any money at the time so I didn't stop, although I did size it up for further expeditions. The blocks flew by and I found myself a mile or two away from home.

At the five-point intersection I was faced with an important decision, to continue up the hill on Fairfield, which seemed very steep, or continue on down Moss. Well, I decided that the hill up was too difficult, and the hill down seemed too far, so I turned right on Oscar Street. This proved to be a good choice because the hill wasn't too steep and it leveled out fairly quickly.

There were many interesting houses on Oscar Street, and for a small boy they were beautiful. Up till that time I had only seen houses on Cornwall and I was easily impressed. All the houses had nice lawns and gardens, which differed from my own house, because my own house had no garden or lawns, only a Laburnum tree which made you very sick if you ate the blossoms. But I really liked that old Laburnum tree; I used to climb it almost everyday. The blossoms looked like little bananas and I would look at them wondering what it would be like living in a country that had real banana trees. I spent many hours in that tree; why, it was almost like a second home to me.

When I was twelve I went to the movie "*National Velvet*" and I fell in love with Elizabeth Taylor. The next day I climbed my Laburnum tree and carved a heart on the trunk with the initials C C loves E T. I dreamed that one day I would meet Elizabeth and let her know how I felt about her, thinking that she would fall madly in love with me too.

It sure came as a surprise that she might meet others before I could get down there to California. By the time I was ready for that great adventure, she had already met and married two or three husbands. The one I truly resented was Richard Burton' I wondered what on earth she saw in him, and what did he have that I didn't.

There were trees all along Oscar Street, different than the trees on Cornwall Street. Our trees had Japanese plums, and you could eat them, but the trees on Oscar had hard, brown chestnuts, that you couldn't eat, but they were sure great for throwing at other kids. When I got older and could throw things, I had lots of fun seeing if I could whack some kid with a chestnut. Of course you had to be careful because other kids could do the same thing to you, and boy did those nuts hurt when they hit you on the head.

As I moved along the street, I didn't see any people, so I thought that only rich people must live there, because rich people never walk on their streets. My mom always used to tell us they don't want to come out and associate with poor people.

The first street I came upon was Linden Ave, although I didn't know it because I couldn't read yet, but I liked it because there was a large cherry tree in the back yard of the corner house, which I figured, would be great to raid just as soon as I got big enough to climb trees.

When I got to Cook Street I turned right, I am not sure why. When you're a kid you sometimes do things without giving it much thought. As I headed up Cook Street, I saw something incredible; it was a huge streetcar coming down the road, toward the ocean. Mind you, I didn't know the ocean was that way, after all I was only three and I didn't learn about the ocean until I was a lot older, and then my mother kept telling me that I shouldn't go near the water because I might drown.

She was always saying that. When I was eleven or twelve I went to *Camp Imadene*, a Bible Camp that was in Maple Bay. While I was there I found Jesus; up till that time I didn't even know that he was missing. When I got home I told Mom that I was saved at camp, she said, "Clifford, I told you not to go near the water".

That was the first streetcar I had ever seen. It was shaking and clanging and ringing a bell as it moved along the street. It looked great, so I pedaled after it, going like crazy, hoping to get on at the next stop. That's when I first met the policeman. He was awfully big. His clothes were so blue they almost looked black, and he had a pointed helmet on his head with a shiny badge on the front. When I got older I found out that he was a Bobby, and looked just like the policemen in English movies.

I saw my first movie when I was five. My Mom was in the Jubilee Hospital having my brother Frankie. My dad took us to visit Mom in the hospital but they wouldn't let us in so we stayed out on the lawn. When my Mom came to the window I called for her to drop little Frank so I could get a better look at him. She wouldn't.

After that Dad took us to a movie; it was scary and had a bad guy named Boris Karloff. After the movie we all stood at the railing that overlooked the foyer, I climbed up on the railing and put my feet between the spindles, leaning over the rail and looking at the people on the lower floor. I never forgot, and many years later when the Theatre was torn down I acquired the whole balcony and built it into my own home in Mill Bay.

Balcony from the Capital Theatre

That policeman who stopped me when I first laid eyes on the streetcar asked "What is your name"

I said "Clifford".

He said "Clifford Clarke?"

"Yeah! How did you know that?"

" Well your mother has been looking all over you and is worried sick"

I didn't know why my mother worried so much, heck I wasn't lost, I knew exactly where I was.

Well, the policeman asked me if I would like come down to the station with him and meet all the other policemen, so I said "sure". I know I was only three, but my Mother always said that policemen were our friends, and I wasn't scared of him anyway.

I sure had fun at the police station. My new friends put me up on the counter and they let me run up and down the top of it, and then they gave me something good to eat, I think it was a donut.

When I got home I remember my mother shouting at me, *"Don't you ever do that again, you had me worried sick"* That was the second time I had heard that, that day. Boy, mothers can sure get uptight.

I often saw my mother get uptight, it wasn't that I was being particularly bad; it was just that everything that I wanted to do was usually forbidden. I had the same experience in school. Boy, the teachers just couldn't get used to the idea that I knew far more than they did, and that I was only there to humor my mother.

I was first introduced to the strap when I was seven; I really can't remember what I did to deserve it, but it hurt like heck. I think teachers were taught to scare the devil out of little boys so that they would grow up to be just like them.

My first grade teacher was short, old, and very ugly. Her name was Miss George. Every morning we would salute her and say, *"Good morning Miss George."* And then we would say the Lord's Prayer and sing God Save The King. They aren't allowed to do that in schools anymore are they?

Miss George wasn't much bigger than I was but she was tough as nails. One day I came to school dressed in some old, wrinkled, hand-me-down clothes that I had selected from a pile that my mother left lying beside the washing machine. You see, my mother went to rummage sales! Have you ever gone to a rummage sale? Let me tell you it was awful.

Those sales were usually held in church basements, or old halls that smelled of mildew and had lots of ladies that smelled of lavender. The second hand clothes were piled on long tables, and mothers, usually with their kids in tow, would hurry down the rows of tables rummaging through the wrinkled piles of hand-me-downs, searching for items that might fit their offspring.

My mother had a system, she would take all the clothes she had purchased at the Rummage sale, and then she would throw them on the floor close to the washing machine, a 1925 Maytag. It was our job to find something that fit us. With four boys in the family it was great to have a chance to try on something different.

When we had made our selection, she would wash and iron the clothes and then we could wear them. On that particular day Marjorie and big brother Clifford were in a hurry to get to school, and so I bypassed the washing machine and iron, and wriggled into some wrinkled garments and hurried off to school without encountering my mother. Of course at that time I didn't know that one day wrinkled clothing would be all the rage.

Miss George wasn't aware that I was starting a trend either, so I guess she can be forgiven for pulling me by my ear to the front of the class, all the while trying her best to get the wrinkles out of my clothing by shaking me and poking at the wrinkles with her bony finger.

When I think back to grade one with Miss George and how she often pulled me to the front of the class and held me up as an example of how not to dress, I realize that that was probably when I first began enjoying the lime-light. All the kids would laugh and tell me how much fun they had watching me dance around with Miss George. I never held a grudge; gosh that's where I first learned the Fox Trot.

As the years of schooling progressed, I found that the best thing to do when getting heck from a teacher, was to keep moving, because this made it difficult for them to get a good crack at you. It certainly helped when they tried to give me the strap. I'd wait till they had wound up and were in full swing, ready for contact, and then I would move my hand to the side. Boy! Did they get mad; they would then try, even harder, to get a good shot in.

Once, when Miss Hiscock, my grade five teacher, was giving me the strap, she held the strap in two hands, high above her head. I waited till she was in full swing. And then I moved my hand. She let it go at the end of her swing; it went right between her legs and hit the cloakroom wall. You know, she never tried that again. For years after, I would proudly show kids the exact spot on the wall where it hit.

But, getting the strap didn't stop for me until I was twelve. Once when all the teachers were home for lunch, I went around and collected all the straps and then took them and buried them in a neighbour's yard. Can you imagine the surprise when they dug those straps up?

When I first started school at six, I met Jack who was only five so I took him under my wing and tried to look after him. The thing that I liked most about Jack was that his family was just as poor as mine and he dressed exactly the same as me.

We started a friendship that has endured for all these years and when we meet we are able to strike up conversations as though time has been standing still. There is something very special about a friendship that begins in school, particularly when that person becomes your very best friend. He tends to overlook a whole lot of shortcomings that will normally drive other kids up the wall.

Our friendship was very special, and though we love each other to bits, we are very competitive. From grade one we would compete to see who could learn the alphabet the fastest, or who would be able to count to one hundred the quickest. This competitiveness allowed us to get reasonably good grades in the earlier years and helped hone the skills that we were to use in later years.

As we grew older we enjoyed sharing things with one another, for instance if one of us got a bruise, we would always try to give the other one a bruise as well. Once Jack picked up a greasy iron bar, as he looked at the grease on his hands, he decided that I should also have the pleasure and immediately passed it to me. I don't know why, but when a friend passes you something you always take it.

When we grew older and started dating girls things changed. We swore each other to secrecy, so I can't tell you a thing, although I will tell you that one of my favorite songs in those days was "Second Hand Rose". Looking back on my association with Jack I realize just how lucky we were.

Schooling in the thirties was quite an experience, and I remember sitting on the curb at the front of my house on Cornwall Street; I was six and it was during the summer of '39'. I remember thinking that within a short time I was going to have to start school. I believed that once my schooling started I was going to lose all my freedom. No more roaming the streets of Fairfield looking for fun, no more scouting out old garages and barns, looking for interesting things, no more pinching candy at the Five Point Store. Heck, my life of freedom was about to end.

Parents often allowed their kids to roam the streets, usually with very little supervision, and I took full advantage of it. By the time that I was six, I had already figured out ways to make pocket money.

One of the first enterprises was collecting pop bottles and selling them to the Five Point Confectionery. I was closely associated with the store through my family. My mom did some of her grocery shopping there, running an account, payable by the month. There were nine members in my family, including my mom and dad and so I was continually running down to the store, picking up necessary supplies.

The owners of that little store were very nice people, and up till that period in my life, had not actually caught me with my hand in the candy bar case. That candy case was right beside the till, and I was careful when they were close to it, which was most of the time. However I did get them to go on the occasional wild goose chase, into the back of the store, which sometimes allowed me enough time and opportunity to snitch a bar. Unfortunately, they quickly caught on, and began watching me like a hawk.

There was a penny candy section, located on the other side of the store near a window, behind a large storage unit and it was possible, when they were busy serving other customers, to help myself to the loose candy, sometimes managing to fill the pocket of my jacket before one them came around the corner looking for me.

My life of crime suddenly came to an end one day. I had just filled my pockets with penny candy, when I heard a knocking on the window, which ran the entire length of the candy bin. A gentleman had been watching me help myself to the candy and was now making animated gestures, indicating that I should put the candy back. My life flashed before me, I envisioned being taken down to the police station for another visit, but this time they would not be feeding me donuts.

I smiled at the gentleman, letting him know that I understood, and I was deeply sorry for my dishonest ways. When I emptied one of my pockets, I again smiled at him. He pointed to the other pocket, again indicating that I should empty it. Ah! Yes, the other pocket. When I had returned all the sweets I carefully chose several more, placing them in a little bag, which were there, just for that purpose, and then took them to the proprietor and paid for them, with the only nickel that I had in my possession. I held my head up high as I left that little store, happy that I had chosen the right path, and would henceforth earn my way in legitimate business.

Collecting pop bottles was an easy way to make a fast nickel. I had my own wagon; it was a Comet Express, newly painted bright red by my Uncle Tom, whose hobby was rebuilding and restoring old toys. I developed a regular route. I would tow the wagon behind me, picking up empties wherever I might find them. One of my greatest sources was the Crystal Spring Beverage Company, which was on Richardson Street at the top of Cornwall Street, just a few doors from where I lived.

The employees of the Crystal Spring Beverage Company stacked empty pop bottles at the rear of their premises. I had discovered this treasure trove on one of my scouting expeditions and believed that they had been discarded.

The beverage plant specialized in Stone Ginger Beer, of course it had no alcohol in it, but it was delicious. The Ginger Beer bottles were stone crocks and were beautifully designed with bold black lettering. I thought that they were wonderful and always treasured them. The company discontinued Stone Ginger by the time I was twelve or thirteen, and eventually the bottles became collector items.

Many years later I had an antique store in Royal Oak, called the Red Barn. Whenever I found an old Crystal Spring Ginger Beer bottle it would bring back many memories, and I could sell it for twenty or thirty dollars. Back in the 30's I was lucky to get a nickel for it. Even their Lime Ricky and Orange Pop bottles only fetched two or three cents. Gosh in the 80's I was getting five bucks each.

Old Mr. Foster, at the Five Point store, used to wonder where I got so many bottles. Mrs. Foster had a suspicious nature and wondered if I was pinching them. Shortly after that the Crystal Spring Beverage Company put all their empties under lock and key.

I never figured that one out. Gosh, the Crystal Spring Beverage Company was at least three blocks away from the Five Point store, and I couldn't understand how they found out. I only knew that my profits had plunged, and I had to work very hard to bring my income back up to its former level.

My collection route took me all the way to upper Linden

Ave, which had a back lane parallel to it, from Richardson to Rockland Ave., and every house had a garage opening on to that Lane.
There was only one of those garages that I had difficulty getting into. When I finally cracked it, I discovered an ancient Stanley Steamer car. Obviously no one used it anymore, because there were cobwebs all over it. Cobwebs didn't scare me until I was seven; that's when I found out that spiders lived in them.

That old Stanley Steamer was a beauty and I sat in the front seat for quite a while before I opened the glove compartment. There wasn't much in the glove box that I collected except maybe, a strip of Nickel-plated metal with the name *STANLEY STEAMER* on it. I didn't really collect that type of thing either, but I was on my collecting route, so I took it.

While I was in the garage, I discovered a number of interesting items, such as, hubcaps, hood ornaments, old license plates, that sort of thing, which helped to make the trip worthwhile.
By that time my wagon was getting pretty full, so I headed for home. I didn't show anyone at home what I had collected, because I thought that they would probably want it for themselves, instead I hid it in my secret hiding place, just outside my sister's bedroom window on the porch roof.
I don't know how my father found that collection, but he did. He knew a lot about cars and he also knew that people didn't just throw those sorts of things away. He listened to my story with keen interest, then explained, that there is a very fine line between finding things or, stealing them; then, he told me to take them back to where I found them, right away.

Collectors do not like the word steal, they much prefer the word discovered, and though I was hurt by his suggestion, I agreed to return the items to the place I discovered them. When I went to return the items later that day, I found that the garage was again securely locked. I decided that it would not be a smart thing to break into the garage a second time, so I took the collection back home, and found a much better storage area, under my back porch. No one ever went there because there were lots of cobwebs with big spiders.

Once, I found a Black Widow Spider and caught it in a bottle that I kept just for that purpose. I showed it to everyone in the family including my mom. That's when I discovered that no one else liked spiders, particularly mom, cause she screamed and almost fainted. She said that if that spider bit me I would probably die. Well I didn't want to die just then, not when I had just discovered the great power I now held over everyone. So I took it out and squished it, under my foot, and then I put the bottle back under the porch so that it would be there ready for the next time I needed it.

I always showed my friend Jack my collections and secret hiding places, and he showed me his as well. His best hiding place was in the basement of his house on Meares Street. The house was as old as mine, maybe older. The basement had wooden floors and wooden walls and Jack and I spent many a day looking for secret passages. The only secret space we ever found was behind a closet that was built into an old doorway, it led to the furnace room with a

Cliff with his friend Bruce

furnace so old it was never used. Jack's dad didn't like me snooping in his basement, so he didn't let me visit too often.

Jack was my special friend. When Jack was seven, while crossing Fort Street, he was run down by a car. He received some bad wounds including a piece of metal that lodged in his chest. I was really sorry for poor Jack getting hit, but he received a lot of money, so he didn't feel as badly as I did, although I secretly was a little envious that he should get all that money for doing nothing. He wasn't able to give me any because it was put into a trust fund until he was much older.

Over the years Jack and I shared many adventures. When we were about ten years old we set out to make our fortune. There was very little spare money available for entertaining young boys, so we had to find our own ways of earning enough pocket money to keep us supplied with the necessities of life. One of our passions was going to the "Movies" on a Saturday afternoon, and having enough money to buy a pocket full of sweets, to tide us over until supper

Cliff with milk wagon horse

Our love for movies developed early in life

The *"Bowery Boys"* or the *"Dead End Kids"* were among our many favorite movies. New York was the usual setting, and the characters including Huntz Hall, Leo Gorcey, and a ragtag group of street urchins kept us entertained with their endless escapades and adventures. For Jack and me, this was the best way to escape from our humdrum existence, and if it meant working for a few hours to earn the necessary admission fee, so be it.

A young boy could earn a dollar or two many ways if he was willing to work, and each season created special opportunities.

Our Newspaper career began one winter, when we were nine and ten years old. We heard that an enterprising individual could turn a fast nickel selling the daily newspaper on street corners in downtown Victoria. All one needed to do to launch themselves into this lucrative sideline was to invest in a few newspapers. The paperboys paid two for a nickel, to the daily press; the papers were then sold on the streets for five cents each.

Sir James Douglas School

Jack and I would leave our school, Sir James Douglas, as soon as possible after the three o'clock bell, run several blocks to the corner of Richardson and Cook Street, and board the number ten Streetcar to Fort and then down to Douglas Street.

If we moved smartly, we would be able to purchase our supply of papers at the back alley entrance of the old Times building, on the corner of Fort and Broad Street, and be on the downtown streets by 4 o'clock. We would approach shoppers and workers as they hurried home, or while they stopped for a bite to eat at one of the many cafes that dotted the streets of Victoria and, hopefully turn a fast piece of change.

Like the other paperboys, we were desperate to get to the customers before they left the town. The competition among these street urchins was fierce, and if you trespassed on another's territory, you were toast. Jack was nine years old and I was ten, and both lacking any of the wiles necessary for survival on the streets, so our first few weeks not only showed a low profit, but were also fraught with peril.

We purchased our supply of papers and tried to get to the customers before we were spotted by the older and more aggressive news peddlers. We quickly discovered that virtually every street corner was controlled by one of the many, other *'Boys'*, and our presence on those corners, by them or even close to them, was a declaration of war. Most of the other boys were older, tougher and meaner. The least we could expect, if we were caught trespassing on their territory, was a swift kick in the pants or a sharp clout on the ear.

Our concern over being caught by one of those War Lords was only surpassed by their reputation as killers. The variety of nicknames associated with those figures of vengeance was daunting. Although I seldom received more than a swift kick in the pants, I was painfully aware that there were indeed boys out there who were to be avoided at all cost.

The *"Reese"* twins were feared by young and old alike, and if you were wise you would cross the street to avoid them. I told my mother about those twins and how they terrorized us. One day they caught me trespassing on their territory. I didn't realize that they were in charge of that particular corner, but I had learned that if they said it was their corner, it was wise to agree with them, and leave as quickly as possible.

On that particular day I was busy trying to peel a large banana that I had just purchased from the corner store for two cents. It was very ripe and had been on 'special'. At that moment my attention was diverted, so I did not notice the "Reese Boys" approaching me. Before I knew it, they were standing on each side of me, and asking why I was on their corner. Of course I tried to explain, but before I could say a word, the one on my left elbowed me in the ribs, and the one on my right grabbed my banana and squished it, and then wiped it on my jacket. Then they calmly walked away, leaving me standing there, holding the remains of an over ripe banana in one hand, and several papers in the other, all the while reciting all the bad words I knew, and even some that I had never heard before.

When I told my mother what had happened, she was furious. She wanted to go looking for those monsters and shake the stuffing out of them. I think she could have done it.

Some of the older kids were okay; we called one of them 'Fast Eddy'. He was great to watch in action; he could sell out a cafe in just a few minutes, but unfortunately it was usually the cafe that I was headed for.

Following 'Fast Eddy' through cafe after café, became very discouraging, for he would sell a paper to everyone in the café, leaving anyone following him with slim pickings. Most of the folk were nice when they told you no, but some of them would say mean things like, "Beat it", or "Buzz off". It didn't take long before I began suffering from rejection, and rapidly developed a life long distaste for any kind of rejection.

Eventually Jack and I found modest success, and if luck was with us, we would be able to sell our bundle of papers, even though it frequently took us until after six o'clock.

Once the papers were sold, we would go to the Olde British Fish & Chip Shop on Broad Street and treat ourselves to five cents worth of 'Chips'. At that time the shop cut the chips from very large potatoes and deep-fried them in real beef fat. The chips were long, thick and crisp and probably the very best chips we have ever eaten.

The Fish and Chip shop usually had a long line up waiting for service. The shop was dimly lit, warm and inviting. Even the smell of the boiling fat was exciting to small boys. We would wait impatiently until we got our turn at the counter, which was just about the height of our large watery eyes, and then take our chips, wrapped in old newspaper, and happily stroll the darkened streets enjoying our dinner. By the time we arrived home we were beat and ready for bed.

While Jack enjoyed the paper-selling year, I didn't. Somehow I never fully appreciated standing on those wet, windy streets, trying to sell papers, all the while hollering, "Get your Daily paper here, read all about it". I felt that it was more than a little demeaning, particularly when you often had to make up the headline to attract attention, and it was definitely a challenge to come up with a headline that would not stretch the truth too much. One of my favorite creations was, "Get your Daily paper here, read all about it, Fat Lady Found Tittering on Park Bench."

Usually no one could understand what you were yelling about, so it seemed perfectly safe to yell anything you wanted to. One day, a man standing near me misunderstood the message; he claimed he heard me say that a fat lady's tit was found on a park bench. Eventually I decided that selling papers was not my bag, so I began looking for other means of revenue.

One day, while strolling down the streets of Fairfield, I realized that many houses heated their home with wood, and the wood dealer would dump it on the street where it would sit until someone moved it indoors. At my house I quite often helped pack it in, so I figured that I had experience and could move their wood in, hopefully saving someone a lot of trouble and meanwhile making myself a buck in the process.

I knocked at a house that had a load of wood sitting at the curb, and when the lady came to the door I offered to move the load in for a buck. Much to my surprise she said that she would love to have me do it, so I went into the basement and got a heavy wooden wheelbarrow with an iron wheel, and started moving that load into the basement. It was not as easy as I figured. I asked the lady how much wood was there and she said "Two cords".

I made a mental note, that in future I would ask how many cords of wood was on the street before telling them how much I would charge them. Thereafter my basic charge was one dollar for each cord, which would include stacking it in the basement, and cleaning the remaining sawdust and debris off the street. Incredibly, I enjoyed packing in wood and found many jobs, keeping myself very busy and always in pocket money.

I learned very early that it did not matter how much you got for doing a job. What was important was doing as many jobs as possible, in the shortest time possible. I would also try to do the best job I could do. Whether stacking wood or cutting lawns, I found that it was fun trying to improve my skills in every way possible. I was never satisfied unless the wood was stacked perfectly, or the lawns neatly trimmed. I also discovered that doing the job properly didn't take any more time than being sloppy and often it was much faster because if you did it right the first time you didn't have to do it over again.

Eventually I became an expert at packing in wood, and discovered many tricks that the wood dealers would play on their customers. One was the old seasoned wood deal. This offer was usually advertised at the beginning of the rainy season. The ad would usually read, *"Seasoned, dry wood, no delivery charge"*. The unfortunate people that had not ordered their wood during the summer months, which would have allowed it time to dry before the soggy winter, would leap at the chance of getting dry wood for their winter needs.

It was delivered in a very large truck, which I suspected was held in reserve for these 'special' loads. It would appear to be piled high with bone dry wood. The delivery man would show the customer a few pieces of nice dry wood from the top of the load, and then ask for payment before he dumped it. The unsuspecting sucker would pay him, the load would be dumped, and before the final piece of wood hit the street, the truck would be driven away, leaving the unfortunate with a load of freshly milled, sopping wet firewood.

It was absolutely useless to complain to the phone number printed in the paper, because that number, invariably, belonged to some distant relative of the driver, who, not only spoke little English, had not seen that particular man for a long, long time, and wasn't even sure that he was back from the 'Old Country' yet.

Of course everyone in those days had, at one time or other, taken delivery of a load of wood that was guaranteed to be Douglas fir. If the customer had been tricked before, he would take the time to climb up to the top of the truck and examine the load himself, often digging down into the truck box, as far as possible, to see that it was indeed fir.

The driver usually stood with an incredibly pained look on his face, all the while telling the suspicious customer that he was an honest man and certainly would not cheat anyone. If the person was satisfied that the load was okay, he would pay the driver and then stand back to oversee the dump. The wood, cascading from the truck, became an object of intense scrutiny as the buyer did the two foot shuffle, while trying to detect any trickery.

Imagine the joy one would experience upon finding that the load was absolutely genuine. Of course this scenario was quite often not the case, and more often than not the customer would be observed shouting unflattering remarks at the rapidly disappearing truck.

There wasn't a household in all of Victoria that could not relate the sad tale of receiving a load of wet, barely recognizable firewood, often buried in wet sawdust and debris that usually yielded fifty percent wood and fifty percent rubbish.

When I had the job of removing this mess from the street, I would often feel great compassion and pity for the victim and do my best to pile the wood in such a way as to make it look like a full load.

The sheer genius required to create this small miracle was a wonder to behold. I would first take several loads of debris into the basement, where I was to pile the wood, and spread it out over the floor several inches thick. I would pile wood on top of this base, taking great care to make it appear that there was more there, than there actually was. The rest of the sawdust and debris was piled in a corner where it could dry, and at some point be suitable for burning.

The look of relief that would register on the victim's face, when they saw the huge pile of wood, and the small amount of debris, lying snuggly in their dry storage area, would give me a tremendous amount of satisfaction. Their words and smiles allowed me a brief moment in the 'Lime Light', plus the joy of knowing that, when winter arrived, the material would be dry and burnable, and the folks, by that time, would have forgotten the disappointment and the shortcomings of that particular load. Happily, they would not have to concern themselves again, until the next load of seasoned firewood arrived.

My friend Jack on the left, sister Sheila and brother George

In those years, there were many Lumber Mills in Victoria and they all required the constant removal of wood slabs, end cuts and sawdust. Each Mill, some of them running two shifts, needed a steady stream of trucks and drivers to carry away the constant flow of cut wood and the sawdust and debris that went along with it.

There were many people employed in the firewood business and many lived in an area of houses situated between enormous woodpiles. This particular area covered acres of land, bounded by Nanaimo, Market and Douglas Streets. Many gentlemen of the 'wood trade' stored much of the surplus firewood that they had collected from the Mills, on these lots, allowing it time to dry before winter.

Customers in need of wood were indeed fortunate to be able to draw upon this stock of number one firewood. Of course, 'old customers' were given preference. Many of these men invited their customers to come over and view the wood prior to delivery, and if lucky, to join them in a meal of delicious curry and roti.

For myself, it was a rare treat to visit that enormous wood lot. There, I would enjoy the mixture of sounds and smells, for the whole area was alive with the sweet aroma of Indian curries, and the mysterious dialects of the Middle East. The smell of freshly cut wood, mingling with the nose tingling aroma of spices emanating from the many homes that dotted the land, was unforgettable.

On special days, when there was no school, Jack and I would hop the #10 Streetcar to town, and then transfer to the #380, at the corner of Douglas and Yates Street. This would take us down Douglas to Hillside. We would then go to that magical wood lot, spending as much time as possible, watching all the handsome men in their neat turbans, and all the beautiful dark eyed ladies in their colorful, flowing saris. We would try to imagine the far off lands that they had come from, and wondered what it would be like to visit those lands. We could only guess at the wonders we would find there. We lingered there as long as possible before leaving to find other places of fun and excitement.

Streetcars

Just before we had arrived at this wood lot destination, either Jack or I would pull the bellcord on the Streetcar, alerting the Conductor that we were getting off at the next corner. We learned, from hard experience, that if you didn't pull that cord at the right time, the Conductor would ignore the bell and continue on to the next stop, which was sometimes several blocks away. There was no point arguing with him, because he was always right. We also found out, that it was a dangerous game to pull that 'Cord', just for fun, because if you did, the Conductor would make you leave the Streetcar right there and then, even if it wasn't where you wanted to get off.

The usual form of revenge for that type of mean spirited discipline was to drop a stink bomb in the "Car" the next time. We obtained those stink bombs from an older boy named George, who lived on the next street to ours. He was an expert at concocting all sorts of chemical mixtures with his chemistry set; these mixtures included bad smells, pipe bombs, and loud noises.
George specialized in stink bombs, particularly ones that might be used on Streetcars. Once I got one of these bombs from George and intended to drop it on a Streetcar for revenge.

It was the first time I had seen one and I didn't know what to do with it. The bomb came attached to a string of butcher twine, to tie to a bench seat so that the conductor couldn't easily throw it off the 'car'. I forgot George's warning to tie it to a seat before lighting it, and pulled it out of my pocket, leaving most of the string still in the pocket. What I didn't realize was that the string had become tangled on something sharp and had caught on the lining of the pocket. I pulled the bomb out, thinking that it would be easy to light, throw under a seat, and then run away from the streetcar before it went off.

Well, I got the bomb out of my pocket without any trouble, waited till the streetcar came to a stop at the corner, then lit it and threw it under the seat.

When the doors opened I jumped off the streetcar, and started running like hell. The bomb was still attached to my pocket and followed me, bouncing around like a string of fire crackers hot on my heels. When I realized what had happened, I tugged at the string to get it out of my pocket, but it was stuck and wouldn't budge. I ran down the street with the smelly bomb following me, leaving a trail of smoke and smell behind me. The bomb stayed alive and stinking for several blocks and I didn't dare stop lest it catch up to me and set me on fire.

People I passed during that mad run, must have wondered what I was doing. No one said anything as I ran by, and they just looked amused, probably thinking that some boys would do anything for a moment in the limelight.

George was also very fond of putting things on streetcar tracks that made loud bangs, the louder the better. We put pennies on the tracks. George put explosives. Once, when a streetcar was standing still at the end of its run, he tied a long rope to the back of it, and tied the other end to the round house that people sat in, while waiting for the streetcar. When that streetcar started moving along the track, it pulled the little house half a block before the conductor realized what had happened.

George pulled a lot of pranks over the years, eventually getting into serious trouble with the 'law'. We younger kids thought that he was brilliant in chemistry but very foolish in many other ways, so we avoided doing anything that might get us into trouble with the law. Although, I have to confess that I did some things that were very close to that fine line that my father warned me about. Jack and I loved riding the streetcars at every opportunity. The cars had the fragrant smell of tobacco, which curled from pipes held by the gentlemen that traveled. The wood panels that lined the cars were stained brown from years of tobacco smoke and the wear of countless hands.

The wooden seats were constructed with hinges, which allowed them to be reversed at the end of the run. Whenever possible, we would reverse them during the run, and then wait to see who would sit in them facing the wrong way, and we would make faces at them until they got up and moved.

We had so much fun on those streetcars. Sometimes we would sit in the back seats and slide open the windows behind us, to face the cars following behind. We would see if we could spit on their windshields. Sometimes we were very successful. Once I spat a great gob on a following car's window, and the driver was so mad he followed the streetcar to the next stop and then jumped on and came down the aisle with fire in his eye, and said," Who spat on my window?" He was looking right at me, so I said, " My friend did it, but he jumped off before you got on." All my friends said that I would make a good lawyer.

That episode taught me a lesson and I never spat out the back window of a streetcar again, although once I was caught short and had to pee. There were no cars following close behind, so I did it out the window, but I was very careful and I didn't hit anyone.

When I was twelve I got my first paper route with the Daily Colonist. I needed to earn extra money so that I could pay a debt that I owed to my brother Bob.

During those War years, Bob saved up four dollars and bought a War Bond. The bond would be worth five dollars at the end of the war. He kept it in a locked cabinet in my Father's room. The cabinet was built by my Father to keep his personal things in and he kept it locked at all times. Bob wanted to make sure that his investment was safe, so my Father let him keep it there.

I was always very curious about what might be in that cabinet, and tried to get into it for a long time. One day I discovered some of my Father's keys, and so I tried to see if they would open the cabinet, and they did. I wasn't foolish enough to take anything that belonged to my Father, so I took my brother's War Bond. I figured that all I had to do was sign Bob's name to it and cash it in. My next mistake was to send it to my friend John, who was boarding at Queen Margaret School in Duncan. I wrote to him, enclosing the Bond, and asked him to send it to the Government so that they might cash it. John said I was stupid to send it to him, because the Sisters at the school opened everybody's mail. Now how was I to know that?

Well, word got around very quickly, and the truth came out. Bob was magnificent. He didn't get mad at me or call me bad names; he merely asked me why I would do that to him. I realized what a low down skunk I had been and begged him to forgive me, and to allow me to pay him back.

The very next day I went to the Daily Colonist and applied for a delivery job. Although I was only twelve, they gave me a route, starting the following day. That delivery route started an association with the paper, which continued until I was seventeen years old.

When I started my route with the Colonist, I was twelve, fairly tall for my age, but quite skinny. I had to go to the Colonist building at the corner of Fort and Broad Street at five in the morning and get the papers for my route.

They taught me to fold the papers into squares, and pack them into a canvas bag that could be attached to the handlebars of my bike. This took about an hour. After that I would pedal out to my paper route, which started at Quadra and South Park Street.

During the winter, it was very dark, and usually very cold. My Mom would get up when she heard me and make sure that I had something to eat and that I was warmly dressed before I left the house. Moms sure worry a lot about their kids. My Mom fussed over me so much that I tried to get out of the house before she woke up. Of course that was difficult as usually she could hear me long before I even got my eyes properly opened. Of course I made it fairly easy for her to hear me, usually banging into almost every thing that I encountered on my way down the stairs. In those days we didn't have lights everywhere in the house, and the ones that were there usually had the switches on the opposite side of the room, and were very difficult to find in the dark.

One morning, shortly after I started my route, I woke up shivering and found that it had snowed during the night. I knew that my Mom wouldn't want me going out into the snow, so I crept down the stairs backwards, on my knees, making sure to avoid everything that might make a noise and wake Mom. Luck was not with me that morning, because she arrived in the kitchen just as I was sneaking out the door. She said that I was not going to go that day because there was too much snow out there. I told her that I had to go, even if I didn't like it, because the papers had to be delivered through rain sleet or snow.

When my Mom got going there was just no stopping her; she said no one should go out in that weather, particularly a twelve-year-old boy. Well she managed to convince me, and then phoned the Colonist delivery room, telling my supervisor that I was sick and couldn't come that day.

Now, I was of two minds, one didn't really want to go, but the other one felt so guilty, that it made me feel sick after all. I went back up to bed, but didn't sleep; I just lay there wishing that Mom hadn't woken up.

The next day when I went to my route, at five in the morning, every one of the boys looked at me in disgust, but said nothing. The supervisor said that he had delivered my papers, as well as his own and that if I couldn't handle a little snow, I should quit.

That episode taught me one of the most valuable lessons that I ever learned, and I swore that I would never again miss a day of work no matter what the weather was like. That day, I sat my Mother down, and told her that I would never miss another day of work, no matter how ugly the weather. I don't know why, but my Mother cried.

The following week, Victoria suffered the worst snowstorm in several years. My Mother came down to the kitchen that morning and said that I shouldn't go, but if I wanted to she would not stop me. My week- kneed mind almost stopped me from leaving, but the other one reminded me of the humiliation that I had suffered the week before.

I put two pairs of socks on my feet, and another two pairs on my hands, and my old aviators cap, the one that buckled under the chin to stop it from blowing off my head, no matter how windy it was, kissed my mother goodbye, who by that time was in tears again, and started on that unforgettable trek.

That weak-kneed mind was sure right. This was the most stupid thing I had done in my life. The snow came up to my waist and was almost impossible to wade through. By the time that I arrived at the pick-up area in the Colonist building, I was almost frozen to death. However, the warm reception I received from the boys already there was incredible, producing enough warmth to thaw, the brass balls on a monkey; and I knew just how that felt. The supervisor gave me the biggest smile you can imagine, and said, "Good boy."

As luck would have it, the paper that day was huge, and the squares that I folded were gigantic and would hardly fit into my carrying bag. By the time that I had them all folded and in the bag I was exhausted. It was still dark outside and the wind was howling so hard it had blown most of the snow off the road. I pedaled my ancient bike as hard as I could against the wind and blowing snow, toward my Quadra Street route. During that seemingly endless trip, I slipped and fell several times. I would have used all the bad words I knew, but it was so cold I was afraid to open my mouth in case my tongue froze, like it did once when I licked a metal bar at the playground, when the temperature was below zero.

When I finally arrived at my route, I found it was impossible to throw the papers up on the porches as I usually tried to do; instead I had to carry them up to the porch, fighting my way through snowdrifts.

The customers must have been amazed that the paper was on their porch instead of the usual place I threw them, because I often missed the porch; sometimes throwing them into the garden, sometimes even onto the porch roof.

The worst times were when I threw them through a window. Of course I would usually continue on as though nothing had happened, hoping that nobody noticed. Usually I was long gone before the customers realized what the crash was that awoke them, and I wouldn't hear a thing about it until the next day when I was informed that I had to pay for the broken window.

I used to dread having to pay for broken windows because it took most of my pay and there was usually very little left as it was. I never did figure out how to get out of paying for those broken windows, but I really tried hard to perfect my aim when I threw a paper, eventually becoming somewhat of an expert and holding the breakage down to a manageable level.

Delivering papers early in the morning, before most people were out of bed, was an education. The most difficult thing was getting out of my own bed. I slept in a room with my three brothers and they would always pretend to be fast asleep when I got up. I couldn't really blame them because our house had no central heating and it was usually so cold in the mornings that milk would freeze sitting on the kitchen table. I learned to dress under the bed covers, in complete darkness. That way I had a chance to get up before I froze a certain part of my anatomy off.

My bed was right beside the bedroom window, and on cold days it always had a thick layer of hoar frost on the inside. I am not sure who told me the name of that frost was hoar, but I know it wasn't my Mom because she didn't like to swear too often, except when she was real angry.
It was an amazing thing, but glass windows did not keep any cold out of the house at all, and so we always left the window open at night because it didn't make any difference.

Even the bathroom was so cold that nobody spent much time in there, except my sisters when they were going out on a date. Once I heard one of them scream when the seat stuck to her bum; of course we weren't allowed in to see what happened.

Sometimes, when my sister Marie wasn't supposed to go out at night she would go into the bathroom and then climb out the window onto the roof, and then down the pear tree. Once I had learned about that exit, I would use it often, not because I was trying to escape, but just for the fun of it. When pears were on the tree I would sit there for quite some time eating them until I was full.

In the winter the house was so cold that the ice in the ice-box lasted a lot longer. I liked that because I was always the first one up and usually cleaned up the water that had overflowed from the ice-box. I always wondered why the people that built them didn't leave more room under an ice-box for larger bowls to catch the water before it ran across the floor.

After emptying the full bowl many times and mopping up the water, I finally took things into my own hands and drilled a hole in the floor, with my dad's drill, which allowed it to dribble into the basement. Fortunately no one could see the hole under the ice-box, and when one of them pulled the bowl out, they would have to mop up the overflowing water which then spilt on the floor. The water that dribbled through the floor into the basement usually ran under my father's metal lathe, which was in his workshop, and along the basement wall eventually disappearing into the dirt floor.

The hole would probably never have been discovered if the water hadn't dripped on my Dad one night while he was working on the lathe. I don't think the mystery of who drilled the hole was ever solved. I'm sure they didn't know it was me, even though I was grilled by my Dad, because my Mom always believed me when I lied. She often said that butter wouldn't melt in my mouth. In summer the house was always hot and full of flies. The flies would gather on the ceiling at night, keeping quiet until daylight. There were usually several strings of sticky fly paper hanging from the ceiling, which caught hundreds of flies. The flies were very quiet when the lights were out, but when the light was turned on they would start buzzing, which attracted even more of the little devils to the paper, where they too would get stuck

The sound they made trying to escape from that sticky paper was awful, and when I arrived down stairs in the kitchen early in the morning, and turned on the light, they would start buzzing like a hive of bees. I would sit at the table, trying to eat my Rice Krispies, which snapped, crackled and popped, almost as loudly as the flies, thinking of the best way to kill them. I was tempted to get a shotgun, but I knew the noise would probably wake every one up, and then I would get heck. So, I sat there, at the kitchen table, developing a life long hate relationship with flies, all the while thinking of gory ways to eliminate them.

I was never completely successful in my war with flies, until RAID came along, which then allowed me to get them with one shot. Unfortunately, in the early days of RAID, the company that made it had not yet perfected the chemical mixture and it was almost as poisonous to humans as it was to flies.

Whenever a person sprayed a room to kill the flies, no one would be able to go back into the room for an hour or two because of the danger. But, when they did go back in, they would find that it had been well worth the wait, because the floor would be littered with a thousand flies, and not a sound coming from any of them. Of course, the next morning, some of the flies would be back including a thousand of their relatives.

Those strings of sticky paper were unbelievable; we could buy them at the grocery store or feed supply stores. They had a funny smell; I guess it was the smell of whatever it was that was on them that killed the flies. We were warned not to touch the sticky stuff because it was not good for humans.

Now that I think about it there was no warning on the package telling us that we shouldn't touch them, just the warning from our parents, "Don't touch them, you might die." Well it sure worked for me, the only time that I touched one of them, was when I put one in my sister's slipper. She didn't know for sure that it was me, but she let out such a scream I decided never to do that again.

My paper delivering years were not necessarily easy, but they kept me in pocket money and allowed me to go to many movies. Sometimes I would get bored in the movie house and think of interesting things to do. I noticed that there was a lot of bald heads in the theatre, and wondered if there was a way that I could hit them with something to see if they were sensitive to the touch. I had a sling shot at home and decided that I should bring it to the movies just in case I got a chance to take a shot at one of those heads. One day, during my summer holidays, I took my slingshot with me to the Capital Theatre. Not many people were in the audience that day, but, there was a bald head glowing in the dark, that caught my attention. I had a pocket full of lead bee-bees with me, and figured that I may as well take a few shots.

I always thought that I was a pretty good shot, and so I took aim at the head and let a bee-bee fly. Well, there wasn't any reaction, so I let fly again. After the fourth shot I was getting desperate, I thought, that either my aim was way off, or that guy had no feeling in his head.

Up till that time I had waited for a noisy moment in the theatre before letting the lead fly. I figured that no one would know where it was coming from, but I guess I let my guard down, because the next time I let one go, a heavy hand clapped me on the shoulder, and I was yanked from my seat and pulled up the aisle to the manager's office.

The manager told me to empty my pockets onto his desk. I pulled out everything I had in my pockets, except the bee-bees. He said, "Is that all you have in your pockets", and I said, "Yes". He then took me to the ticket booth, gave me the money - I had paid for my ticket - and said that I should leave quickly and not come back.

I sure had fun that day, I got several shots at a bald head, and I got my money back from the theatre as well; mind you, I never did that stupid thing again, because there was one thing that I had learned in life. 'Quit while you're ahead'.

After my brothers and I had gone to our beds at night, we would lie there telling stories about what we had done that day. My brothers never seemed to get involved in the same type of escapades that I did, and I often wondered if there was something wrong with them. Usually I had more adventures to tell than they did.

They would lie very quietly, sometimes asking me to repeat the story, that is, if it was interesting enough. When I told them about the bee-bee episode they said I was lucky that the manager hadn't called the police. I said that if he knew that I was shooting lead pellets he probably would have.

After listening to my brother's comments, I decided I was going to turn over a new leaf, and help others. For the longest time I went about saying nice things to people, helping old ladies to cross the street, whether they wanted to cross or not. I even decided to help my little brother Frankie broaden his knowledge, and learn about adult life.

The first thing that I did to help Frank, was to tell him that there was no Santa Claus, and that it was our Mom that crept into the bedroom at night and left stockings stuffed with good things for us. Frank didn't want to hear about it because he always had so much fun going to bed on Christmas Eve and lying awake as long as possible, hoping to see Santa Claus.

Now, in our family, we always tried to encourage every child younger than ourselves, to believe in Santa Claus for as long as possible for, in that way, the joy of Christmas would stay for a long, long time.

I understood exactly how Frankie was feeling. I explained to him that it was a wonderful thing to believe in Santa, and that I didn't want to spoil his dreams, but he was, after all, at the right age and it was time for him to enter into the next level of life. Frank always believed in me, and he said that he would try his best to understand what I had told him, even if it meant disappointment next Christmas.

The reason that I told Frankie the truth about Santa went back to the time that I learned the truth about Christmas myself, that Santa was merely a story invented for little children. I didn't want my little brother to learn from some smart kid who didn't care if he hurt someone, the way I had. On that day before Christmas, he told me that the whole thing about Santa Claus was a hoax, that he didn't live in the North Pole or have a sleigh with reindeer that would bring presents every December 25, to all the children in the world, that he didn't live with Mrs. Santa Claus, and that the elves didn't make all the toys that he brought with him on Christmas Eve, that he didn't climb down the chimney loaded with toys and goodies for every good boy or girl, and that he didn't even eat the cookies or drink the milk we left for him, that it was probably Dad. In fact the whole story was a big fat lie.

That Christmas had been very sad for me, and I felt that my childhood had come to an end too soon. I swore that I would never try to puncture anybody's dreams, like mine had been punctured.

My reward came the next year. One day, shortly before Christmas, Frankie announced to the whole family that there really wasn't a Santa Claus, because Moms and Dads loved their kids so much, that they wanted an excuse to give them presents on another day besides their birthdays. He was very happy that the day was finally near, and that he could hardly wait for Christmas morning, and that everyone should be careful not to let our little sister know that there really wasn't a Santa Claus, because she would be very disappointed.

For years after, my Mother continued leaving a stocking full of goodies at the foot of our beds on Christmas Eve, and we continued to wake up in the middle of the night feasting on all the goodies in those stockings and we always closed our eyes when she came into our room, pretending that Santa was still alive and well.

Living in that old house was an experience not soon forgotten. There were four rooms that were used as bedrooms, but there were two adults and seven children to share them.

Little Frank slept in my Mom and Dad's room, Marie, the oldest, had a small room to herself just off the dining room. Marjorie and Nell shared a small room upstairs, next to the room that my two brothers and I shared, and Mom and Dad had the room at the end of the upstairs hall.

I remember only one or two closets in the house, one in our room that doubled as a dark room for my Dad's photographic hobby. I wasn't supposed to go into that darkroom because I caused too many accidents; at least that's what my Dad always said. I guess he was referring to the time that I dunked a hot light globe into the toilet to see how fast it would cool down, but it exploded. I really don't remember doing too many things wrong in that closet, except the time that I lifted some of my Dad's film out of the developing tray before it was fully developed. Of course I was only trying to help Dad, but he didn't seem to understand that, and I caught the devil and never did it again. The kitchen had a pantry off to one side, which had all the food cupboards in it. My Dad got tired of us kids eating all the food in those cupboards, so he put locks on them to keep us out and only opened them at meal times. Of course there was always something we could eat when we were hungry. One of the best things to eat was dripping and bread. The drippings were collected from the roasts that Mom cooked on weekends. She would get extra fat from the butcher, to cover the roast, and then let it drip into the pan as she roasted it. When the grease cooled she would scoop the top off and let it solidify into a buttery mass. It was delicious. We would slather it onto a thick slice of bread. This was not only delicious, it was filling, and normally would hold us over until suppertime. Whenever we had bread at meal times, my father would show us how to butter half the slice of bread, and then fold it over, to make the butter go further. We would listen to his directions; nodding our heads in agreement and then double the amount of butter on the whole slice, and fold it over, all the while smiling at Dad, and indicating how pleased we were to do as we were told.

In the war days we were lucky if we got enough food, so, we learned to eat everything that was put before us. Of course there were always some things that we didn't like. I personally hated turnips and cabbage, and when I was forced to eat them, I became nauseous, and threatened to throw up over everyone. My Mom would always say that there were millions of kids in the world that would give anything to have what we had, so I suggested that she send them my cabbage and turnips. One of the most delicious things mom made was Yorkshire pudding. She mixed flour, eggs and milk into a pan near the roast. She stirred in the drippings and cooked it until golden brown.

I read stories about Medieval times, that described how cooks would mix flour, eggs and milk into the grease dripping from the side of beef roasting on the spit, and then serve it, when cooked, with thick slices of meat. Every time that we had Yorkshire pudding and beef I would imagine I was a Knight, just home from 'The Wars', and that all the others at the table were my Squires and servants. I always believed I had lived in the days of Knighthood, and that I had gone about the countryside dedicated to the ways of the Knights, rescuing damsels in distress, slaying Dragons, and doing incredible good throughout the country.

I would tell everyone in my family about my adventures and often made up stories describing my exploits. My amazed brothers and sisters always seemed to enjoy the stories, and at night when we were all in our beds, with the lights out, I would return to those days of 'Yore', telling all within earshot wonderful fables from the past. My young sister Marjorie would call out from her room asking me to speak louder, sometimes slipping into our room. She would sit at the foot of my bed, and listen to the stories of Chivalry and Knighthood, until Mom came up the stairs and shooshed her back to her own room.

When I was twelve, John moved into a house on Cornwall Street. He was thirteen and knew a lot more about life than I did. We became great pals and spent many hours together. One of the first things that I learned about John was that he was a terrific businessman and, even though he was only thirteen, he knew how to make a buck. Everyday during the summer he would tell me that he couldn't play until he earned a dollar, because his father said so.

I enjoyed playing with John, so I would help him make his dollar as quickly as possible so we could go have some fun. I often took him to one of my own jobs if there wasn't anything else available. The only advantage to sharing one of my jobs was that we got it done very quickly, even if I didn't make a red cent on it. We cut lawns, packed in wood, picked black berries, which we sold to neighbours, and did almost anything we could think of to make that dollar as quickly as possible.

My friend John

The agreement we made was that he would get the first dollar we earned and I would get the second one. Often, after earning that first dollar, John would suddenly remember that he had to go do a chore for his father and then leave very quickly. I slowly came to believe that the dice we were playing with were loaded in his favor and, being a rather slow learner, it took me most of that summer to come to the realization that John was a heck of a lot smarter than I was.

One day, shortly after becoming friends, John and I decided to run away to some distant place in order to start a new life far away from the rules and regulations of our own homes. John's father owned a small cabin on the Old Island Highway, just above Goldstream Park. We figured that it would be a good starting point for our world trip.

We hitched a ride up to the cabin and attempted to get in through the front door. John brought a key that he thought would open the door; unfortunately he brought the wrong one, so we broke a window and got in fairly easily. John was afraid that his dad might come looking for him there, so we took whatever food and supplies we could find, quickly made our exit, and headed back to Goldstream. We crossed the river, by walking over a fallen tree, near the park, and set up camp, erecting a tent from some black building paper and tree boughs.

That night we lay awake listening to the sounds of the forest. We were sure that most of the sounds came from bears that were snuffling around looking for dinner, and we were terrified that we might be the main course. As we lay there listening to the strange sounds around us and the steady drip, drip of the rain which was slowly seeping into our tent and onto our bed covers, and the hum of an occasional car traveling along the narrow highway, I began wishing that I was home, safe in my own warm bed. The idea that John and I had about seeking fame and fortune in a far off land was quickly losing its appeal. In the morning we cooked pancakes over our campfire with a mixture of flour and water from the river.

Suddenly I noticed a sharp pain in the area of my willy and discovered the half buried body of a tick in the part that little boys hold very dear. John said that the only way to get it out would be to put a red hot knife on the part of it's body sticking out. I was very concerned that the red hot knife could slip and cause more harm than the tick itself. While we discussed our dilemma the tick was rapidly disappearing into my privates. John applied the knife which was glowing hot by this time, but the tick didn't back out as we had hoped, he seemed to be heading in the wrong direction. John suggested that we cut off the whole apparatus, but I said, " No, I might need it someday." Finally, in desperation, I caught the tick between my fingernails and yanked him out. John wanted to cauterize the wound, but I said, " No way, I'm going home."

Surprisingly, our folks were so relieved to see us back home safe and sound we escaped with very little punishment, although John's father made him pay for the window out of his own savings.

Introduction to Beautiful Antiques.

The Rithet Estate was several blocks from our home at the corner of Moss St. and Rockland Ave. It covered about ten acres, and had at one time been a beautiful estate. There had been a mansion on the property before I was born, but it had caught fire, leaving it partially destroyed, it was dismantled, and many salvageable items saved.

There was a three-story barn on the property, which was still standing when I was a boy. It had been used to store all the magnificent stain glass windows and doors that had been salvaged from the house. The barn was a grand structure, which stood at the end of a long gravel driveway. The drive was lined with enormous poplar trees, and was accessed through great cast iron gates, just off Rockland Ave.

The main floor of the barn had housed all the horse drawn carriages on the estate, plus all the necessary harness and equipment. The stable, where the horses were kept, was on the floor below, and was accessed by a door, on the lower level at the back of the building. The stables had at one time been well kept, but over the years they had become overrun with cobwebs and dust, and, as I later discovered, were very spooky.

My brother Bob took me to the Rithet estate when I was very young and I was absolutely entranced by the curving driveways and beautiful lawns and gardens. Evidently an old Chinese gardener maintained the gardens for the first few years after the fire, however, in all the time that I enjoyed the estate, I never encountered the gentleman, and he always remained a phantom figure to me.

As the years passed, the estate fell into disrepair, and the garden shed and teahouse became overgrown with brambles and wild grape vine, and the lawns and gardens gradually succumbed to weeds and wild grass. I spent many happy hours sitting in the overgrown shed and teahouse, imagining myself living on such an estate, and promising myself that one day I would have my own estate, perhaps even more beautiful, and if I did I would never allow it to fall into such disrepair.

Over the years I explored every inch of that property, playing hide and seek with my friends John and Jack and other close friends, climbing the majestic poplar trees, playing in the lily pond, searching for the hidden passageway, that supposedly lay between the foundation of the house and the barn, but never finding it.

During all those early years, my friends and I were constantly trying to break into the barn, but it was securely locked and all the windows boarded up. Of course the challenge remained uppermost in our minds and we attacked the doors and boarded up windows at every opportunity.

One day when I was twelve, one of my friends and I played hooky from school. I had formulated a plan in my head. This was the day that I was going to get into that barn. I borrowed a steel bar and a hammer from my Dad's tool chest and with my friend set out for the estate. That day will stand out in my memory as one of the blackest days of my life.

We attacked one of the covered windows that opened into the stalls. Over the years we had tried every possible way we could think of, to get through that particular window, but always without success. On this day, however, fate had its way. I managed to jimmy the covering off the window, allowing me a small slit, barely wide enough to crawl through. I had read somewhere, that if one could get their head through an opening; the rest of the body would follow. If I ever meet the fellow that wrote that little white lie, I will have a lot to say to him.

My head hurt for days after that episode, and everyone asked me what the scratch marks were on the side of my head. I couldn't tell anyone where I had been, because I was supposed to be in school that day. My Mother and Dad were very concerned about the scratches and questioned me closely. As I mentioned before, My Mom knew that butter wouldn't melt in my mouth, and so believed whatever story I concocted that day.

My head was stuck in that small opening for quite some time before my friend was able to push me all the way through. When I finally squeezed through, into the basement of the barn, I fell six feet to the floor. Fortunately I fell on my head, so I was all right. It took about fifteen minutes for the stars to clear and my eyes to get accustomed to the dark, during that time, I wondered if, perhaps, I should have gone to school after all.

The stalls loomed ominously in the dark like the walls of some medieval dungeon. I slowly inched my way through the dusty stable, brushing countless cobwebs from my face and hair, all the while wishing that I had gone to school, and wishing that my father had kept all his darn tools locked up.

After a few steps I bumped into what appeared to be a stairway leading upwards, I cautiously climbed the stairs, on my knees, until my head again banged into something solid, which appeared to be a trap door.

With all my strength I forced the trap door upward, pushing with all my might, until it finally opened. When I climbed the steps, I found myself in a small darkened room; it was probably the feed room, as there was a metal chute leading down to the stalls, where oats and other feed could be poured down to the horses below.

When I opened the door leading to the main part of the barn, I was overwhelmed. The huge room was filled with the most beautiful stained glass that I had ever seen, or would ever see in my entire life. An opening in the pigeon loft far above, allowed light to pour into the room, illuminating an incredible collection of doors, stained glass windows, banisters, fireplace mantels, wood carvings, and other interesting items. I stood in total silence for sometime, wondering if this was just a dream.

I had never seen such beautiful things in my life. Finally, I was jolted out of my thoughts, by the voice of my friend frantically calling to me, wondering if I was still alive.

Common sense told me to retrace my steps and leave the barn the same way that I had found it, and to replace the window covering so that others would not be able to get into it after me. But my friend was calling to me, and so I called that I was okay and that I would open a sliding door on the side of the barn, just above where he stood.

I knew that I shouldn't open that door, for something was telling me to leave right then before it was too late. I was torn, should I tell my friend that there was nothing to see, or should I let him in, and swear him to secrecy.

During my lifetime, I have found that no matter what you swear to, no matter how sincere you are when you swear to it, somehow you forget everything when you are talking to a good friend, and eventually you blab the whole thing.

Now, I am not saying that you shouldn't tell your good friends secrets. I am just saying, that if you do tell them your secrets, be prepared for them to share them with all of their good friends. After all, what is the point of a secret if you can't share it with a friend?

Well, I swore my friend to secrecy, I told him that he must never let any one know what he was about to see. We spat in our hands, and then pressed them against each other's, holding them tightly as we repeated the sacred oath, "May I die before I tell."

Three days later there was a line-up of friends to see all the treasures in that barn. I wasn't there because my parents grounded me once they found out that I had played hooky.

I thought that I had been very careful. I had written a note to the teacher, Miss McNab, telling her that I was very sick that day and couldn't come to school. I had spent a lot of time practicing my mother's handwriting, and was certain that Miss McCrab wouldn't know the difference. When I gave it to her that morning, she didn't say anything right away, so I thought that I was safe.

Later, during that class, when I had completely forgotten playing hooky, she came over to my desk and casually asked me who wrote the note. Without thinking, I said, " I did."

She then said, "Take this note to the principal."

As I walked up the hall to the principal's office, I wondered if I was really cut out for crime. It seemed that no matter how well I planned something; there was always something that screwed it up.

Old Mr. Wilson read the note, and then asked me if I deserved the strap. I thought about it. If I said no, he would probably call Miss McCrab to the office, and then we would have to debate the whole subject, and probably they'd both have a go at me. I knew that all the teachers stuck together, so I said, "Yes, I deserve it."

Over the years I did discover that when you did something wrong, the best thing to do, when found out, was to confess to the whole thing; that way you got it over with very quickly, and very likely with less pain.

Mr. Wilson looked at me quietly, his brown eye's twinkling, and then pulled the strap from his desk drawer. I made a mental note that one day I was going to get rid of every damn one of those things. He then said, *"Hold out your hand."* There was definitely something in his eye that said, *"Don't try any tricks."* So I didn't.

I took a deep breath and then held out my hand, expecting the worst. Mr. Wilson lifted his hand up to his shoulder height, and then let the strap fall gently onto my hand. He repeated this movement several times, and then said, "*Clifford, truth will always triumph."* I never forgot Mr. Wilson, and when he passed away I felt that I had truly lost a friend.

The following week I returned to the barn. The side door was wide open, and inside, every stain glass window lay smashed to bits on the floor. The glass was several inches thick on the floor. Large cut-glass emeralds and rubies lay everywhere, glass of green, pink, amber, yellow and every color of the rainbow lay in ruins at my feet. I walked among this carnage, picking up several rubies and emeralds as I shuffled through the rubble. What had once been a beautiful treasure now lay like a thousand shattered dreams. I swore that I would never cause, or allow the destruction of any object of beauty ever again. In later years I established an antique store, and spent many years restoring things to their former splendor.

That magnificent barn remained standing for many years, although completely empty, and I played there at every opportunity.

Class Photo 1946

Langham Court

The barn was situated close to an old private school, which had been converted to a small theatre and was known as *Langham Court Theatre*. I often played in the yard, imagining that one day I would become an actor and join the theatre group and perhaps act upon its stage. In later years I did indeed join the theatre, often performing on that very stage, even installing the first sloping floor in the auditorium.

At that time, a large Bing cherry tree stood at the front of the building. I had enjoyed the fruit of that tree many times during those years, and always looked forward to visiting it as soon as the cherries had ripened.

I patiently awaited the day that I could again enjoy the fruit of that wonderful tree, and when that day arrived, I hurried to the Langham Court yard intent on plunder. But there was a sign on the tree warning people not to eat the cherries, as they were poisoned. I could not believe my eyes, how could that delicious fruit be poisoned? After all, I had eaten from that tree many times, and never suffered more than a sore belly from overeating.

There was a man gardening at the side of the Theatre, so I asked him why they thought that the cherries were poisoned. He explained that the tree was situated on top of the Theatre septic tank and that the roots had penetrated it, sopping up all the nasty liquid in the tank.

As fate would have it, I had just recently read about plants and trees, and how they got their nourishment from the earth, and how manure often helped produce an abundant and delicious crop, particularly when used on strawberries. I figured that if manure was okay to use on strawberries, what was the problem using septic on cherries?

As soon as I returned home, I looked up the telephone number of the city health inspector and phoned him. During those years, officials would usually answer the phone themselves, and this was one of those occasions.

The inspector was a very nice man, and he listened to my story about the cherry tree and the septic tank and told me that as far as he was concerned those cherries would be just fine to eat, as a matter of fact they would probably be a whole lot better than any that one might find in a grocery store.

Well, that was good enough for me. I hurried back to that tree, and perching on one of the many branches, I ate my fill of the most delicious cherries I had ever eaten. I returned every day until every cherry was gone, of course I left the sign on the tree, so that anyone else, who might be tempted, would be aware of the possible danger from eating poisoned cherries.

On the last day there, the same man that had warned me about the tree, said," What are you doing eating those cherries when I told you that they were poisoned." I told him that I had phoned the Health Inspector, and he had assured me that they were alright to eat, and so I had been enjoying them every day for the past week.

The gardener was probably very upset that I had enjoyed so many cherries, and he had not even had one, because he said a bad word and left very quickly.

Camp Imadene Bible Camp

About that time in my life, a wonderful Lady by the name of Miss Munday made herself known to me. She was a Christian and had somehow heard about me and my friend Jack. She introduced herself to my mother and to Jack's mom as well, and asked if she might send Jack and me to a Christian Bible camp called 'Camp Imadene'

Our mothers were very proud ladies and did not like charity, but Miss Munday assured them that her church often sent boys to the camp during the summer time, and she would love to able to send us. Neither Jack, nor I had anything against charity, so we pleaded with our moms to let us go. They reluctantly gave their permission for Miss Munday, to send us to the camp, and we could hardly wait for the summer to arrive. All Jack and I talked about that winter was going to camp. Miss Munday suggested that we go to church, so that we could spiritually prepare ourselves for camp. We told her that we already went to church on Sundays, and were certainly full of spirit, but she had a different spirit in mind, and wanted us to go to her church. Well, our moms figured that one church was as good as another, so we started going to her church on Oak Bay Avenue.

While I was growing up in Fairfield, we seldom got to visit Oak Bay, because only rich people lived there, and my mother didn't want us associating with any snobs. The first Sunday that we went to *'Bethesda'*, on Oak Bay Avenue, I felt out of place. Nobody except Miss Munday said anything to me, and I thought that my mom had been right after all, snobs, really did live in Oak Bay. Miss Munday assured me that I was very welcome in that Church and that God knew I was there and was very pleased.

We continued going to that Church all winter, learning about the Spirit and the Bible, until summer arrived, and then we went off to Camp Imadene and had the time of our lives. The leaders in the camp were super and they spent a lot of time with us boys, teaching us the joys of Christian fellowship, and showing us the scriptures and teaching us about the life of Christ.

Jack and I both came to know the Lord as our personal Saviour while we were there, and vowed to spend the rest of our lives serving him.

For the next few weeks butter truly would not melt in my mouth. I did my best to spread the word of the Lord to all my family and friends, beseeching them to take the Lord as their own personal Saviour. My parents, and brothers and sisters, were wonderful, they listened to all my sermons with great patience, assuring me that they did indeed believe in the Lord and that they would cast all their sins away and try to live a life without sin.

Gradually, life in the *'Clarke'* house at 633 Cornwall Street, returned to normal; my sisters resumed dating boys, my older brothers continued their search for lively girls, and I stopped preaching to them. About that time, I overheard my brother Bob making plans with some of his friends, to go to the lower part of the Governor's estate, on Richardson Street, to smoke cigars. I had forgotten that a good Christian would never smoke a cigar, and begged him to let me go with him. Brother Bob was a very wise boy, he knew that he shouldn't let me go with him, but thought that it might be a good time to teach me about the utter foolishness of smoking cigars, and so he agreed to my request, allowing me to join him and his friends when they went through the secret opening in the fence behind the Government House. It was a secret place where older boys did sneaky things. Of course, Bob did not want me to actually smoke a cigar, because he knew that it would probably make me sick. My problem was that I was younger than Bob and didn't know that those stinky things were actually devised by the Devil to tempt rotten little kids like me to sin, so I begged him to allow me to puff on one. I promised that it would not make me ill, and, that I would never tell anyone what I had done.

After a few puffs on Satan's disgusting invention, I suddenly felt very giddy, my legs seemed to turn to rubber, my eyes lost their ability to focus on any one object, and my stomach suddenly rebelled, discharging all that was left of my breakfast and lunch.

Bob said that he knew he shouldn't have let me puff that cigar, and said that he would get heck if Mom or Dad found out about it. I assured him that no one would ever find out about this foolishness, and that I would never touch one of those horrible things again, even if I did live.

In the early stages of my life I discovered that when I did a stupid thing, I didn't want to tell anyone about it, and so I did not tell my Mom or Dad what I had done, even though they did ask me why my skin looked so yellow. I told them that it could have been all the cherries that I had eaten. Bob was sure pleased that I had kept our little secret, and always remembered what a great little guy I was.

Old Cars and Lots of Junk

My older brother Harold was my idol. He was very good looking and always wore nice clothes even when he worked underneath his car. I asked him one day why he wore his new suit when he was working in all that grease. He told me that he had a date and didn't have time to change into work clothes. I watched him while he rolled around under the car, listening to the strange language that he was using, remembering that it sounded just like the language that my Father used when he was working on his car. I thought that a person had to learn a whole lot of new words to become a mechanic.

My Dad used a tremendous number of strange words while working on his car, I eventually learned that most of them were swear words. I guess my brother Harold was using the same words that he had learned from Dad and I always thought that there were a lot of parts on a car starting with the F word.

My Dad tried to get me interested in mechanical work, but I just could not get excited about putting my hands into greasy motors or transmissions or gear boxes or almost any other part of a car, except the parts that didn't get you all dirty.

It seemed that every weekend my Dad had his car apart; he was either replacing the clutch, overhauling the transmission, grinding the valves, redoing the breaks, repairing the gas tank or turning back the mileage on the speedometer.

My brothers, Bob and Harold, loved working on cars and, took every opportunity to take some car apart. In those years a person could pick up an old Model T or a Model A for fifteen or twenty dollars, and then work on it, get it running and then sell it to some one who needed an inexpensive vehicle.

There was always some old junker in our yard and I didn't like it at all. There was so much clutter: old engines, transmissions, gear boxes, worn out tires, bumpers, radiator grills, most of them covered in so much grease that I developed a dislike for any greasy piece of old equipment, and eventually refused to ever touch anything resembling an old car part.

During my life I never worked on any vehicle I ever owned, and even though I spent one whole year in high school trying to learn the mechanical make-up of a motor vehicle, I managed to avoid any internal relationship with the automobile. However, I always enjoyed getting behind the wheel of any vehicle whether it was new, old or vintage, and managed to drive some of the greatest relics of that era.

When I was sixteen, Brother Bob owned a beautiful 1931 Chevrolet Coupe, his pride and joy. I had just secured a driver's license, after twice failing the drivers test, and was anxious to try my hand at driving. Bob was more than reluctant to let me set foot in his little gem, and managed to keep me at a distance for some time. However, I worked on him, pleading for the chance to drive the Chevy and to prove that I was a responsible, caring individual. Eventually I wore Bob's resolve down and I managed to get his permission to borrow that classic little car, and take it out for a drive with some of my friends.

I recall driving along Quadra Street and out into the country, which at that time was Royal Oak. The road was very bumpy with many potholes; although I managed to avoid many, there were some that somehow managed to inflict damage on the Chevrolet's undercarriage. Finally, the worst possible thing happened, there was a loud clunk, the car shook violently and, lurching from side to side, slowly came to a halt at the side of the road. I jumped out and immediately noted that the car was leaning heavily to one side. My heart sank. How would I ever explain this to Bob?

We walked back to the closest store, where I phoned Bob and gave him the sad news. There was complete silence on the other end of the phone and I was not sure whether Bob had fainted or not. Eventually, he said to wait by the car and he would come out to tow it home.

When Bob towed it to the garage to get it fixed, the mechanic said that he had never seen a broken frame like that before, and could not figure out why it had happened. I did mention that we had come upon some potholes, but I tried to avoid them wherever possible, and was sure that we hadn't actually hit one.

Once again Bob was magnificent, he never raised his voice in anger, or said any of the bad words that I had so often heard others use, and once again I vowed never to do anything to upset him again. Over the years Bob loaned me different cars that he owned, and I managed to avoid any nasty accidents, eventually gaining his complete confidence. Sometimes life plays a dirty trick on one, and allows the unthinkable to happen.

When I was older, I bought a beautiful 1941 Plymouth sedan from my brother in-law Wally. He had restored it to mint condition. After driving it for some time, he purchased a new car and decided that I should have his old Plymouth. He allowed me to pay for it over a number of months, with no interest. I loved that car and was very careful to keep it in good condition, always avoiding any road hazard that might harm it.

One day I stopped at a confectionery store on Esquimalt Road for a loaf of bread. The store was situated at the top of the hill at the corner of Esquimalt and Dominion Road. I parked in front of the store, carefully setting the handbrake on the old Plymouth, and then went inside to make my purchase.

When I returned, my car had disappeared. Somehow it had slipped its break and rolled down the hill, crashing into a rock wall at the bottom of the hill, and then rolling over. I was devastated. The policeman who attended the accident was very sympathetic and did not charge me with any thing.

Telephoning Wally, and telling him what I had done, was one of the most difficult things I ever had to do. Wally was of course very disappointed that his beautiful car had been wrecked, but he realized just how heart broken I was, and the following month he cancelled the debt.

During the War years almost everything was rationed including gasoline. Each car owner received a certain number of ration tickets, which allowed him to purchase a small amount of gasoline. If he was careful he could make this last until the next allotment day, if he was not careful he might run out.

My Father was very clever. He discovered that white gas, which people used for various things, including cleaning greasy car parts, also worked in motorcar engines. White Gas was not rationed, and could be acquired from hardware stores and gas stations. Practically everyone in our family was enlisted to make trips to the gas station or hardware store, to buy a gallon of this white gas. After many trips to get the gas, the proprietors began asking questions. We were all programmed to say that my Father cleaned a lot of engines and needed a steady supply of it.

I believe that many people had the same idea, because it soon became very difficult to get a steady supply, and before long my father had to drive all over the city, burning up gallons of the precious liquid in the process, searching for more white gas.

Eventually, it came to the attention of government officials that apparently, there were too many people in the business of cleaning car engines and so, by some mysterious government decree, white gas became hard to find and our search became even more difficult than it had been before. I always wondered if our insatiable thirst for White Gas prolonged the war in any way.

Rations Were a Way of Life

War was declared in 1939 when I was six years old and didn't understand what it was all about, but I soon found out that many items the family used or needed, quickly became difficult to acquire.

Gasoline was strictly rationed, and so were many other items such as butter, sugar, bananas, and foods from other countries. Even silk stockings were rationed and though I seldom wore them, it was a major inconvenience in our town and, I suppose, an inconvenience in almost any part of the world.

Over a period of time I came to understand that anyone who had a supply of silk stockings, particularly men, wielded a great influence over the ladies, and even though I really didn't understand the significance of the silk stocking, I developed more than a passing interest in them.

My interest in the hosiery business remained firm, because I had two older sisters that loved them and often said they would die for them, and so, silk stockings, as well as other rationed articles, were often the subject of conversation at the dinner table.

My father did not like my sisters wearing silk stockings; he thought that it was an "open invitation to boys", whatever that meant.

My mother was always arguing with Dad, saying that silk stockings were not the invention of the Devil, and furthermore they made a woman or young lady, feel wonderful. My Father asked how it was possible to feel good in stockings that generally had large runs in them.

It really didn't matter how much he argued against them, the girls still wore them whenever possible.

After hearing many arguments about silk stockings, I began to take an interest in what ladies wore on their legs and, as years passed, I noticed that most men like myself paid a whole a lot of attention to them as well.

Shortly after the war, silk was replaced by a wonderful synthetic fiber known as nylon, and soon after, nylon stockings became readily available to anyone, young or old. Unfortunately that nifty product, though welcomed worldwide by the entire female population, completely ruined the silk stocking black market, and ultimately ruled out any thoughts that I had regarding that enterprise.

The passing of the silk stocking era did not remain a concern for me for very long, because by that time in my life, most young ladies, were wearing ankle socks and loafers, commonly known as *Bobby Socks and Saddle Oxfords.* I never did know why they were called by those names; however, the socks never developed runs, and the Oxfords held up to the highly energetic 'Jive' dancing, then all the rage among the younger population.

There was a grocery store on the corner of Fairfield and Cook Street where I had a job as delivery boy. I was twelve years old, and holding down two jobs, the paper route in the early morning, and the delivery job after school and on Saturdays.

The Colonist did not print a paper on Mondays, but the delivery job did include deliveries on that day. Well, this helped develop my early habit of working seven days a week if necessary, a habit that I maintained my whole working life.

The grocery store would get their deliveries of canned and packaged goods on Monday morning and as soon as I arrived at the store I would start unloading the goods from their wooden crates.

First I would remove the nailed-on lids from the crates, and then remove the nails with a tool that was used as both a pry bar and a hammer, carefully saving each nail for future use. I would then take the goods and stock the shelves in the store. When the shelves were full I would gather items that customers had ordered, and then get them ready for delivery.

Before I left on my deliveries I would check the rat-trap in the basement for dead rats, and report the find to the store owner, who would then pay me five cents for each body. To this day I still get excited whenever I see a rat.

Once the floor was swept and the outdoor sidewalk cleaned, I would be free to make my deliveries. On a normal day I would be finished my deliveries by six o'clock, which enabled me to be home just about the time my mother put supper on the table.

Suppertime was a great event; my dad would take his place at the table and invite us to "dig in". Usually the whole family was there, and often someone that was passing by, possibly it was George, the milkman, or one of the other interesting characters that had been adopted by my mother.

The stories told by those colorful characters, kept us kids entertained for hours. 'Old George', as we knew him, had come from the old country as a fifteen year old after working as an apprentice in an iron works factory. Evidently he had to sleep under a workbench in the factory during his apprenticeship and had lived a completely miserable existence for several years.

George would spend hours telling us about his life in England, and about his long and painful trip across the Atlantic in steerage class, eventually landing in Halifax, and then continuing his journey by train to Vancouver and finally, Victoria. The cheap ticket cars on the trains in those days had no dining facilities, just little charcoal stoves for the passengers to cook on. George made friends with a family on the train, who had several kids, and had run out of food and were very hungry.

At one of the station stops, George went out into the fields with one of the boys and managed to snare a rabbit, which he turned over to the family so that they might have something to eat.

They cooked the rabbit and then ate it without giving George any. He never forgot that incident and related the story many times while visiting our home. We kids would listen wide eyed as he described the scene, and how he sat there yearning for a taste of that rabbit, watching it quickly disappear without so much as a morsel for himself.

'Old George' had many exciting tales to tell, and we were a very willing audience. He even invited us to his farm on Shelbourne Street where he raised cows and chickens, and sold eggs, meat birds, and milk from the cows, which he

An old time milk and produce wagon

delivered himself. He even allowed us to try our hand at milking a cow.

The most important thing one had to remember was that the cow would flick her tail around while being milked, and often that tail was laden with manure accumulated while she was out in the fields. The effect of a wet tail, laden with all sorts of unmentionable material, lashing out every few seconds, often wrapping itself around your head, and occasionally upsetting the milk pail, was an unforgettable and of course, sobering occurrence.
George often left the barn at these moments, obviously trying to control either his laughter or his tears. He eventually showed us how to tie the tail to the rail of the stall before beginning milking, which helped to make the whole experience an enjoyable one.

The milk was rich and creamy and had not been pasteurized, which made it even more delicious. George would strain out all the straw and hair and other materials that had fallen into the metal pails during milking, and pour the thick milk into glass bottles that he had collected on his route. The bottles were from different dairies in and around Victoria, and they were really works of art. Many became collector items and can still be found in antique stores.

At that time there were several dairies selling milk in our town, among them the *Northwestern Creamery, Palm Dairy, Royal Dairy, and Shepherds Dairy,* plus a number of small dairy farms such as the one owned by George.

Sometimes, when the temperature was below freezing, I would go out to the porch before anyone awoke, to see if the milk had frozen, and if it had, the cream would have risen up out of the bottle two or three inches. I would break the frozen cream off, replacing the bottle cap before mom caught me, and then eat the delicious cream stick.

Of course when the milk thawed, most of the cream would have disappeared, and my mother would ask me where it had gone. I never liked owning up to the fact that I had eaten it, so I would suggest that George probably hadn't filled the bottle before dropping it off on our porch. I often wondered if my mother thought that perhaps, I was not as perfect as she liked to believe, and maybe the unmelted butter in my mouth should be exchanged for soap.

It seemed to me that if you did something wrong, but managed to come up with a reasonable excuse for doing it, you would likely escape serious punishment, and perhaps even escape unscathed. The more I studied this subject, the more I realized that I was on to something that could be very beneficial in my life, and I resolved to try to live as close to perfection as was possible, making sure that if I did slip, however, I always had a good excuse at hand.

A Family Divided

As far back as I remember, my mom and dad fought over almost anything, including a few things that didn't even come close to being worthy of fighting over. When I was fourteen, I came to the very painful conclusion that they were truly not happy together.

I had always felt that they loved each other, and always hoped that they would find a way to happiness. But one day, mom told us that we were going to move to my uncle's house on Denman Street, near the Jubilee Hospital, and that we were going to do it while dad was at work.

When that fateful day arrived the whole family waited until dad had gone to work, and then began packing our belongings into cardboard boxes and moving them out to the porch ready for pickup. Within a short time my mother's two brothers arrived and they quickly moved our boxes and furniture into a large van. By noon we were on our way to Denman Street.

Years later, our next door neighbour told me that when my father came home that day, he had stopped outside the house for a minute, standing very still, and then had rushed up the back steps and thrown open the door, only to find empty rooms. I can only imagine the pain that he suffered that day. I never forgot that we had hurt him deeply, and I swore to myself that I would never do a thing like that again, as long as I lived.

Our life was very different, and while it was a relief that we did not have to see or hear our parents' endless fights, there was always the feeling that somehow this was not a happy ending, and that there should have been some way for them to settle their differences and remain together.

Over the years the two fighters did call a truce, and eventually dad started visiting, often joining us at the table for lunch or dinner, and it soon became the normal thing to have both of them at the table, sharing a meal, though seldom saying a word to each other.

I never gave up the romantic notion that they belonged together, and even though I tried many times to talk some sense into them, they never did reconcile. Many years later, when my father died, my mother was torn by grief, and until her death, at age ninety four, she never shared her life with another man.

The house we moved into, in my fourteenth year, was my dream home. It was three stories high with two turrets on the upper floor, one on each side of the building. The one on the right side of the house contained one very small room, which became my own private bedroom, and though it was only large enough to hold a single iron bed and a small dresser, it was a dream come true.

The turret on the other side of the building was part of a very large room that became both our living room and kitchen, the social center of our life. There was hardly a time that the room did not teem with the many members of my family, plus many characters that enriched our lives.

One huge room on the upper floor must have been originally designed as a bedroom, but it was converted to a bathroom, with one toilet and a large

Casa Grande

cast iron bathtub. It was the first bathroom I had ever seen with its own walk-in closet.

On the other side of the upper floor was another large room used as sleeping quarters for several of my siblings, a smallish room for my brothers and an unfinished attic space which doubled as a storage room and sleeping room for any homeless stray that my mother might bring home.

Several rooms on the floor below us accommodated my aunt and uncle, and my cousin Frank. There was also a room with a piano, that I tried to play but never managed to get the hang of it, plus a room for an old fellow, Sam.

Old Sam was one hundred years old and had twelve children by five or six different wives, and was one of the most colorful characters I ever met. We had many interesting conversations, and I was always very careful not to refer to him with a four letter word, although once I did ask him some very personal questions which caused him to jump at least three feet in the air, at the same time letting a loud fart.

I didn't know why he was so upset by my questions, although it may have been when I asked him if he was paying alimony to all his wives. I don't know why, but he was always very grumpy around me after that.

The house was very old, built on a brick foundation with a dirt floor and was very musty and damp. I always suspected that bodies were buried somewhere in that basement, and so I seldom went into it.

A wide curved stairway led up to the front porch, which was framed by several ornate pillars and 'CASA GRANDE' was carved over the doorway.

I often wondered if a Spanish Grandee had once lived there and perhaps lay buried under the ancient foundation. I considered digging around to find out, but decided that the whole place might collapse around me.

Beautiful carvings and ornate railings surrounded the windows and porches, while conical spindles and finials adorned the turrets. An enormous front hall was lined with rich wood panels, and ornate brackets supporting woodcarvings and picture rails. The stairway was very wide with deep treads leading up to a spacious landing that featured a large colorful window, similar to the ones that I had seen in that old barn years before.

Whenever I climbed that magnificent stairway I would imagine the days when ladies in long dresses and gentlemen with long mustaches and silk cravats walked upon them. I envisioned them leaving the house and climbing aboard a black carriage pulled by a pair of white horses decked out in shiny leather harness, perhaps on their way to a fancy ball at the Governor's mansion. That was the same estate that had the garden where I used to snitch daffodils and tulips and smoke stinky cigars.

Often I would climb to the shingled roof of the *Casa Grande*, and sit on one of the many peaks, and enjoy the rugged splendor that surrounded me, like a King in his castle. Sometimes I climbed to the top of the gigantic Sequoia tree on the east side of the building which soared over one hundred feet above the ground. From that lofty perch I would survey the castle below and dream of the life ahead.

At the front of the house was a large lawn that I treasured, and spent many hours cutting and maintaining. After living in a home that had absolutely no grass in the yard, this was a dream come true.

Cutting the lawn was no easy task, for the lawnmower was an old single reel mower that needed frequent sharpening; unfortunately I never did learn how to sharpen that mower. It took special tools, and all I had was an old rusty file that had outlived its usefulness. Consequently the job of lawn cutting became more and more difficult, and what was once fun became a real chore. Fortunately my brother Frank still obeyed my commands, and soon took over the job, although somewhat reluctantly.

Eventually the yard began to show signs of neglect, but nobody really noticed or cared because that is how it looked before we moved there and, as I was to learn over the years, people seldom appreciate something that is free.

Going Into Business

When we moved to the *'Casa'*, I quickly scouted out the neighborhood for potential friends, and was pleased to find several likely candidates. One of the boys I met enjoyed raising guinea pigs and had several of the little rat-like creatures.

I immediately took a liking to the furry little beasts and soon acquired some of my own, which multiplied very quickly to twenty something animals.

When I discovered how easy it was to raise them, I figured out that I could make some extra pocket money by raising and selling them to pet stores for a dollar each. This worked very well for me, and I soon had several cages in the back yard where I bred and raised the little rodents.

My job at the Colonist newspaper as a delivery boy helped finance the venture and helped me with other day-to-day expenses. It did not occur to me that it was anything but natural that a boy of fourteen should earn his own pocket money, after all I was not born with a silver spoon in my mouth and, in reality, if I didn't earn my own money, it was very likely that I would have gone without the little luxuries.

The rodent business, while not hugely profitable, did allow me to put aside a little nest egg to launch my next venture, rabbit farming. I thought that guinea pigs multiplied very quickly, but to my surprise, rabbits broke all the records of reproduction, and I soon needed other cages.

Eventually I realized that though it might be easy to raise rabbits, it was no easy task to sell them, and I found I had to supplement the operation with funds from the paper route. It soon became apparent that I would need to increase my income if I was to keep the sex crazed little critters well fed.

My next step came a short time later when I saw a sign in the window of Gibson's bowling alley on Yates Street. Evidently they needed a pin-setter, and as I had nothing better to do after school and on weekends. I applied for the job. The manager of the bowling alley was delighted and so, the next weekend, I started my career setting pins.

Setting pins was an exciting way to make pocket money. As soon as a bowler knocked the pins down, the setter would jump into the pit and reset the pins, pick up the balls, and then get out of the way as fast as possible before the bowler launched his next projectile.

Normally a setter had to attend to two alleys and on the odd occasion three alleys. When in charge of three alleys, the pin-setter would have to move at the speed of light if he valued his life, for he faced three bowlers that might have one purpose in life, to maim as many setters as possible before the game ended.

Sometimes the setter was not as fast as the bowler, and he would face the daunting experience of having to dodge one rock hard ball after another, as they hurtled down the waxed lane at the speed of sound. Often the approaching ball would send one of the pins flying into the next pit, catching the setter before he had time to reach safety.

I quickly discovered that the main reason that the bowling alley needed many setters was because the mortality rate exceeded that of any known industry. After a very short time I decided that those maniacal bowlers were getting extra points for every kid they maimed, and I began to develop ways of getting even with them.

When a setter picked up the balls from the pit, he would place them on a grooved channel that ran back to the bowling station, and gently send them on their way. However, I soon discovered that with an extra strong push, they would hurtle back to the offending bowler with incredible speed, often jumping out of the groove at the moment of impact with the other balls, and, with any luck, give the offending bowler a taste of his own medicine. I quickly became the object of retaliation, and the most fearsome bowlers would often be assigned my alleys.

Eventually I began to believe that pin-setters were worth a lot more than they were being paid and so, one night, I organized a work slow down. When the bowlers saw that we were deliberately slowing down, they started shouting at us, but we started to go even slower, finally coming to a stand still.

For the first time in my life I beheld a mob of angry people, most of whom seemed to be focusing their blood shot eyes on me and, though I craved the lime-light, I rapidly lost my enthusiasm for their attention.

Finally, some of the bowlers marched down the alleys, first scaring the dickens out of us, and then setting their own pins, completely ignoring the now subdued strikers. The other bowlers cheered them on.

The setters, now wholly subdued, began looking at me as an object of scorn. Then the manager came down and confronted us with the ultimatum, "Get back to work, or leave the building."

The other boys returned to the alleys, and then the manager suggested that I should leave the building as I was obviously not satisfied with the job. That was the first time that I was fired, and it was not a pleasant experience. I believe that it was at that time that I developed an intense distaste for strikes, and from that moment on I never liked the word, 'Strike', and always avoided anything to do with labour unrest.

One week before this regrettable night that ended up costing me my job I had purchased my first three-speed bicycle. It was a beauty, and though second hand, was my pride and joy. I had looked forward to owning a 'three speed' for as long as I could remember, for it would make my paper delivery job so much easier and faster.

That week was like a dream. Time flew by while I was delivering my papers on the 'three speed', and the ride to school was pure joy. There was never a prouder boy than myself when I rode that bike.

When I left the bowling alley, after being fired, I returned to the place I left my bike, but it was gone. I searched for it, down back alleys, in every conceivable place, but no bike. Finally, realizing that I had seen the bike for the last time, I sat down on the sidewalk and cried my eyes out.

The next day I pumped the tires on my ancient, single speed bike, and once more delivered papers on the poor old thing. I never again possessed a three-speed bike.

Girls A Hard Learned Lesson

My life on Denman Street was more or less happy. There was a beautiful girl, Elaine who lived three houses down. She reminded me of Elizabeth Taylor, and I fell madly in love.

Every day I would go out of my way to talk to Elaine, offering to carry her books or give her a ride to school on my antique bike. Once I even managed to dance with her at a lunchtime dance at Victoria High, and it was pure joy.

I was involved in boxing at school, and I did my best to impress Elaine with my prowess. Eventually I won my school's welter-weight division and I was on cloud nine. But, my joy came to a sudden end, for I discovered that Elaine had fallen in love with some guy that had just moved up from California. Even though he was much better looking than I was, and was able to twirl a rope as well as any cowboy, I felt terribly let down.

It was at that sad moment that I met Nadia. She lived on the next street over and where Elaine was petit and demure, Nadia was quite large and a little gruff, but as I was suffering in that awful state of rejection, and willing to settle for any type of friendship, I went for her like a ton of bricks. Before long I was visiting her at every opportunity, before school, after school, before lunch, after lunch, on Saturdays and Sundays. Life was good.

Nadia had an uncle who shingled roofs and was very busy and needed a helper, so I offered to work for him. The work was very hard, but I was now fifteen and fairly strong, so I managed very well. I carried heavy bundles of shingles up to the roofs, some two and three stories above the ground, tore old shingles from roofs, cleaned up the mess when the shingles were removed and did any other job that he asked. He taught me how to lay the asphalt shingles, which he purchased from a roofing plant on the inner harbour.

I worked all that hot summer, happy to be helping Nadia's uncle, even though he was only paying me twenty-five cents an hour, very low pay for such heavy work. However, I was in love and it all seemed worthwhile.

At the end of summer, just before I returned to school, Nadia informed me that I was a pain in the ass, and that she often joked with her family, even her uncle, about how I never let her alone. She was fed up with me coming over, and she could hardly wait to see the back end of me.

This revelation hit me like baseball bat, and I felt betrayed. After all I had worked very hard for her uncle at unbelievably low wages the entire summer, just because I loved her. Being twice rejected in a few months left me feeling I was just not cut out for love, and so I decided that from then on I was not going to be taken in by any sweet talking girl.

That state of unrequited love slowed me down for a while, but before long I once again fell madly in love with another delightful girl. From that day on I never faltered in my appreciation of the warmth and sensitivity of the opposite sex.

During that period of unrequited love, I discovered muskrats in Bowker Creek. They looked similar to the common everyday rat, but their tail was longer and broader and their features were more endearing.

The fur on this larger than rat creature was prized by many furriers because of its brilliant sheen and silken quality. Sensing a new business opportunity, I acquired several leg hold traps from an old family friend, and set them in the creek. I was soon rewarded with my first catch.

I had read books on skinning and tanning, and had already skinned and stretched a few rabbits, plus a guinea pig that passed away after becoming one of my favorite pets. So skinning and tanning the muskrat was an easy task. I quickly applied myself to the task of acquiring more skins. I would have tanned my mothers Persian cat as well, but she put her foot down and warned me not to get any ideas about the family pets.

My interest in furs began the year before, while I was attending Central Junior High School, at the corner of Fort and Fernwood Street. During my year at that tired old school, I studied fur farming as a class project, with the idea that it could possibly result in a future career for me.

My teacher, who nurtured a certain dislike for me, due to a few episodes of my unruly conduct and naughty tricks, considered me a lost cause and probably never entertained the idea that I might come up with any credible idea for my future, probably assuming that I was destined to end up in reform school.

In an attempt to prove to him that I was not a complete waste of time, however, I researched fur farming and animal husbandry with all my energy, and soon discovered I had a great passion for fur bearing animals, and particularly for the silver fox, which had been developed by breeding the red fox to the gray fox. Both were natives of the far north.

This cross breeding produced an animal of unsurpassed beauty, which possessed a magnificent coat of long silver hair, highly valued by furriers everywhere.

During my research I contacted a family in northern B.C. that was raising the beautiful animals, and found that they were delighted that I was interested in the fur industry. They immediately sent me a large package of information regarding the fur farming business.

For several months I immersed myself in catching and skinning animals and tanning the hides. The beautiful muskrat pelt was a prized addition to my rabbit skin collection and I proudly displayed the pelts in the piano room at Casa Grande.

When I presented my essay on fur farming to my grade nine teacher, he could hardly believe that I had done it myself, and asked me to tell the class all about the process of raising the animals and also how to skin and tan them. When I stood in front of the class that day, I was petrified, because up till that time the teacher had never shown any interest in me and quite often derided me in front of the other students.

Usually I would play jokes on kids and try to get them to laugh at my antics; however, this time the tables were turned and I had to tell them a straight story, hopefully keeping their interest and attention long enough to satisfy the teacher's doubts.

Once I overcame my fear, I launched into my story about fur farming and my dream of one day having my own farm, and all about the muskrats that I discovered in Bowker creek. I told of the joy of holding a beautiful fresh pelt in my hands, feeling the soft silky fur, knowing that it would continue to give pleasure to people for a long, long time.

The time flew by, and I kept talking till the bell rang. The kids gave me a standing ovation, the teacher hugged me, and we both wept. From that day on I tried my best to apply myself to school and, while never becoming a brilliant student, I did enjoy my remaining two years in school.

Though fairly strong, I was rather a skinny kid, and so I ate every thing I could lay my hands on, with the exception of muskrat, hoping to put some meat on my bones. My paper delivery route included a stop in the kitchen of the Jubilee Hospital in the old wing of the hospital, the same building where I was born.

Each day I would deliver the newspaper to the cook, and he would allow me to eat my fill of bacon, eggs, toast, sausage, milk, peaches, and anything else in the walk-in fridge that caught my fancy. Breakfast usually included five or six fried or boiled eggs, half a dozen strips of bacon, three or four sausages, a stack of toast, followed by a huge bowl of peaches and cream, and several glasses of milk.

The cook never ceased to marvel at my capacity and perseverance, even suggesting that perhaps I should leave something for the hospital patients. Of course I did my best to keep on his good side so I might continue the daily ritual of gorging myself. However, I eventually lost my place at the table by making a grave mistake, a mistake that cost me dearly and gave me one more painful lesson in life.

One day I broke the cardinal rule of never telling anyone but your best friends about good fortune that comes into your life. A fellow delivery boy had heard that I had breakfast at the hospital each day, and asked me if this was so. Not wanting to lie, but wishing that I had, I told him that I did indeed stop for a snack each day, but it was a very modest amount and due to certain restrictions there was only room for one paper boy in the kitchen.

This particular boy was very charming and friendly, and soon won my confidence and friendship; however, I soon discovered that his main interest was not necessarily becoming my friend, but rather gaining access to the larder of that kitchen.

Not fully understanding the art of subtlety or machination on the part of others, I allowed him to join me one morning when I made my daily visit, and then introduced him to the cook. This proved to be a major blunder, because he soon won the cooks friendship, overwhelming him with his charm and personality, and soon displaced me.

I did my best to retain my place at the table, but the cook, probably admiring him for his self control and willpower when faced with all that food, gave me the old heave-ho.

For months I would weep each time I passed the hospital, for in spite of the abundance of food in that kitchen, I truly missed the cook and his helpers. However, I eventually accepted my fate and relegated the sad episode to a place in the far back of my brain, and vowed to be more careful about my friendships in the future.

Learning to Drive

About that time I became interested in cars, not working on them but rather driving them. My brother Harold, seven year older than I was, always had a car either under repair or in reasonable driving condition.

He was an inspiration to me. He was very good looking and even though he had a girlfriend he tried very hard to find the time to teach me to drive. Although this proved to be a major task he valiantly kept trying, no matter the setbacks.

Sometimes Harold would drive me out into the country, where it would be difficult for me to do much damage, and show me the general rules of the road.

After I had mastered the brake, the clutch, and the accelerator, remembering exactly when to take my foot off the accelerator and place it on either the clutch or the brake, he allowed me to try my hand at the wheel. This step was a little difficult, because his old Essex had certain mechanical shortcomings. Probably the worst flaw was in the steering column, because sometimes, usually while the car was in motion, the steering wheel would become loose and fall off.

The first time that this happened while I was on the road almost brought my driver-learning program to an end. The wheel came loose and fell onto the floor, and I was so terrified I didn't know what to do. In fact I almost jumped out of the door. The only thing that stopped me was that the door wouldn't open. Of course I should have known that the door wouldn't open, because I had to crawl through the window to get into the driver's seat.

There were other hazards as well, but my brother Harold kept a close eye on things and he was able to overcome most of the problems before they became catastrophic.

One other critical problem was the braking system. While the brakes did slow the vehicle down, they did not actually bring it to a halt. This was only accomplished when someone pulled on the hand brake at precisely the same time that the foot brake was applied.

The driver normally did this; however, in my case, it took all of my energy and concentration to step, or stand, as it was in this instance, on the brake pedal when trying to slow the car down, while trying to keep the wheel on the steering shaft, where it belonged, and all the while, fighting the urge to jump out of the open window, wheel and all.

When the wheel came off, Harold was always ready, and would calmly reach down, pick it up, and easily return it to the shaft of the steering column. The Essex usually didn't alter course during this free flight mode because the steering mechanism was very stiff, and it took almost super human strength to turn it in the first place.

The old Essex remained in a state of uncertainty for as long as Harold owned it, however, after several hair-raising incidents, he did find the correct nut which held the wheel onto the steering column and managed to take most of the terror out of my driver learning program.

Eventually, after many near disasters, I became skilled at handling a car under difficult and trying circumstances, probably the worst difficulties one might ever encounter while at the wheel of a car.

After many months of patience and understanding my brother Harold drove me to the motor vehicle building on Menzies Street, to pick up the manual to study for my driving test.

My theory was that I would study the manual for a short while, get my license, and then borrow brother Harold's car whenever I needed it. However, Harold had a theory of his own. If he helped me get my license, he was off the hook and he could then resume his own happy life with a minimum of bother from me.

By the time we returned home I had read that little book from cover to cover. When I thought I had all the questions down pat, I badgered Harold to take me for my learners test. Unfortunately he always seemed to be too busy to take me to the Motor Vehicle Office, but finally, after months of badgering, pleading, sniveling, and whining, he consented, and one memorable day he drove me down to that old brick building on Menzies Street.

When I was ushered into the room where the test was to take place, something came over me. My hands became clammy. My tongue became very dry. I felt as if the room was turning and when the test paper was put before me I had difficulty focusing my eyes on the printed page.

Eventually my eyes became focused, the room stopped spinning, and I was able to begin writing that test. I'm not sure where they got those questions, but I swear that virtually none of them came from that little book. At least I couldn't remember reading any of them.

The gentleman that gave me the written test studied my answers for a short while, and suggested that I wait a while before I took the road test, but I assured him that I was okay and ready for it.

When we walked out to the old green Essex, the man stood, looking at the beast, and muttered something under his breath that I didn't quite understand, and then reluctantly pulled on the door handle of the car. After a few tugs, the door opened and he carefully climbed into the front seat

While he was opening the door, I reached in through the open window, on the driver's side, and picked up the crank that we used to start the car. Happily the old brute started on the first turn of the crank, which in itself was an unusual event. I then jumped into the driver's seat, through the open window, ready and willing to give the gentleman the ride of his life.

My brother had parked the car in a space that would allow me to drive away without too much trouble; however, another driver had parked his vehicle right in front of our car leaving me with a minimum amount of space.

As I stated before, the brakes did not function as normal brakes should, and when I tried to put the transmission into gear, which was not an easy task at the best of times, as the clutch was badly worn, the whole vehicle shuddered, and the gearbox produced a loud grinding sound.

When I finally accomplished the gear change, the car jumped forward just far enough to bounce the vehicle in front ahead a few inches. After three such starts, the car in front had moved ahead a foot or so, which made it a little easier to get out of our space, and finally we were on the road ready for the test.

The gentleman sat very still as we started out, although, in retrospect, I realize that his stillness was probably a state of quiet panic, possibly even desperation. However, I was fully confident and ready for the test, so I stepped on the accelerator, and hung on as the old thing lurched forward. As we gained momentum, I managed to shift gears with a minimum of grinding, finally settling into third gear.

During this part of our journey the man never said a word, and I imagined that everything was going rather well, but I was very wrong.

I had read in the instruction book, that one should always gear down when turning corners, as it slowed the vehicle enough to ensure safe turns. However, I forgot that part of the book, and while making every effort to slow down when I felt the need, I did turn corners a little faster than I should have.

We traveled down Menzies Street and then turned left onto Superior and drove down to Beacon Hill Park, where I spent a lot of my time trying to catch ducks, back when I was a little kid, and then right onto Douglas Street. In those days there were very few stop signs, which was a blessing as I had not yet fully mastered them yet.

Evidently my stops were very similar to the famed ' California stop', which had become very popular with many drivers. Unfortunately the government agent soon brought to my attention that he did not agree with this system of 'slow and go'.

As I approached the stop sign at the intersection of Douglas and Dallas Roads, I stood on the brake pedal just long enough to slow the Essex down a little. Unfortunately I miscalculated the distance and ended up on the grassy slope leading down to the beach a hundred feet below. I then forced the car into reverse, catapulting the old beast back onto the road.

The gentleman made some strange rattling noises in his throat, and asked me to stop the vehicle, which I did, right in the middle of the road. When he recovered his voice, he suggested that we return to the testing station as quickly and safely as possible.

I said that I wasn't frightened and that I would like to continue the drive, however he said that he was not feeling very well and that we should return to the station. So I carefully turned the Essex around and reluctantly returned to the station.

Before I managed to bring the car to a complete stop in front of the Motor Vehicle Office, the man flung open the door and departed without a word. I quickly followed him into the station hoping against hope that I had not failed the test.

When I finally caught up to him, he turned and smiled at me although, in retrospect, I don't think that it was actually a joyful smile. He suggested that it would be better for me to come again, some time in the future, and give it another try and perhaps by that time another vehicle might be available.

One day when I was with my brother in his car, he stopped at a friend's place for a visit. I sat in the car cooling my heels. As I whiled away the time, I moved into the driver's seat and began playing with the gear shift, and in general fooling around, putting it into and out of gear.

When I became bored with this play I started tinkering with the different knobs and gadgets on the dashboard. The cigarette lighter, a new gadget that my brother had just installed, caught my attention. I pushed it in and watched till it popped out glowing and red hot.

I found this intriguing and wondered if it would burn a hole in anything other than the end of a cigarette, so I tried it on a piece of paper from the glove box and found that it burned a perfectly round hole in the document.

After burning several holes in the car's registration papers, I turned my attention to the dash itself and was amazed that it could even melt the hard metallic finish. But not wanting to upset my brother, I stopped before completely ruining the dashboard.

The idea that this little round gadget could burn holes in almost anything was fascinating and I wondered that if it was held in a little longer, would it get it hot enough to burn a hole in a rubber tire.

Unfortunately, when I held it in, it became so hot that smoke started pouring out of the dashboard, and I panicked and tried putting the fire out with my brother's wool sweater.

I almost had the fire under control when my brother returned to the car. He yelled and reached under the dash and ripped out some wires, which quickly stopped the smoke, but unfortunately didn't stop the smoke that was coming out of the top of his head. He was so mad I got out of the car and walked home.

After that somewhat disastrous event, brother Harold became even more reluctant to allow me behind the wheel of his motor vehicle, and many months passed before I was given another opportunity to drive, and even then, it wasn't in brother Harold's car.

The paper route manager, who was in charge of the paper pick up station, was a really great guy and he had a new 1948 Chrysler. He was very proud of that car and didn't like it when I started to show an interest in the beauty. Of course I asked him to show me how to drive it, but he was even more reluctant than my brother to let me behind the wheel.

However, I used all my charm and persuasive powers to win him over. I assured him that I genuinely loved the vehicle, and that I would care for it as if it were my own.

Eventually I gained his trust and love and then, one day, he allowed me to sit in the driver's seat, though it was obvious that he was very concerned that I would somehow damage the car. Of course, he had absolutely nothing to worry about, as far as I was concerned, for I had truly learned my lesson and was more than careful whenever I sat in that luxury vehicle. Over a period of three or four months, he came to look upon me as a favorite brother, and one day he asked me if I would like to drive the car.

During my entire fifteen years I had never wanted anything as much as I wanted to drive that car. That day arrived, and as I sat in the driver's seat preparing myself, I truly believed that God himself was with me.

I eased the Chrysler into gear, gently touched the accelerator and slowly it began to move as though pushed by the wind. My friend was smiling, and I was almost overcome with the joy of it all. We drove around in the car for a very long time but to me it seemed to be such a short while. At last he suggested that we should be getting back, so I retraced the route we had taken, and brought the vehicle safely back home, completely unscathed.

When I turned sixteen, my friend drove me to the Motor Vehicle Branch, parked the Chrysler outside, and confidently passed me the keys. Strangely enough, the same tester that I had those many months before, called me into the testing room. Fortunately he did not remember me and I wrote the test again, answering every question correctly.

The road test was like something out of a dream. The car performed flawlessly, I came to a full stop at every stop sign. I remembered all my hand signals. I backed in and out of a parking space. I reversed along a road without running into anything. I parked at the top of a hill, remembering to turn the wheels into the curb and also remembering to set the hand brake. I even remembered to thank him when he said, " Well done". All in all, I performed brilliantly. That day was the proudest day of my life, for now I was an accredited, licensed, driver.

Riding and Running

The house that we lived in at 1712 Denman Street was a mile or so from Victoria High. Everyday, depending on the weather, I would either ride my bicycle or run those many blocks to the school.

Each day I would try to improve my traveling time, by using different streets to find the fastest route. I eventually decided on a certain course, and thereafter did my best to improve my performance.

My bicycle had a single gear axle, which was just fine when you were pedaling on a level surface or possibly downhill, but when you had to go uphill it was a killer. I would stand on one of the pedals, using all my strength to exert enough pressure to keep the wheels turning, but sometimes the downward force of the leg even with the full weight of my slim body, wasn't enough and the bike would slowly grind to a halt. Then I would be forced to make the crucial decision to get off the damn thing before it fell over.

Fortunately I had ridden such a bicycle for the better part of my life, and was fairly successful in forcing the reluctant pedal machine up most hills. There were certain hills that even I could not master, however, and at those frustrating times I would often resort to using my father's mechanical vocabulary when forced to get off that damn contraption.

As the school year slipped away, the residents, on that hill had witnessed my frustrated exertions many times, and would await my appearance, and either make wagers as to how far I would manage to ascend the hill without dismounting, or quickly lock up their young children to shield them from my highly descriptive and colorful language.

When the weather was favorable, I would leave my bicycle at home and run to school in the morning, run home for lunch and then run back to school hoping to reach it before the one o'clock bell sounded.

After school I would sometimes run down to the bowling alley on Yates Street to make a buck before it was time to return home, and if I successful, I would take a bus back to my castle, the 'Casa Grande', on Denman Street.

Running back and forth to school, and running a mile or two after school, was very enjoyable for me and helped develop a strong heart which increased my physical strength and endurance, and ultimately gave me the stamina to work very hard all my life.

At the beginning of each school year I usually purchased a new pair of shoes, which made running a great pleasure, but as the year wore on so did the shoes, and by mid-year they had just about given up the ghost. The first thing to go were the soles, which usually developed small holes that gradually enlarged, finally becoming as large as silver dollars.

Of course there were certain things one could do with holey shoes, either throw them away in the garbage, or try to patch the holes hoping to increase the shoes life span. There were several ways to patch holey shoes. One way involved using the patching kit that every boy who had a bike always kept on hand. This worked very well for a short while, but eventually the rubber patches wore through and allowed moisture to enter the shoe, particularly on a rainy day.

Eventually the constant friction between the soggy foot and the pavement caused even larger holes in the socks, making life increasingly miserable. However, holy shoes were not my only form of torture. It seems that old shoes are inclined to sink even lower, often developing more devilish ideas to further complicate life.

The 'Fall Dance' was the highlight of the year; it offered the opportunity to invite the 'Lady' of your dreams to help you trip the light fantastic.

For several months I had been looking forward to inviting a certain young lady to the dance. But every time I saw her she was surrounded by friends, and I was not fully prepared to take a chance of being publicly rejected.

Two weeks before the dance I made the decision to approach her, no matter the outcome. Unfortunately the best laid plans of mice and men often get screwed up. On the day that I had planned my approach, the sole of my shoe came adrift, separating from the body of the shoe like a partially peeled banana.

Usually an event like this would not be life shattering; however, the sole belonged to the only pair of shoes I owned and, as I was flat broke, there was no possibility of acquiring another pair before the dance.

The only remedy that my feeble brain was able to formulate entailed wrapping butcher twine around the shoe, hopefully securing the sole. Unfortunately butcher twine was not designed for this purpose and either slipped down to the heel, or wore through and broke.

After several futile attempts failed, I decided that I could not possibly

Victoria High School

invite my dream-lady to the dance; therefore I would avoid all contact with her. Of course fate would not allow this painless form of escape.

That very day I had lashed the flapping sole to the body of my shoe. I knew by experience that the twine would not hold the sole in place for long, so I walked the hallowed halls of our school carefully and gently, avoiding any place that I might encounter the lady of my dreams.

As I carefully shuffled along the hallway, past the general office, the door opened and my 'Lady' suddenly appeared, walking directly toward me. There was no place to hide, nowhere to run to; I was trapped, flapping sole and all, I desperately wanted to disappear into a hole in the floor but no such luck, she saw me and smiled.

I will never forget that smile, meant for me and only me. For months I had dreamed of an opportunity to talk with her with no one else around, I could even ask her to go to the dance with me.

She was even more beautiful than I had imagined. I wanted to hold her in my arms, tell her how wonderful she was, tell her that every time I looked at her my heart skipped a beat, and tell her that I would be honored if she would go to the dance with me. Before I had the chance to ask her, she asked me! I was elated, I could not think of anything to say.

Suddenly I remembered the sole of my shoe, and that no matter how careful I was, the damn thing would start flapping the minute I started moving. I could not go to the dance, I would be the laughing stock of the whole school, she would laugh at me, everyone would laugh at me, there was nothing that I could do, so I told her that I was busy that night. Thereafter she was very cool toward me and I never had another opportunity to invite her to a dance or even speak with her. Eventually I earned enough money to buy another pair of shoes and once again enjoyed going to dances.

There were several halls in Victoria where a young person could dance. They included the 'Newstead Hall' on Fort, the 'YMCA' on Blanshard, the 'CCF Hall' on Douglas, the 'Eagles Hall' in James Bay, the 'Golden Ballroom' on Broad Street, and a number of other places including school gymnasiums. Every week there were at least one or two dances, and I took advantage of every opportunity to 'Go dancing'.

I developed a love of dancing that stayed with me throughout my life and I attended dances at every opportunity, though often enduring the bleak reality that shoes do wear out, for over the next two years I missed several dances due to the lack of proper shoes.

The Girl of my Dreams

One of my all-time favorite dance halls was the "Newstead' on Fort. I went there at least once a week, honing my skills, overcoming my fear of rejection, and meeting beautiful young ladies. On one of my weekly Wednesday night dances I met Barbara, a girl who changed my life forever.I had just turned sixteen and she was fifteen. She was a former Victoria Majorette, wore brown saddle oxfords, white ankle socks, a pleated skirt and blouse and she danced like a dream, and best of all, she attended Vic High. During the previous few months I had not run across her at school or even seen her at the school dance, so it was a wonderful thing to suddenly become aware of such a beautiful young lady. I took every opportunity to seek her out at school, watching for her at lunch time, searching for her in the hallways, using every excuse to run into her after school.

Early the next Wednesday, I arrived at the Newstead hall hoping to see her again, not knowing that she also would arrive early hoping to see me. When I set eyes on her my heart stopped for a moment. She immediately saw me and quickly walked over to where I was sitting and said hello. From that moment on we were inseparable.

Over the next year Barb and I were together as often as possible. We went hiking, dancing, and met after school almost everyday. When she got out of school before me, she would wait for me by the fence, near the 'Technical building' where I took carpentry.

If I got out before her, I would watch for her, and then we would walk downtown or catch a bus to her home in Vic West. Sometimes I was able to borrow a car from my brother and take her out in style, often stopping at the drive-in restaurant The Monterey by the round about at the junction of Hillside and Douglas Streets.

In the summer we often swam at Thetis Lake, a magical place. We spent many wonderful hours walking the trails around the lake, holding hands and dreaming of the life before us. The year flew by and our love increased dramatically, and then one day Barb told me that I was going to become a father.

When I was very young I always dreamed of getting married and spending my life with the one I loved, and I could barely wait until that wonderful day arrived. Little did I know that momentous day would arrive just after my eighteenth birthday.

After a period of trepidation, I took the bull by the horns and informed my mother and Barb's mother and father that they were in for a pleasant surprise. At first they did not seem very happy at the prospect of becoming grandparents so soon, never mind within a few months. Once the shock wore off, however, and they had partially recovered from the mortification of the whole thing, they sprang into action and began planning our wedding.

In those early days there was not much money to spend on a lavish wedding, and so a great deal of thought went into the arrangements, and how best to pull it off without piling up a lot of expense. Eventually we decided that it would take place in Barbara's home.

It is very surprising how quickly a mother can spring into action once her daughter announces wedding plans. My future mother-in-law moved so quickly my head began to spin. I don't know why, but I somehow fostered the peculiar notion that things would move slowly, and allow me time to catch my breath. However, once the wheels of matrimony were set in motion there was no stopping her.

I found that the best thing to do was to sit quietly, occasionally nodding my head in agreement, as it rapidly became obvious that whatever ideas I might proffer, would be looked upon as completely irrelevant or even fatuous. For example, when I suggested we elope, I felt a certain amount of hostility, and then and there I resolved not to cause any more embarrassment to my blushing bride.

Finally we decided on April 28, 1951, the church was booked, the invitations mailed out and Barb and I joyously contemplated our future together.

It was surprising how many friends or relatives suggested that we were really too young. Even my own mother suggested that we wait a little while, possibly a few years. However Barb and I knew we would be okay, and that we had everything we needed to succeed. We could get by, even though she did not know how to cook anything other than hamburger.

Once the plans for our wedding were well on their way, the question of a honeymoon came up. A friend's parents owned a very rustic, summer cottage on Shawnigan Lake, and as they were aware that we were practically penniless, offered it to us at no charge. Barb and I thought that it would be a wonderful place to honeymoon and thanked them for their kindness.

When we ran the idea of a country honeymoon past the members of the planning board we met a great deal of resistance. Most felt that the location was too remote and the facilities were not exactly as they had hoped for. One of Barb's aunts, a colorful, wonderful, and caring lady, suggested that the cabin was definitely an unworthy place for our honeymoon and that we would be well advised to book a room in the Empress for a night or two instead.

I pointed out that Shawnigan was a wonderful place to spend a honeymoon, and though the cabin had no running water, or electricity, it did have a very nice wood stove to cook on, and as I had grown up in a house that had few modern conveniences, this cabin would be just fine.

During my formative years I had developed a rebellious resistance to most variations of authority, and while I quietly went along with the wedding

Our Wedding

plans, I had no intention of having anyone tell me where I was going to honeymoon, and I let my feelings be known to one and all. This caused great suffering among the board members, some of whom released their frustrations with an out-pouring of tears and wails.

There were of course some who stood behind our decision. This minority included Barb's father Barry, a smallish man with the heart of a lion. He stated the fact that, if we were old enough to get married, we were certainly old enough to decide where we would go on our honeymoon.

In my lifetime if a friend, a companion, a teacher or a father-in-law stood up for me, I would do everything possible to repay them for their support. When Barry stood up for me, I knew that he was okay, and from that moment on I always did my best to show my appreciation for his understanding and confidence in me.

The wedding day arrived. I wore my best and only suit, gray herringbone, and I think it was wool. My best man wore his blue, go-to-Sunday-school suit. Barb was a dream in her white dress, and her beautiful bridesmaid a vision in pink. Altogether it was a fabulous wedding party.

My brother Bob generously loaned me his 1942 Dodge sedan for our honeymoon. We then made the long trek over the Malahat to Shawnigan Lake.

The rustic cabin was even more rustic than either of us had imagined. There was no insulation, no electricity, no running water, there was however, a load of fire wood beside the old wood stove, and pots and pans and cutlery. What more could we need?

Barb and I packed in our supplies, three-dozen eggs, two pounds of bacon, four quarts of milk, several loaves of bread, hamburger, cheese and cookies, and we set about making ourselves comfortable. The first thing we did was to try out the bed and it was just fine.

For one week we slept, ate, and made love. Once in a while we would go out onto the float on the lake and bask in the early spring sun. Then we would go back and make love again. The week flew by so quickly we wondered where it went. All good things come to an end, and so did the most wonderful week of our lives. Over the years we often laughed as we remembered that little piece of heaven on Shawnigan Lake.

Employment beginnings

Several months before our wedding, I had found a job in an upholstery shop on Johnson Street. The shop supplied custom upholstery for the Standard Furniture store on Yates Street, and I was hired as an upholstery apprentice. The wage for the first year was set at twelve dollars a week, almost the same amount that I earned as a paper-boy.

The previous year I had worked for a company that was installing a new forty-eight inch pipeline from the 'Humpback reservoir' in Goldstream to greatly increase the supply of water to Victoria. My wages were one dollar and twenty-five cents per hour, wonderful for a young man just out of school.

This job had been secured for me by my cousin Charlie, who was a terrific worker. He impressed the pipeline foreman with his tremendous energy and drive. The man believed him when he said that his cousin Cliff would also be a great worker.

My first problem was trying to perform as well as Charlie. Charlie had been out of school a couple of years before me and had learned, by hard knocks, just how to perform on the job. My experience, while varied, did not equip me with the same fortitude as cousin Charlie.

The terrain that the pipeline passed through included solid rock and sometimes very sandy soil. The rock was not too difficult to work in, however the sandy soil presented an entirely different situation, often requiring safety walls to keep the sand from falling into the trench.

Charlie and the foreman reveled in such trying conditions, and worked as though possessed, while I was prone to cower on the edge of the ditch, preferring instead to watch from above. This reluctance was noted by the foreman, and eventually brought to my attention in a rather profane way.
On that particular occasion, a member of my family stopped by the work site to visit me. We were laying pipe through a particularly dangerous vein of sand and I was doing my very best to direct the crew from above, occasionally shouting encouragement to them. My guest showed a great deal of interest in the proceedings, so I did my best to give him the 'Grand Tour'.

The foreman, noting my seeming lack of interest in the pipe-laying program, let out a shriek, using the same four-letter vocabulary that my father excelled in. Needless to say, I was astonished at his use of the colorful adjectives, and quickly descended into the trench, setting off a small avalanche. I was amazed at how quickly the workers got the hell out of the ditch while I, completely at ease with the situation, did my best to stop the avalanche. Fortunately the foreman returned to the ditch just as the sand reached my waist and managed to extricate me from the ensuing landslide.

By that time my visitor had disappeared and presumably missed my heroic efforts in the trenches. The foreman, on the other hand, seemed speechless and was unable to utter another word for the rest of the day, which coincidentally was my last day on that job.

After several weeks of job seeking, I applied at Standard Furniture, and after a very interesting interview, the interviewer suggested that I might suit a job in the upholstery department. The upholstery owner, Jesse Smithson, was a wonderful fellow and offered me an apprenticeship, starting immediately. I jumped at the chance. I probably would have become a very successful upholsterer, because I thoroughly enjoyed the work. A few weeks later, however, I was faced with the reality that I would not be able to support a family on twelve dollars a week, so after a heart wrenching talk with Jesse, I left and once more began the task of finding employment.

After a week or so, I found a position as a delivery man with Weston Bakeries, on Viewfield Road in Esquimalt. The pay was very generous, and I did my best to live up to the expectations of the company.

My bread route covered an area in the Fairfield district and included parts of Foul Bay and Oak Bay. Each morning at six o'clock I would load up my van and then drive to my route and start deliveries.

After a few weeks I began to feel that being a delivery man was not unlike being a delivery boy and quickly re-affirmed my conviction that sometimes people can be very demanding and often quite rude. Many of these types of human beings tend to look down their noses at others less elevated than themselves, and usually make no bones about their feelings.

Unfortunately my feelings have always been very sensitive to this kind of treatment, and I usually find it difficult to accept this form of abuse without introducing my own form of retribution, or as it is sometimes referred to, 'revenge'.

Unlike delivering newspapers, delivering bread pretty well demands front door delivery, or what is considered in the trade, soft landings. It is of course almost impossible to throw a loaf of bread through a window, so there really are very few ways of getting even with a nose-in-the-air customer, other than subtle verbal assault or crafty insinuation.

Salesmanship

The fact that I was now an adult and married precluded childish action, so I developed the attitude that if you can't beat them, sell them. This launched my career as a silver-tongue salesman.

A prerequisite of good salesmanship is a full understanding of the product and conviction that it is the finest available. So I proceeded to learn everything that I could about the bakery business and in the process I developed a sincere liking for the product. Thereafter it was easy to sell many products that my customers actually cared less about or possibly would be better off without.

In the following months I found that when I became truly sold on the product, I was able to sell it to almost anyone, and win them over in the process. Many of the people that I thought looked down on me, actually were very special, and I absolutely rejoiced in setting their souls free.

Every other week the bakery would feature a special item. One week it was a delicious raspberry layer cake. I tested the product, and was overwhelmed with the quality and mouth watering appeal and immediately went out and sold over one hundred.

The management could not believe that this very same delivery man who received more complaints than any driver sold so many cakes. This moment of success however, did not secure my position with the company, and we soon parted ways.

While I was still employed at Weston's Bakery and we were getting along fairly well financially, Barb and I had a lovely daughter we named Marilyn Louise. When Marilyn was born it was not general practice to allow husbands into the delivery room and even though I asked I was not permitted in. This was a great disappointment for me because Barb was in labour for twenty-four hours and I was beside myself with worry.

Feeling very frustrated and left out, I went for a long drive in the country and then drove to a confectionery store in Victoria where I delivered bread every day. The owner of the store was a nice fellow and we got along very well. What I did not know at that time was that his sexual preferences were directed toward men.

When my friend heard that I was not allowed in the delivery room he embraced me and indicated how sorry he was to hear that. His next move was to bring out a bottle of his finest whiskey, and I at the low end of self-pity, joined him in a few drinks. During the past twelve hours I had not had any thing to eat, and as you can imagine I got thwacked very quickly.

My friend, ever anxious to console me, continued to feed me that intoxicating brew. Within a very short time I was unable to think or to stand, and so my friend ushered me to his bedroom above the store and proceeded to put me to bed.

In my saturated condition I was a sitting duck, so to speak, so I did not protest too much when he removed my shirt and pants, as my only interest was sleep. His interest however, was rising by the moment, and within a very short time he became most anxious to remove my under-garments.

When my brothers and sisters and I were very young our mother constantly emphasized that it was not nice to remove your clothes when others were present, and particularly not nice to allow anyone other than your mother to remove them for you. So, remembering this, I suggested that he get the four-lettered–word off me.

For some reason my demands fell on deaf ears, I thought that perhaps he had either not heard me, which seemed unlikely given the close proximity of our bodies, or that he was so intent on making me comfortable that he had not completely understood the command.

During my early years I witnessed many instances of alcohol related problems, becoming painfully aware of the danger in over drinking, and swearing that I would not allow myself to become a victim of alcohol. So, you can imagine the ungracious thoughts that were coursing through my mind, whilst my friend was hot on my tail.

It seems that time passes very slowly in a crisis. It almost comes to a standstill, and frantic thoughts race through the mind a mile a minute. After what seemed a very long time, I vomited on the bed. This quickly brought this ambivalent adventure to an end, and also helped to clear my foggy brain enough to realize that I should definitely be elsewhere. After a hot shower and a complete scrub down, I managed to have a hearty laugh at my near folly and mentally added another page to my book.

My Beautiful Child

I arrived at the hospital just after my dear wife had given birth and I was allowed to see them both. Baby Marilyn was the most beautiful child I ever laid eyes on. She had reddish blond hair, and the prettiest dimples imaginable. Over the years she became even more beautiful, winning a beautiful baby contest and in later years, becoming a runner up in the Miss Victoria contest.

Barb and I had been staying with her mom and dad while I was taking my upholstery apprenticeship, as my salary was so low it would have been impossible to rent accommodation and support my little family except below the poverty line.

Her parents were very kind allowing us to move into their home. Considering the amount of money I was making, I was unable to make more than a token gesture toward room and board. Their house was on Wilson Street in Vic West, and was quite comfortable though very small. We were happy there, however, and under the circumstances got along fairly well with her folks.

When I left the upholstery trade and found the job with Weston Bakeries, our life improved dramatically. I was able to pay her folks a little more, although it was still very low, and I was able to pay the many bills that I had accumulated over the past few months and even purchase a 1932 Ford coupe, with a rumble seat. The Ford coupe cost one hundred and fifty dollars, but it was worth every penny, and we enjoyed the freedom that it brought us.

Baby Marilyn was growing quickly and developing her very special personality. Unfortunately, it included a considerable amount of fussing and tears. This caused some strain and one evening, after several sleepless nights, the whole situation reached the point of no return. After some very highly charged opinions were exchanged between the son-in-law and the parents of the bride, we decided that new accommodation should be found forthwith.

Fortunately it was not raining that night, so we packed all our belongings into the coupe's rumble seat, made a late night call to my sister Marie, asking her if she was still up and how would she feel if we drove over immediately and stayed for a day or two.

Marie had never let me down during my entire life and she was not going to start just then, so she told us to come right over, and that she would prepare the guest room for us so that we could all go straight to bed the moment that we arrived there. One week later we found a small apartment on the second floor of a some-what run down house on Bay Street.

There is no doubt that the apartment was shabby, but Barb and I did not mind in the least, and I quickly repainted and wall-papered all three rooms, including painting the floors, the bathroom, and the old wooden icebox that was suspended just outside the kitchen window. It coincidentally, overlooked a work yard belonging to a group of Chinese vegetable merchants, who began their workday each day at 3:00 a.m.

When we moved into the apartment on Bay Street and I discovered the outside cooler, I was very excited at the prospect of reliving some childhood memories. Barb too, could remember a similar cooler that was on her house when she was very young, and so she greeted this discovery with relatively good humour. This happy disposition lasted approximately one week and then all hell broke loose, and I went on an urgent hunt for an electric refrigerator. When I located a second hand Frigidaire, life took a turn for the better, and once again, we began enjoying food that had not yet soured.

About that time I parted company with the bakery and, with no job offers in the near future, money once again became very scarce. For several weeks we got by on very little, but finally the barrel ran dry and we found ourselves stony broke.

Somehow we managed to scrape enough money together to buy food for our little daughter, but for several days there was nothing left for us and all we had to eat were pickled beets from Barb's mom. We never forgot those days, but we were always able to laugh at the situation, and certainly appreciated any success that we achieved in the future.

The little apartment was quite comfortable, and always looked clean and bright, though the furniture was a tad shabby, even considering the fact that I had reupholstered some pieces. Of course nothing really matched anything else, and the colour scheme, was definitely not the fashion of the day, but we loved it and really, who cared if it was not upper class, it was our home.

A Job in a Mill

One day I arrived home with the wonderful news that I had found a job in a mill, at the Dalziel Box Factory on Bridge Street. Miraculously I had managed to land a job that paid a very good wage, and I was beside myself with joy. Hopefully I would now be able to supply more than canned beets for my family.

The mill was located on the banks of a small bay in the Bridge Street area. Though it was old and run down it was a busy little mill, producing dimension lumber for building and also thin wooden strips of lumber which were used in the manufacture of wooden boxes.

At the back of the mill, there was a pond or boom yard as it was known, where raw logs were kept before they were milled into the required lumber.

The logs were brought up from the pond by securing them with heavy chains and dragging them up a chute to the deck above, where they were cut to size by the head sawyer.

My job for the first week was on the green chain, obviously a position on the very lowest rung of the ladder. After the logs were cut into the desired dimension and length, they were carried along a conveyor belt to the green chain. The lumber was then disgorged onto the green chain by way of another chute.

The quantity of lumber cascading down that chute depended on the dimension of the lumber. Smaller dimension lumber would arrive in a steady flow, which required the green chain worker to work as fast as possible to avoid the chain getting clogged up. If it were a larger dimension lumber, the flow was considerably slower since the green lumber was so heavy and sopping wet, due to the time that it had been immersed in the water. It took the strength of a heavy weight wrestler to manage the monster planks, which then had to be stacked in different piles according to their size.

Fortunately I was in very good physical shape, considering the fact that I had existed on canned beets for so long and was, for the most part, quick witted and agile. Maintaining a green chain required all of the above attributes, and I prided myself on my ability to overcome almost any stumbling block.

The green chain however, was the most diabolical devise ever created. It did not matter if one possessed super-human abilities. That devilish contraption could outwit and outrun even the most formidable adversary. No matter the resolve, it would turn the poor unfortunate victim into a whimpering shadow of his former self.

At times the lumber would appear to be giving the green chain worker a fighting chance, and it would move along its track at a reasonable pace. However, in the twinkling of an eye it could turn into a raging monster and the lumber would hurtle down the track at the speed of a locomotive.

The lumber would suddenly come cascading down the ramp much faster than before, defying all the human efforts of the worker to get it under control. The poor fellow, now going full tilt, would frantically try to pull it off the track before the rest of the lumber began piling up at the end of the chain. Then hopefully he would stack it on the correct pile, often finding that much of the lumber had somehow found its way to the wrong pile.

On the fifth night I sought out the foreman and suggested that I was being wasted on that soul destroying apparatus, and would be more profitably used in some other department. He studied me for a minute or two, possibly trying to decide if I was cut out for the lumber business, and then said that I was right, I would be very useful on the log deck.

The log deck was the entry point for the log before it was hauled out of the water and up the chute. My job was to fasten a chain around the log and start the winch that would take it up to the head saw. There the head sawyer would cut it into suitably sized boards and send it on to the boys on the chain gang.

My shift began at ten o'clock at night and continued till six in the morning. And even though it was a difficult shift, I loved it.

It was a very challenging job because I not only chained the logs and sent them up the chute. I also sorted the logs in the pond during the time that it took the head sawyer to mill them. The job required the sorter to jump from log to log, moving them around and lining them up before the chute, until a good supply was ready for the trip upward. It did take a while to get the hang of it, but eventually I became very good at it and was able to jump from log to log with no difficulty, except on the odd occasion.

One night at about two o'clock, as I was working on the pond, I threw a seventy-pound boom chain over my shoulder to take it across the pond where I intended to anchor a group of suitable logs. The prescribed method was to leap from log to log as quickly as possible, keeping up the momentum to ensure that you reached the other side safely.

When I began my trek, the logs were fairly close together, but by the time I reached the middle of the pond, some of them had drifted apart, and the only log available to me in the circumstance, was partially submerged. As I was totally committed to the operation, which was akin to walking on water, I found that I had no other choice, but to jump. Unfortunately, the log turned out to be a floating slab of heavy fir bark that had dislodged from one of the logs in the pond. Time passed in slow motion as I propelled myself and that heavy boom chain toward the floating piece of bark.

Many years before, when I was quite young, I had enjoyed both broad jumping and high jumping, developing strong legs in the process. Almost every day I practised on the jumps, and though not by any stretch of the imagination a champion, I was able to hold my own in competition providing, of course that the competition was not too stiff.

One of the disciplines in broad jumping was the ability to fully concentrate, and move the legs in a motion similar to a man running on water, which, in turn, allowed the party to propel themselves as far as possible before hitting the ground.

The instant that I propelled myself off the log toward the floating bark, not knowing of course whether the piece of stuff floating in the darkness was actually a log or not, I suddenly remembered my experiences in broad jumping and the sense of floating that I had developed, and the unbelievable ability to soar like a bird in flight. I began kicking my legs furiously, as though my life depended on it, which come to think, it did.

My legs were moving so fast when I landed on that wily piece of bark that it seemed that I only sank to my knees in the water, before managing to lift, like a bird, into the black night. During that wild leap my legs were going like a buzz saw, but finally, I gained a solid footing on the next log, the heavy chain still draped across my shoulders.

My foreman was standing on the deck watching me, doing what appeared to him, the dance of death across the pond. Once I reached the other side I noted that I was soaked right up to my neck. Just how that happened is still a mystery to me, although the foreman did say that he thought that at one point I completely disappeared beneath the water, and suddenly reappeared like a Phoenix rising from a watery grave. Noting that I was soaked through, he sent me home to have a warm bath, and kindly suggested that I take the rest of the night off. But in future, if the same thing occurred, be sure to drop the damn chain.

My career at the box factory was progressing nicely and the foreman asked me if I would like to be trained as a sawyer, which would double my wages and provide a secure future for me and my little family.

As I noted before, the best laid plans of mice and men often get screwed up. One night, just before I was to begin training on the head saw, a union organizer came into the lunch room, where I was enjoying my peanut butter sandwiches, and told me that we were going on strike. I told him that I was perfectly happy in my job and I preferred not to go out on strike at that time. He left little doubt that he did not give a tinkers damn whether I wanted to go out on strike or not and quickly let me know that his remarks were not meant to be a question but rather a statement

For some reason I have never been able to understand why it was necessary to strike in the first place. The mill owner certainly did not want a strike and the workers really couldn't afford a strike. Our wives got sick worrying about it. As it turned out their concern was entirely warranted, for the mill did go on a strike that lasted three months, and when it was finally over the wages were raised by only five cents an hour.

The workers that stayed with the company during that period, lost several hundred dollars over the three-month strike, and with a five cent an hour raise, never had a chance to recover the lost money. The union organizer so infuriated me, I quit the job two days later, and once again began the task of finding a new position.

My First Hot Rod

I took different jobs to tide me over, sold my coupe and bought a 1936 Ford sedan. I installed a rebuilt engine in it, which increased its power dramatically.

This proved to be a bad move, for one freezing night in February, while testing the power and speed of the car over a stretch of road north of the Malahat summit, I spun out of control and after a series of barrel rolls, landed upside down on the top of an embankment, at the foot of Bamberton hill.

Fortunately my good friend Don who was riding in the passenger seat, was uninjured except for a sprained shoulder. I was thrown through the window ending up in the ditch. I managed to break my ankle and sustain a number of other minor injuries. The car was an uninsured write-off.

The next few months were difficult and once more I turned to my family for help. Barb and I and our little family that now included Maureen moved into the basement of my mother's house on Ash Street. My mother and three brothers lived on the main floor.

When my ankle and the other body parts that hurt recovered, I began searching for new employment. Having spent the better part of my life as a delivery person, it was only natural that once again I would seek similar employment.

Shepherd's Dairy

At that time, my brother Harold was working for Shepherd's Dairy, a family run business at 1818 Chestnut Street, on a large property which was part of the original farm. The cluster of buildings where the milk was processed was on the next street, behind my mother's house. Harold put in a good word for me and I soon began a new career in the *'Milk'* business.

Herb Shepherd, who ran the family business, was as nice a man as I ever had the pleasure to know. He had an extraordinary sense of humour, and truly enjoyed his employees. We thought the world of him, and enjoyed every minute we spent with him.

Our workday started at four o'clock each morning. I cut through the property just behind my mother's house, and then crossed Chestnut Street to the dairy where we loaded our truck with fresh Jersey milk.

The milk had been collected from the Shepherd farms and pasteurized in the processing room behind the old farmhouse. It was then bottled in beautifully embossed bottles, loaded on vintage Dodge trucks and delivered to customers.

My route started in Esquimalt, continuing through View Royal and into Colwood and Metchosin, and finally finishing up again in Esquimalt. On a normal day I was able to finish my route by mid-day, and on Saturdays I was usually finished by two o'clock.

The hours were fairly long but no one really minded because the

Shepherds were great people to work for, and there were certain perks available to us, such as free milk for our own consumption. As I was still fairly slim and wishing to put on a few pounds, I usually drank four or five quarts a day.

Surprisingly, I did not gain much weight while working the milk route, as I used up an incredible amount of energy running up and down stairways all day long. However, over the year or two that I worked as a milkman, I noticed that my legs became so used to running up and down stairs I had great difficulty running on flat ground. It felt as though my legs were stiff at the knees and unable to completely straighten out. This caused a great problem for me, as I still loved running long distances, but it was very difficult, because my legs refused to extend properly on flat ground.

The sight of a man running along a flat course, moving his legs up and down, as if he was climbing stairs, was no doubt hilarious, but it did provide me with a great background experience that I was able to draw on while doing comedy routines later on in life, while involved in the theatre.

The early hours did not bother me at all as I had developed a love of early mornings delivering papers on the many paper routes that I had from the time I was twelve right up until I was seventeen. There was something magical about early mornings; everything was always very still and quiet, with few people up and about. The quiet and peace was always a wonderful thing to experience, and I always enjoyed early mornings on any job.

My Introduction to Smoking

When I was seventeen cigarettes were widely advertised in magazines, papers, and even movies. Almost every actor, from Humphrey Bogart to Clark Gable puffed on cigarettes, and I wanted to be just like them, so I took up smoking the 'Weed'.

Most actors would make a huge production when lighting one. First they would remove the packet of cigarettes from their shirt pocket with incredible grace and fluidity, and then casually open the pack. With careful deliberation they would draw a cigarette from within it, tap the end of it on their wrist, and then gently place it in their mouth. With great flair they would ignite a match, usually managing it with one flick of the thumb, and finally, cupping the match and the end of the cigarette with both hands, inhale deeply, allowing the tobacco smoke to completely saturate their blackened lungs.

The overall effect was very dramatic, and though it likely added several minutes onto the length of the movie, every macho kid in the audience was eager to perform the ritual just as their heroes had done. It was a definite mark of sophistication to be able to accomplish the feat without catching your shirt on fire.

For weeks I quietly practiced this dangerous exercise, intent on perfecting my performance before performing it in public. The most necessary item was a shirt with fairly large pockets, because the whole presentation depended on successfully removing the packet of smokes without tearing the shirt. If the shirt had a flap over the pocket, as was often the case, it would take a tremendous amount of practice to get the packet out of the pocket without the blame thing getting tangled up. This, of course, was of paramount importance if you wished to impress people.

My first tentative efforts to nonchalantly remove the packet of cigarettes from my pocket were very frustrating. Firstly my shirts either had flaps over the pocket or the pocket itself was too small. The solution for small pockets and large flaps, was to carefully remove a certain amount of the thread that held the pocket onto the shirt. This enlarged the opening and allowed a much easier retrieval of the packet. However, after a period of time the rest of the threads would either break or disappear, and then the whole pocket would fall off. Eventually I mastered the art of drawing a packet of cig's from my pocket without dropping them or catching them on the pocket flap, and also managing to remove one of the tobacco sticks and then tap it on my wrist with flair and precision.

Kids would often stand around, just to see me perform the ritual of '*the smoke*', amazed at the artistry of the exhibition, watching in fascination as I inhaled enough smoke to fell a moose, intrigued at the yellowish hue that would envelop my face, as the smoke seeped through my every pore.

It soon occurred to me that I enjoyed the *'light up'* ritual far more than actually smoking those cigarettes, and no matter how often I smoked them, they always tasted like old socks. Most mornings my mouth would taste awful, my mind conjuring up wild thoughts that compared the sensation to kissing a logger's armpit at high noon.

Over the seven years that I smoked that noxious weed I came to despise the habit and tried my very best to quit. However, as everyone who has ever smoked will tell you, quitting is not as easy as it sounds.

There were many occasions that I threw a package of smokes away in disgust, vowing to quit then and there, but, no matter my good intentions, I would keep going back, going through the very same ritual that attracted them to me in the first place.

Finally, after at a least hundred tries, I concluded that the only way that I would ever be able to quit, would be to follow the same ritual each time I lit up, except that I would not inhale the smoke. As you can imagine, trying to stop inhaling, was every bit as difficult as trying to stop smoking.

For one week I stopped inhaling, even promising myself that I would go back to inhaling the next week. This of course was a lie. The second week was almost as difficult, but this time I assured myself that I was winning, and if I could last another week the self-torture would end. It took me a full month, however, to get to the point that I actually was able to resist the urge to light up, and then, whenever I did light up, I found that my convictions were correct, the cigarettes tasted as foul as anyone could imagine.

I was working for Shepherd's Dairy when I had finally found success with my strategy of not inhaling. It began on my daily milk route, where I had chosen two stopping places to put my plan into action. One stop was on Atkins Road in Colwood, the other was on Constance Street in Esquimalt.

I decided that I would be very methodical with the application of my theory of ritual versus habit, and the stopping spots were an important part of the ritual.

At each secluded spot, I parked the truck, always taking care that there were no witnesses, got out of the vehicle, and slowly performed my act. Not wanting to waste any more time than necessary, I carried out the cigarette routine while at the same time taking a pee, which was also a necessary ritual by the time that I reached that special place.

As I stood smoking the cigarette, I usually relieved myself on a beautiful and luxuriant flowerbed close at hand. Day-by-day, the flowers seemed to wilt, but as my attention was solely involved in the ritual, I never took much notice of the destruction in the flower patch.

Over a month I reached that stage where I no longer needed to light up, and I was able to throw the cigarettes away, never lighting up again, except on stage. The flowers however never recovered.

Shepherd's Dairy was a wonderful chapter in my life and I enjoyed most of the memories associated with the job. A year after I joined the dairy team, the plant relocated to a lot near the Oak Bay Avenue and Fort Street intersection. For several months I remained with the dairy enjoying the work, but something unfortunate brought the position tumbling down about my ears.

My supervisor was a wonderful fellow and I looked up to him with a feeling of admiration and respect. He likewise was quite fond of me, even overlooking the rough edges that seemed to make up the better part of me, and we spent a fair amount of time together laughing and enjoying each other's company.

One of the employees in the office was an attractive woman, several years older than I was, and my supervisor was very fond of her, perhaps even in love with her.

My usual behavior included flirting with any lady that I encountered. Whether she was young, old, beautiful or plain, made no difference, as I enjoyed all women equally. This habit which could be, and usually was, deemed a character-flaw, managed to get me into a whole lot of trouble over the years. It almost caused a divorce between me and my beloved Barbara. Fortunately I was able to control that part of my life and I remained married to Barb for over forty-seven years.

Over a period of time I began paying more attention to the lady, probably much more than I should have. This flirtatious escapade did not escape the attention of my supervisor and his attitude toward me changed a little. One day, while I was engaged in an innocent though very humourous discussion with her, he walked through the door. At that very moment, something extremely funny was said and we both broke out in laughter. At the same moment, hearing the door open, we both turned and looked directly at my friend. He stood for a moment, as though stunned, looking in bewilderment at us, and then turned and walked out.

Instantly I realized that he thought that we were laughing at him, and so I went after him to explain the cause of our laughter, but he refused to listen to me, and in the days ahead did not speak a word to me. No matter how hard I tried to reassure him that the laughter was innocent, our relationship ended. From that moment on, he looked with suspicion upon everything I did and my good relationship with the company quickly deteriorated.

About the same time, one of the other drivers, a boy several years younger than I, left the dairy to start a job on the Graving dock at Naden. One morning while driving on the dock he accidentally drove the car over the edge, into forty feet of water, and by the time they got to him he had drowned.

That young fellow was very well liked, and his death cast a pall over all of the employees in the dairy, particularly me, for I was very fond of him. The loss of my friend over a simple misunderstanding and the loss of this great young kid through a tragic accident was a very moving experience and it served to remind me just how tenuous life can be.

Within a very short time I again found myself unemployed and once more began the chore of finding a job to support my little family, which now included three children. Those little people were my pride and joy; they were Marilyn, Maureen and Michael.

A Carpentry Career

I had several fill-in jobs over the next year that included delivering laundry, dry cleaning, and even a short stint washing floors at the Hudson's Bay Co. These were merely temporary situations while I looked for something more promising. Finally destiny caught up with me when I landed a job as carpenter's helper with a small building contractor.

During my two years at Vic High, I had taken carpentry as my main course, thoroughly enjoying it and thinking that it would be a very good trade, but never really pursuing it until the day that I happened to see the add in the Colonist.

As soon as I saw the advertisement, I phoned and spoke with the owner of the business. By that time he had already fielded several calls and didn't really seem too impressed with my credentials, even though I told him all about the model house that I had built to scale while in school, and also about the wooden soap box that I built and entered in a race when I was only seven. He told me that he had taken several calls that morning and that he would phone me back if he thought that he might be able to use me.

After sitting near the phone most of the day and not hearing from him, I decided that I should call him again to jog his memory and so about seven o'clock that night I dialed his number again.

George answered the phone, and I quickly told him who I was, and that I was sorry to be calling again, but I really wanted the opportunity to show him what I could do. He sounded very weary but did take the time to speak with me.

Evidently, that day while pouring the concrete foundation of a house, he stepped off the two by four's that were used in the construction of the concrete forms, and without thinking, jumped down, without first removing his arm from behind them. He broke his arm and was now unable to work.

At that particular time, he and his wife were in the process of hanging wallpaper in a rental house they owned on Hillside Avenue. The tenants were to move in that weekend and it was imperative that the job be completed by the following day. In a state of desperation he asked me if I knew how to hang wallpaper. Well, did I know how to hang paper!

One of my favorite uncles was a master paperhanger and painter, and years before had trained me to spread paste on the rolls of wallpaper. While he hung the paper, firstly on the ceiling, and then on the walls, I would work as fast as I could trying to keep ahead of him, spreading the sticky flour paste on the rolls with a huge brush that was almost as heavy as I was, ever fearful of stepping into the paste can, or worse yet, getting paste on the front side of the paper.

During those early sessions he taught me many tricks of the trade and on a few occasions he even allowed me to hang a roll or two. When I told George that a master had trained me, he was overjoyed and asked me to start work the next day.

Right away I phoned brother Bob, and told him that I had led George to believe that I was a master paperhanger, and what could I do now? Good old Bob, had never let me down before and he wasn't going to let me down now.

That night, as late as it was, he went over the whole business of paper hanging with me, refreshing my memory and giving me the confidence to hang wall paper, which I did all the next day without a slip-up, and George, very happy with the results, hired me.

My first day on the job was exciting. The concrete had dried enough so that we could remove the two by fours and boards from the cribbing that held the concrete in place.

There was another young man on the job that George had hired the day before; evidently his idea was to keep the one who performed best. Even though I had no idea that I was being watched, I worked as hard as I had ever worked before. The other fellow couldn't understand why I was working so hard, and even suggested that I slow down.

One of the traits that I had developed during my early years was the burning desire to get a job done as fast as possible in the best way possible, no matter the job. It was always a personal challenge for me to get on with the job at hand so, while the other chap sat and smoked, I worked like a man driven. The next morning the other worker was no where to be seen, so I picked up my tools, and continued the work at the same pace I had set the day before.

George had a brother Pete who was a master carpenter. Over the next year he taught me everything that he knew about carpentry, and I sopped it up like a sponge. Within the year I could hold my own with any framing carpenter and then one day, with no warning, Pete quit.

We were in the process of constructing a duplex on Kings Road and had it framed up to the point where we would be able to put the roof on it. George did not know how to cut a roof and suggested that he would have to get another carpenter. As I had learned the practical theory of cutting a roof while attending school, and as I had actually worked on several roofs with Pete, I was confident that I could cut it myself.

That night I called an old carpenter friend, and asked him to help me figure out a roof that I would like to cut the next day. He was extremely helpful, showing me the best way to do the job, and the following day, much to the amazement of George, I cut the roof while he and a helper nailed it in place.

For many months I acted as head carpenter on many of the construction projects handled by George, and with his guidance I learned everything I possibly could about the building business, from framing to finishing.

As my building expertise increased so did my ego, and before long my arrogance got the better of me and I began to act as though I was the boss. As anyone with the sense that God gave geese knows, bosses do not like employees who think that they are superior to them, and before long he suggested that it was time for me to try my wings, preferably far from him.

Before very long I found a job with a larger construction firm that was building a seventy-suite apartment complex on Fort Street, across from the Jubilee Hospital. There were several carpenters and I was just one small cog in a very large wheel, and I did not like it at all so, one week later I quit.

My friend Griffin was a dynamic character who knew very little about building, but he was a great go-getter, and an even greater talker. So we began a small construction firm, Griffin and Clarke. I realized that the name wasn't alphabetically correct, but he assured me that it would be far better if we called it that, rather than my suggestion of CC&G Construction.

We found work very quickly by going around door to door, asking house owners if there were any repairs that we might do on their houses. We only visited houses that were obviously in need of repair, so there were many opportunities.

Within a week we had several jobs lined up: gutters, porches, stairways and even fences, and we were very happy with our progress. For my part I was earning more money than I ever had, so I tended to overlook the fact that Griffin was a better talker than a worker. Eventually Griffin arrived at the conclusion that he was not cut out for manual labour and decided to go back to school.

This was an excellent decision, because he excelled in school, getting excellent grades in every subject, and soon decided to study law. He eventually became a very good lawyer. I never doubted his ability to talk himself into anything and was thrilled that he had found his true calling in life.

Finding jobs for myself was not the easiest thing I had ever done and I certainly discovered many pitfalls along the way. One of the first lessons that I learned the hard way was to always put everything in writing before starting a job.

My advertising in the Colonist suggested that I would do anything for a buck. The owner of a lawn mower shop on Douglas Street needed a shed built on the back of his store to hold equipment and inventory. He answered my ad and asked me if I could build the addition. I informed him that I was a specialist in shed building, and could start immediately.

My drafting experience was somewhat limited but I managed to draw a fairly decent set of plans and then acquired and paid for the building permit.

The price of building the shed and drawing the necessary plans amounted to approximately six hundred dollars. This was a substantial amount as I was just starting out and did not have a lot of money to spare. The shed took me a week to construct and turned out to be very good structure. When I had finished I approached the owner for payment, but he informed me that he did not have any money to pay me, however I could have a lawn mower in lieu of money.

Even though there was no lawn to cut at the house I was renting on Vining Street, I felt that I had no choice but to accept the mower in payment. This of course was a great disappointment because I had bills to pay and a family to support.

In spite of that setback I managed to survive, and in the process learned a very important lesson. For the rest of my building career I never did any job without money up front, and always put it in writing.

While working for George I had learned a great deal about building and was I able to take on almost any construction job. While I would never be considered a first rate draftsman, I managed to put my limited training to good use building many structures over the years, most of which are still standing today.

Our First Home

When I was twenty-three years of age, we rented an old junker of a house on Henry Street in Vic West. The rent was fifty dollars a month, which was not out of line for such a house. A year or two later the landlord asked me if I would like to buy it for twenty five hundred dollars and I said yes. Of course I did not have that kind of money so I asked him if I could buy it on time and he said yes. My mother loaned me five hundred dollars and we were able to buy our first home. Within a year or so I renovated the house and managed to pay off the mortgage. Barb and I were off and running.

Before long we bought the vacant lot next door and moved a house onto the site and added a suite in the basement. Two years later we purchased five more houses, all surrounding our original twenty-five hundred dollar house.

Early one morning, while living on Henry Street, Barb visited the Jubilee Hospital once more, returning a few days later with my third daughter Marlene. Coincidentally, it was my birthday that day and I was overjoyed to have yet another beautiful daughter to add to my lovely little family which now consisted of one son and three daughters.

Eventually we acquired several old houses in Victoria, renovated them, and then rented them out to a variety of interesting tenants. One of the houses which we purchased for seven thousand dollars, was very large and we were able to renovate it, creating eight rental units.

Our next move came when we purchased a half-acre lot on Glanford Avenue and built our first, almost new home. I say almost new, because I actually dismantled an old home and used the lumber to construct the new house. The house was large with five bedrooms.

The old home that I tore down was near the junction of Cloverdale and Douglas. The owner wished to have the house removed so that he might build a new structure. I suggested that I could pull it down for nothing, and realizing that this was a good deal he allowed me to dismantle the house and to also keep some antique furniture that was in the house at that time.

A man by the name of Ronald Hopkins recognized that the furniture was collectable and made me an offer that I could not refuse. Ron was a very colorful acquaintance, who built homes 'on spec', usually having me do the building. I believe that we had more fun talking about life in general and specifically voice production than actually building homes.

He had a rich tenor voice and he would break into song at the slightest provocation. I was taking vocal training at the time and encouraged him to serenade me whenever he felt the urge to do so. Often while performing his favorite operatic piece Paggliacci, he would become so involved he would cry and I, deeply moved, would also break into tears. Quite often these touching moments would occur while we were driving. I often wondered what people in other cars must think as they observed us singing at the top of our lungs and weeping like unhappy lovers.

Ron had a quick temper, and would sometimes heat up and explode like a rocket. I would do everything that I could to calm him down, including telling him that his emotional outbreaks showed such depth and feelings he should definitely have been on the stage. At this he would break into gales of laughter and perhaps even into song.

Once, in a fit, he refused to pay me for a job that I had done for him at a home on Locarno Lane. I told him that I did not look kindly on people who refused to pay me for my work, and suggested that he pay me immediately. He refused and suggested that I go to a place from which there was no return. That night I returned to the house that I had been working on and removed all the doors, light fixtures, and anything else that was not secured to the floor.

The next day he called demanding that I return all of the items that I had removed the previous day. I said that I would consider his request if he paid me in full and added on a little for my efforts. He began to laugh at my audacity and promised that he would pay me right away. Once again we became friends and I was able to enjoy his vocal powers to the fullest.

The structure on Douglas that I dismantled to construct my own home was a two-storey house with many interesting features. The front of the house had a large verandah that stretched across the entire face of the building. It was supported by large decorative posts, which held up the shingled roof. I reasoned that if I removed the posts, the roof would slowly descend to the porch floor and I would be able to dismantle it easily.

Using a very heavy sledgehammer, I quickly removed several posts

Our Family

while standing on the porch under the overhanging roof. As I approached the last post and prepared to knock it off its base, I suddenly realized that I was not standing in the best place. So I stepped off the porch and picked up a two by four. Just as I touched the post, the whole roof fell with the sound of an earthquake.

My first thoughts were of my brother Frank who was helping me. I could not see under the collapsed roof as it now lay absolutely flat on the porch floor, and I was sure that the roof had flattened my little brother.

I frantically called his name expecting the worst but, to my joy, he poked his head out of an upper window asking me what the noise was. If I had been able to reach him that instant, I would have kissed him. My dear little brother worked with me for many years and continues to this day constructing homes and additions, and often helps me out with projects.

Bitten by the Acting Bug

While in my early twenties, I was bitten by the acting bug and never fully recovered. My first production was "A Kiss For Cinderella", a humorous play staged by St. Luke's Players at the church of that name on Cedar Hill Road.

One of the actresses was *Margaret Martin*, a very talented and busy lady. She made quite a name for herself over the years on stage, in film and television, particularly when she portrayed the character of Emily Carr, the famed artist. Margaret was a wonderful person to work with, and she quickly recognized the ham in me and encouraged me to continue performing, preferably on the stage.

My interest in 'the stage', soon took over my life and I began devoting most of my waking hours, performing a variety of roles both on and off stage. During those years I took every role that came my way, and performed in every venue in and around Victoria.

Almost every church had a hall that allowed stage productions; however, very few halls had more than rudimentary stage facilities so the productions, while commendable, where not always memorable.

When I was very young I used to steal cherries from the tree in the front yard of the Langham Court Theatre, on a lane just off Rockland Avenue. While gorging myself on the cherries, I dreamed of one day becoming an actor on its stage.

After honing my skills in practically every church hall in the town, I joined the Langham Court Theatre and auditioned for a role in a play directed by Jim and Phil Dulmage. The play, 'The Matchmaker' was a comedy and the part I read for suited me perfectly, so I was given a small role in the production.

The Dulmages were a super couple, both schoolteachers, and absolutely committed to theatre. They shared the responsibilities of selecting the plays and directors for the productions, often directing the plays themselves. This theatrical couple became dear friends, helping me wherever possible and directing me in several productions during the next year or two. I certainly enjoyed their style of directing and greatly benefited by working with them.

Every two years, the theatre would hold general elections and the members of the group would select and then vote for the chairs for the various departments. For some reason, that I never fully understood, there was a move afoot to oust Phil and Jim from their position as production chairmen.

The first that I heard of this was when a member approached me to run as production chairman. Naturally I declined, because I liked Jim and Phil and thought that they were doing a fine job, and hoped they would continue in that position for many more years.

Human behavior and its inherent weakness has always been a mystery to most human beings, and particularly to myself, and so what happened next always perplexed me to say the least. Evidently the person that invited me to run for the *'Dulmage'* position was aware of my own weakness and persuaded me, far too easily as it turned out, to run for that coveted position. They applied the age-old technique of flattery to convince me that I was perfect for the position, and in the process managed to inflate my already robust ego to even further heights of self-importance.

Every fiber of my body told me to decline this Machiavellian attempt to dethrone my friends, but the power of flattery destroyed my sense of fair play and I entered my name in the contest, and to my great surprise easily won the position. Jim and Phil were very gracious, and continued to be very supportive of me in many ways, even though I had let them down. Over my term as production chairman I did my very best to make it up to them, often consulting them when I needed advice or assistance and they, with their usual generosity, never let me down.

Many lessons are learned as we travel our path in life, and the lesson that I learned from this event was indelibly imprinted on my mind. Never again would I listen to, or entertain, any offer or suggestion to undermine a friend.

The years that I appeared on stage were wonderful, the different roles that I played were both exciting and rewarding and with the encouragement of my inflated ego, I even began to believe that I was a pretty good actor.

Hollywood Beckons

When people offered words of praise for particular roles that I played, I wallowed in the glory of it all, never getting enough adulation or praise. Eventually I believed that I had what it takes to make it in the movies, so I made plans to go to Hollywood.

At twenty-eight years of age I thought that I had it made. I was reasonably good looking, at least that is what I thought. I still had my hair, my teeth, some muscle and a tremendous reserve of energy and conceit.

Barb, ever supportive, allowed me to make plans for my assault on Hollywood, and though she never gave full support to the move, she never actually vetoed my plan.

After a long period preparing for the Odyssey ahead, finishing jobs that were underway, paying bills, and making financial arrangements with my bank manager to ensure that my wife had funds for her survival while I was gone, I began my quest.

Initially I wanted to go to New York to try my hand at acting, hopefully on the Great White Way, however, Joan, an old theatre friend of mine, had moved to California and wrote that it was a land of opportunity for any one with talent.

Ignoring the obvious innuendo, I changed my plans and headed to Hollywood. The first week I stayed at the Nickerbocker Hotel, and then moved to a little apartment on Yuma Street just behind the Capital records building.

The apartment building was strategically situated just under the Hollywood freeway and provided an uninterrupted stream of traffic sounds including, the roar of truck engines, police and ambulance sirens, exploding tires, blaring horns, traffic jams and frequently, vehicle accidents.

Joan was an accomplished opera singer. She lived in an apartment building right next door to the 'madhouse' I called home. She was unemployed, awaiting the phone call that would revive her operatic career.

Evidently she had been waiting for several years, and though she was confident that the call would come soon, I was not entirely convinced myself, and so I suggested that she should come to auditions with me, once I found out where those auditions were.

She promised me that she would do just that, But as time went by and little came of her promise, I began to realize that she had become totally discouraged and no longer believed in herself. I did my very best to encourage her, but I found that she no longer had the desire to perform, and would or could not bring herself to try.

Everyday I would try to audition for a part in a play, often answering 'cattle calls', that movie studios staged when they were looking for actors for crowd scenes or mob scenes. If the casting agent asked if I could ride a horse, or drive a bus, or milk a cow, I would answer in the affirmative.

Unfortunately they never asked me if I could hang wallpaper or cut a roof, so I had no opportunity to say that I was an expert in anything, although I did begin riding horses when I was six years old. On that particular occasion my family and I were at the 1939 Worlds Fair in San Francisco. We were driving down to Los Angeles to visit my grandparents who lived there, and since we were in San Francisco we all went to see the fair.

There were horses there, some were big and some were small. I wanted to ride on the biggest horse because I thought that it would go the fastest. So when the man asked me if I had ever ridden a horse before I said "Yes", although truthfully it was only a wooden horse on a merry go round in Victoria, but what the heck, a horse is a horse, isn't it? Even though they gave me the biggest horse, I was still disappointed, because the darn thing was the slowest animal they had on that circle and I couldn't even get it to break into a trot.

While in Hollywood I discovered the magazine 'Variety'. It listed every play, musical, or movie that was casting that day, and I answered every call I could, in the process becoming a very proficient auditionee, although not necessarily a successful one.

Once I auditioned at the 'El Capitan', an old theatre on Vine Street, a block up from Hollywood Boulevard. They were casting a play called 'Under the Yum Yum Tree'.

I had previously directed it at Langham Court Theatre, and thought that I would be right for one of the roles. I wrote all my particulars, including Joan's phone number and the fact that I lived just around the corner on Yuma Street, not that it impressed them that much, but what the heck, it wasn't a lie.

They said that they were very interested and that they would give me a call when they had decided on the cast. Of course when you auditioned, you would often get such words of encouragement, so I took it with the usual grain of salt.

Several months later, after I left Hollywood, the director called Joan and said that the actor they hired had not worked out and they wanted me for that role. When Joan phoned and told me of the call, I laughed and said that there was nothing that would ever entice me away from my family again.

Years later they converted the El Capitan into a major television studio calling it the Hollywood Palace, and produced many big name shows there including the highly successful *'Jerry Lewis Show'*.

One night I was having a nightcap at a bar on Santa Monica Boulevard and was sitting next to a huge man who kept plugging the jukebox and playing Frank Sinatra records. A man on the other side of me took exception to his choice of songs and started giving him a hard time. I told him to stop picking on him; after all he was the one who was putting all the money into the machine.

The man who was plugging the box put his arm around me and hugged me. At first I thought that some bear had grabbed me from behind, but the guy started whispering in my ear and saying what a great fella I was for standing up for him. The other man finally got up and left the bar.

The bear introduced himself as Stormy Minkle, a bodyguard for none other than Frank Sinatra. He told me that he was the one who punched out the fellow who insulted Frankie in the parking lot at the Moulin Rouge, a well-known nightclub in Hollywood. Evidently Frank did not like what the man had said to him and had Stormy put out his lights. This incident had occurred a month or two before I arrived in Hollywood, and had made the front page of newspapers all over North America. I read it one morning in the Daily Colonist and so it was fresh in my mind.

Stormy invited me back to his apartment for a drink and also to see his collection of Frank Sinatra memorabilia. I figured that he probably was partial to girls rather than boys and so I agreed to go with him, but on the condition that he didn't hug me anymore.

He lived close by so we walked to his place chatting all the way. He was a very animated character with a good sense of humour, and I liked him in spite of his gruff manner and shuffling gait. He somehow reminded me of the cartoon character Yogi Bear, although his face reminded me more of an over the hill prize fighter.

His apartment was well kept though relatively small, considering that he was such a large man, and true to his description was filled with every conceivable piece of Sinatra memorabilia that I had ever seen, or thought existed.

His collection of Sinatra records was nothing short of amazing. Evidently Frank made sure that all his hired hands were well stocked with his latest hits and also signed photos of himself and his many friends. I couldn't help but wonder if the bathroom held any special *'objects de Arte'*, or special pictures, but thought better of broaching the subject just in case it rubbed him the wrong way. My sense of adventure often led me into some very interesting situations, and this was one of those special events, and I enjoyed every minute of it.

Stormy asked me if I would like to talk to Frank himself, and I, thrilled beyond reason, responded with a resounding yes. He pulled a card from his wallet with Frank's number in Palm Springs on it, and dialed while I frantically tried to think of something intelligent or witty to say. Unfortunately I was unable to speak to Mr. Sinatra because he was not at home that night and his buddy, another hired hand, who answered the phone, had no idea where he was or when he would be back. Undaunted, Stormy dialed several other numbers trying to track him down, but was unable to contact him.

While I was somewhat disappointed at not getting the chance to talk with 'Ole Blue Eyes' , I actually felt relieved that I wouldn't have to make a fool of myself by saying something inane or downright silly to Frankie. My new friend Stormy was even more disappointed than I was at not being able to talk to his idol, and he all but wept when he ran out of numbers to call and finally had to give up.

It was revealed to me that Mr. Sinatra had hired hands in most towns that he would visit, and they were always ready and waiting to do his bidding. The teary eyed Stormy was no exception and was keenly looking forward to seeing him again or at least talking with him on the phone, but this was not going to be the night and he was devastated. The evening with *Stormy* was a lot of fun but it was getting late and I thought that I should be going but he was still in a talkative mood and would not hear of me leaving just then.

It had been my experience, that some people would expect you to stay and listen to them all night, or at least until they grew tired of talking, at which point they would quickly send you on your way. On one such an occasion a fellow that I used to build houses for in Victoria invited Barb and me to a small party, actually there were only the four of us there as it turned out. He expected us to drink rum, talk, drink more rum, talk even more, and then get down to serious drinking.

Unfortunately, or fortunately, depending on whether you talked to my wife or me, I have never been able to hold more than a small amount of alcohol. I either become comatose, or an aggressive competitor in the *'Greatest Lover in the Universe'* competition. Then I ended up with nothing more than an extended stay in the 'doghouse'.

On one particular occasion I was intent on limiting my consumption of demon rum to a minimum, only swallowing the amount I could safely handle. My host, on the other hand was convinced that I should drink even more than usual, and kept refilling my glass. Finally I resorted to an old trick, and deposited most of the fiery liquid into the potted palm in the corner of the front room. But as luck would have it, he observed me during one of the potted palm maneuvers, and flipped his lid.

He then filled his own glass with rum, and in front his wife, my wife and me, poured his drink on the rooms beautiful, thick white carpet, and then, not satisfied that I was completely chastised by my indiscretion, he pulled the phonograph player compartment out of his expensive stereo cabinet, and stomped on it, knocking it to the floor.

When describing this incident to a friend the next day, saying how upset I was at his complete lack of concern over the beautiful and expensive piece of furniture that he had all but destroyed, my friend said that I was lucky, because on one occasion when someone refused to drink with him, he chased the man out to his car and then shot at the tires of his vehicle, using a large caliber rifle.

Remembering this bizarre episode, and the odd behavior of some people who drink to excess, I was trying to be very careful not to rouse the beast that I suspected lay just beneath the surface of my friend Stormy. I began telling him about my wife and how I missed her and would he mind if I phoned her. He agreed to this call, not realizing that it was a very long distance. Once I had her on the phone I told her all about my friend Stormy, and how he had punched some body's lights out in the parking lot of the Moulin Rouge at the request of Frank Sinatra, and that he had tried to phone Frank so that I could talk with him, and also that I was trying to get out of his apartment before he punched my lights out. At length I asked Stormy to say a word to her, but by this time he was beginning to suspect that this was not a local call, and after a few short words with Barb, he suggested that I had talked enough and that I should hang up. Good old Stormy became somewhat upset that I had phoned all the way to Canada, and I quickly offered to pay for the call. This had a very calming effect on him and so I was able to thank him for all he done for me and said that hopefully we could get together again very soon, and that if he was ever up in Canada he should be sure to look me up. Shortly after that I took my leave, happy that Stormy was still my friend and delighted to have met such a likeable rogue.

During the few months that I stayed in Hollywood I went to every audition I could manage, sometimes two or three a day, and though not successful at most auditions, I did gain a lot of knowledge about the professional theatre business. There were always a number of people at these auditions and many became quite familiar to me. Often as we sat around waiting for our turn in front of the casting director we would chat about the different roles we had played and our hopes for the future. It became obvious to me that most people involved in theatre would probably never make it professionally, and that likely, I belonged in that category.

One day after reading the 'Variety', I phoned for an appointment to audition for the play *'Blood Sweat and Stanley Poole'*, at the *'Players Ring'* on Santa Monica Boulevard. My appointment was booked for an early afternoon three weeks hence. When that day arrived, I went to the theatre and gave the person in charge my resume and photo. I really did not expect to get a role but I did my best and was delighted to be able to have a chat with the director, who just happened to be Canadian. We had a fairly long chat about life in general, but strangely, very little about theatre.

When I left the audition I felt very confident that I would get a role, and happily, three weeks later I was invited to join the *'Second Company'*, in a very good role. During rehearsals with the cast of *'Blood Sweat'* I discovered that a fairly well known actor, whom I had seen in different movies over the years, was performing my role in the *'First Company'*. The director evidently thought that I looked like him, and probably thought that I could also act as well as he could. At the first rehearsal of the play I was shocked to find that every other actor knew all of their lines and most of their moves while I knew very few of my lines and none of my moves. It seemed to me that either these actors had already received direction or they were geniuses. Unfortunately I did not have genius in my resume, so I had to stay up most of the next few nights learning my lines and moves.

One of the cast had been in the movie *'Breakfast at Tiffany's'* and was terrific on stage. His role was fairly large, but most of it was left on the cutting room floor. He was very disappointed but still happy that he had at least appeared in the film.

When I saw the movie the next week, and realized that the major part of his role had been discarded, I began to feel that perhaps the life of a movie actor was not all it was cracked up to be. I remembered my short roles in the two movies, and the disappointment of seeing only a fleeting moment of myself on screen, and began to believe that the energy I spent chasing roles, and the mind sapping boredom of entire days waiting for a brief moment on film only to end up on the cutting room floor, was the beginning of the end of my movie career.

By this time my money had nearly run out and I was beginning to understand the true meaning of poverty, so I made the decision to go back to the real world and to get a temporary paying job, to help with my hard pressed finances, and to tide me over while I pursued my questionable future in the movie business.

The first move that I made was to locate the Carpenters Union office in Hollywood. I know that I swore never to talk to a union representative ever again; however, it is surprising just what a fellow will stoop to when on the verge of starvation.

The moment I approached the reception desk, my sixth sense warned me that this was not a place that I should be. A secretary, surrounded by a cloud of tobacco smoke, was concentrating on her lacquered nails, seemingly unaware of my presence. I hesitated, imagining that I was in the wrong place, and seeking employment where I might meet an underworld boss.

At last she acknowledged me giving me a quizzical look as though she was mystified at the interruption, and asked me if she could help me. My immediate response was to tell her that I was looking to put out a contract on someone; however I managed to pull myself together and informed her that I was looking to join the union.

Her response was that the union was not accepting any new members at that time, and it wasn't likely that they would accept any new members any time soon, but, after a moving display of theatrical eloquence on my part, she did manage to reveal a glimpse of compassion, and suggested that I could talk with the boss. At that, she turned to the intercom on her desk, pressed the right button and announced that Clifford Clarke wished to have a word with him.

Entering the inner sanctum of the great man was an experience and, as a man of the theatre, I absorbed every moment and minute detail of that smoke filled room.

The *'Boss'*, as I had expected, sat in a patent leather swivel chair. He was visibly overweight, dressed in a bright floral shirt and smoking a large smelly cigar. He seemed to realize that I was a foreigner; it may have been the way that I was dressed, or possibly the way I said "Eh!" whenever he asked me a question that I didn't understand. Eventually I made it known that I would like to find a job as a carpenter and how did I go about joining the union.

He repeated the story that I had just heard from his secretary, adding that the first thing I would have to do in order to join the union would be to file intent to become an American citizen. Then I would pay the dues, which I thought were exorbitant, and put my name on the list. Finally I could join all the other hopefuls at the union hall each day, waiting until every old timer was hired before I would get my chance at a job and, by the way, there were thirty three locals in LA and thirteen hundred men out of work. I suggested that I could visit work sites and find my own job. He responded in a very negative manner, suggesting that I had a snowball's chance of getting around the rules of the hallowed union institution, and if I tried that sort of thing he would not be responsible for what might happen, and that I would be better off looking for work in Oklahoma. After my unhappy encounter with the union *'boss'*, I decided that my chance of getting work as a carpenter was close to zero, so I began looking elsewhere for employment.

The May Company

One of the first places I tried was the 'May Company', a department store on Whilshire Boulevard. That district had a particularly large Jewish population living close by, and they were probably the major source of business for the store. The company itself was Jewish owned and relied on its employees to keep up good relations with the their customers, particularly those of Jewish descent.

There has always been a soft spot in my heart for the Jewish race and I was delighted to get a job at the May Co., even though the job paid far less wages than I was used to getting. When I applied I did not know just how much they paid, but quite frankly I really didn't mind as I was close to starvation.

The lady in charge of hiring had me fill out an application form which asked, among other things, how much I earned at my previous job, and I so filled out the form including the amount I used to make as a building contractor.

When the lady read my application, she noted that the wages paid at the May Co. were nowhere near the amount that I had previously made. When I explained that I only needed enough money to pay my rent and buy the odd loaf of bread, she patted my hand and said that she understood my situation, and that I could have the job starting right away. When she told me that my starting wage would be one dollar and twenty-five cents an hour I almost burst out laughing, but I mentally worked out the amount that I would receive and decided that if I was very careful I would be able to manage on that amount, at least for a short time.

My position in the hardware department suited me very well. As a carpenter I truly did understand the hardware business and so I fit in rather well. Whenever a job was given me, I would always do my very best to make it fun, and though this position paid very little money I wasn't going to let that stand in the way of any enjoyment, and so I applied myself to the work at hand and also applied myself to the golden rule, *'If it's not fun, it's not worth doing.'*

This hardware store was different than most other hardware places I had dealt with, and it handled a variety of products as well as the expected hammers and saws, plumb bobs and levels, including wooden furniture, paints, garden implements and an assortment of kitchen gadgets.

After a very short introductory message from the department manager who was, as it turned out, a Canadian from Saskatchewan I was given a key to the cash register, a receipt book, and finally, a nudge in the right direction with the instructions to go get them.

From the very start I had a ball, and I found that I truly enjoyed selling the products and so I made it a point of meeting as many customers at the door as I could, welcoming them to the May Co. and asking them if I could help them.

Within a short time I was selling more merchandise than any of the other salespeople on the floor, and having fun doing it, of course not realizing that my energy and the application of the golden rule was giving them a royal pain in the butt.

One day, a classic Yiddish mama entered the store and without replying to my cheery greeting informed me that she *"Vanted a scrrew"*. I avoided the obvious cliché and the normal response to such an opening line and, with all the seriousness that I could muster, informed her that she had come to the right place.

Leading the way to the *"scrrew"* section of the store, I kept up a lively discussion regarding the well stocked shelves in this department, and the likelihood that we would be able to satisfy her needs, possibly even her desires if absolutely necessary, although that particular part of the discussion was barely audible.

At that time, screws only came in boxes containing a gross, and most users would buy the full box using whatever was necessary to complete the job, and then keeping the remaining screws for future use. After a short search, we located the size that she required and I suggested that I would carry them up to the cash desk for her.

At this point the dear lady informed me that she only *"Vanted vone scrrew"*. I began to wonder if I had misunderstood her and so, asked her exactly what she wanted that screw for. She explained that she had an article in her home held together by these little screws and one had fallen out and had ultimately disappeared, and she was sorry for the inconvenience, but she only *"Vanted vone scrrew"*.

By nature I am a hugger, and I have discovered that pretty well every person on the face of this earth loves a hug once in a while, and this lady was no exception. When I looked at that dear soul, and saw the concern that came over her when I suggested that she purchase the entire box of screws, my heart melted, and I was unable to stop myself from stretching out my arms and enveloping her in my embrace.

For a moment all activity in the hardware department came to a halt, as every eye in the store turned toward me, amazed at the sight of an employee of the May Co. hugging a Jewish lady, and even more amazed at seeing the Jewish lady returning the hug with all her being. Finally, while still in that embrace, I whispered in her ear that she could have one screw.

She whispered, *"How much vill that cost?"*

I whispered, *"Nothing, but when you need a full box, please come back to the May Co."*

It seemed that at the May Co. staff did not hug customers and so, after having several words with the manager, words that I suspected were near reproachful, I gave him a big hug and told him that hugging was an old family custom handed down from our Greek ancestors, who lived in Brighton England during the days of Augustus, and I found that it was a difficult habit to break as I feared the wrath of our forefathers.

The following day the anticipated announcement came over the stores loudspeakers, *"Will Clifford Clarke please come to the office."*

The trip up to the office on the fourth floor was uneventful, although one

Cliff 1964

of the staff that worked in my department did give me a peculiar look as she passed me on the stairway. I wanted to hug her too, but she was moving too fast. Once in the upper office, I was relieved to see several smiling faces looking my way. My first impulse was to hug all the bodies attached to them but darn it, the hugging episode was getting out of hand and I wasn't all that sure that those Greek ancestors were too keen on hugging anyway.

When I was ushered into the office manager's quarters I was shown to a seat, which faced a large mahogany desk, and asked to wait a moment please. I began to wonder if hugging was a criminal offence and if I was there for interrogation.

My mind was running wild and I was considering whether I should mention that hugging was an old Jewish tradition handed down in my family over the centuries, or whether it might be better to confess that I was so lonely I needed some human contact to keep me from going insane.

The manager was a lovely lady with flashing black eyes and a smile a mile wide. She spoke with a hint of a Yiddish accent, and asked how I was, and if I was enjoying the work at the May Co. I told her that I was having a ball and loved having such close contact with so many wonderful people.

She laughed at that comment and said that the company was pleased with me and that even though I had only been there for three weeks they were going to raise my wages to one dollar and fifty cents per hour.

"Then you don't mind my behavior on the floor, and my propensity to hug customers", I said, "*In the line of duty of course."*

She laughed again, and said, *"The lady you hugged yesterday was my mother."*

My trip down from the fourth floor took me a little longer than the trip up, and strangely I was not feeling the joy that perhaps I should have, given the raise and all. But somehow I felt it would have been better if they had fired me, because by that time I was close to deciding to go home, and I was feeling very guilty that they had shown such faith in me and I, in all probability. would not be there for very long

When I returned to the hardware department the manager immediately came over to me and asked me what they had wanted upstairs. I tried to think up some reason, other than the truth, because I knew that he would not be happy at my good fortune, and as it turned out I was right.

Usually I can think up logical excuses or alibis in an instant, but at that moment I was completely at a loss for words and I began to mutter and stammer inanely, all the while trying to come up with some brilliant answer. Finally, bereft of any intelligent thought, I mumbled that for some reason they had given me a raise. He of course would not settle for that short answer, and pressed me for more details.

Reluctantly, I confessed that they had raised my wages to one dollar and fifty cents an hour. At that he angrily told me that he had been here for nine years and all he was making was one dollar and fifty cents per hour and how the hell did I rate that much of a raise after only a few weeks.

It has always been my custom to avoid any form of bragging or gloating when good fortune happens my way, for others are never truly happy unless they can have a share of it and so I once again came to the realization that no matter how careful you are, jealousy will always cause ill feelings and misunderstandings and will ultimately destroy almost any relationship faster than any other type of disagreement. The once happy atmosphere seemed to change and I found that I really did not enjoy my work there as I had before.

Whenever possible I would spend time walking the historic streets of Los Angeles, poking about in every well known building, restaurant, drugstore, looking for famous people, all the while hoping that I might have the opportunity to speak to some of them. My efforts were often rewarded and I did indeed speak to many well-known characters that I had enjoyed in the movies over the years.

Many mornings I would have breakfast at a restaurant on the corner of Hollywood and Vine two blocks from my apartment. Some mornings, I would sit next to Percy Kilbride, the well-known star of the 'Ma and Pa Kettle' movies that I watched years before. He was exactly the same in real life as he was on the screen. We had many interesting chats and I never tired of hearing him talk of his days on the farm.

Once an acquaintance offered to take me to meet Marion Anderson, a former star of the Metropolitan Opera, and I jumped at the chance to meet this singing icon. My acquaintance was writing an article on opera and had an appointment with her one afternoon, and I tagged along like a schoolboy going to the fair.

Ms. Anderson was most gracious and treated us royally, serving us tea and cookies and also sparkling conversation. It seemed that she was deeply committed to the art of human communication, and spent an enormous amount of time attending seminars around the world.

The subject of human communication was extremely interesting and of great importance to the world, particularly between different nationalities. I was particularly interested in her knowledge and understanding and the gift she had in that area. I was completely taken with her genuine love of that subject. That wonderful afternoon passed by very quickly, but I never forgot her sincerity and inspirational wisdom. I tried my very best to learn more about human communication, and to hopefully apply it in my own life.

There were many more encounters with a variety of actors and actresses during my stay in Hollywood and I enjoyed every one of them. My friend Joan was acquainted with an actor by the name of Rex Reason. He had starred in many movies and television shows and was incredibly good looking and talented. She often had him over to her home for visits and thought that I would also enjoy his humour and wit.

We spent several afternoons together, visiting and enjoying his stories involving other famous stars, and hearing the account of his long running tiff with Charlton Heston. Evidently, he frequently found himself competing for the same roles with Heston, and usually lost out to him. In the process, he was able to study the star's movements and gestures and eventually developed a brilliant and hilarious impersonation of him and, while in our company, he would act out the various scenarios he had developed and keep us in stitches for hours.

Rex had been a champion athlete in his early days and sometimes entertained us by performing terrific physical feats. The one that stands out was his ability to stand on one hand, do a full press, and then hop up and down on the same arm, moving about the room like a pogo stick.

Going Back Home

One day on a drive along the ocean toward Malibu I encountered heavy traffic on all three lanes heading north. After one hour breathing engine fumes and fighting traffic I had enough. The next day I resigned my position at the May Co., said goodbye to Joan, paid my phone bill, hugged my landlord, regretfully gave up my role in 'Blood and Sweat', packed up all the little goodies that I had acquired while in Hollywood and jumped into my 1956 Chevrolet convertible and headed North.

The first day I traveled from LA to Red Bluff where I stopped for the night. Early the next morning I continued my drive north. Shortly after on the outskirts of Red Bluff I picked up a hitchhiker. He was on his way to Seattle but had no money. I bought him two or three meals that day, loaned him a toothbrush and gave him a few dollars. He said that he would send the money as soon as he was settled and got a job. I did not expect to get anything back and so I was not disappointed that I never heard from him again.

My mother was the most generous woman that I ever met, and always stressed the point that one should always be willing to help out another human being, whether they were ever able to repay it back or not. The fact that I was able to help the young man was payment enough for me.

When I arrived at the Canadian border, an agent asked me where I had purchased the car. Without any hesitation I told him that I bought it in Los Angeles and that I was hoping to keep it in Canada. The agent informed me that it was not permissible to bring it into Canada and that I would have to leave it in the U.S. or sell it before returning to Canada.

The trip had been very tiring, and when he told me that I couldn't continue my journey, I was extremely disappointed. My options seemed very bleak, and the thought of not being able to go straight home to Barb and the kids was devastating. As I looked him in the eye, I suddenly remembered Marion Anderson and her powerful conviction that communication is the best solution to most problems.

Normally I would try to overcome a situation like this with subterfuge, storytelling or even my own form of logic. But this was an entirely different situation. I was faced with the realization that I was not going to be permitted to pass through the border unless I got rid of the car.

The car itself was filled to overflowing with all the stuff that I had acquired over the past few months, and the thought of having to find a way to get it to my home without transportation, seemed an impossibility, and the fact that I only had a few dollars left and no way to get anymore, caused me near panic.

Whenever I look back at some of the seemingly impossible situations I have found myself in over the years, I realize that my life has been touched with many small blessings, and that some force or power has watched over me, helping me whenever I have been in need. From that early age when I was saved at camp, I always believed that prayer and faith would pull me through most difficulties.

As that agent and I stood looking at each other, I suddenly found myself telling him all about my trip to Hollywood, and how I had met so many interesting and famous people, and how I had tried my best to break into the movies, and also about the many disappointments I had experienced while pursuing this dream.

Leaving nothing out, I told him that I had finally come to the realization that my place was with my family back home. I told him I was broke and had no money to stay away, for even one more day. I also promised him that if he would allow me to take the car back I would return it to the U.S. as soon as I possibly could.

The agent listened to my story and my plea to allow me to take the car home, and then turning away from me, he walked to an office in the back of the building. After a few minutes he returned and said that they would allow me to take the car over the border if I would promise to return it within the month.

In all instances, when I have been blessed, I physically sense the weight being lifted from my shoulders and experience brightness in my soul that outshines any earthly light. The joy I felt at that moment must have shone like a beacon, because that agent broke into the most wonderful smile I have ever witnessed and wished me the best of luck.

A feeling of euphoria enveloped me during that final stage of my trip home, and I knew that coming home was the wisest decision of my life. As I approached my home I saw a little girl in a *'Brownie'* uniform walking along the road, and I recognized her as my own beautiful daughter Maureen. When I stopped the car and asked her if she would like a lift, she shook her head no, so I said, *"Would you like a jelly bean?"*

Maureen looked at me as though she had seen a ghost, *"Are you my dad?"* she said, and she ran to the car and threw her arms around me unable to say anything except, *"Is it really you?"*

The rest of my homecoming is a blur, I only know that my family were overjoyed to see me and made me promise never to leave again.

Barbara's aunt Bea lived in Port Angeles with her husband 'Biz'. He was a prominent businessman there and had many connections. When he heard the story of my trip and that I would have to take the car back to the U.S. he made a phone call to a friend who owned a car lot, and arranged for him to purchase the car from me.

The car was a beauty, which I had purchased for five hundred dollars. The friend of 'Biz' thought that the car was in excellent shape and paid me six hundred dollars for it.

Today, one could name their own price for that little beauty, and I was always sorry that I could not have kept it as a souvenir of that memorable adventure and also the reminder of the valuable lessons learned while attempting my shot at fame.

Though I returned from Hollywood satisfied that professional theatre was not for me, I always loved the stage and continued my involvement with many different theatrical groups in and around Victoria, often performing in several shows each year.

Our Revival of "Mr. Toad"

Before my trip to Hollywood I had performed in a wonderful play called 'Toad of Toad Hall', adapted from *'The Wind in the Willows'*, written by Kenneth Grahame. My dear friend Anthony [Tony] Burton directed the play several times over three or four years, and each time I played the role of Mr. Toad.

'Toady' was an extraordinary character filled with adventure and spirit who wished to experience everything that life could offer, and more, much, much more. Somehow the character of Mr. Toad suited me perfectly and I enjoyed my association with him throughout my life, eventually building a little theatre on my property in Mill Bay and calling it *'Toad Hall'*.

We first produced *'Toad of Toad Hall'* in the Langham Court Theatre in Victoria, with Tony Burton as director. The show was a great hit with both the young and old, and especially with children. Because of our success of this classic play, we decided to do it again, and over the next few years we did mount it in several theatres and venues.

On one occasion a visitor from Port Angeles saw our production at Langham Court, and asked us to bring it over to their town for three days. We of course were delighted with the invitation and immediately began modifying the sets and making preparations for our first national run.

Crossing the border with our load of costumes, sets, and props had not seemed a problem while we were making our plans to take our show abroad, and so we did not make any preliminary inquiries as to whether we could or could not take the overflowing truck load of stuff, and the bus full of actors over to the U.S.

We approached the border with no inkling that there was even a possibility that the officers in charge would be anything but delighted, at the opportunity of helping our group bring a little culture to their town. However, it appeared that the gentlemen who interrogated us, had either

Cliff as "Toad"

no experience with live theatre or perhaps thought that we might be the advance troops for a foreign take-over.

For one hour they gave us a thorough going over, inspecting every piece of equipment, set, and costume, that we had managed to cram into that five-ton truck. As the sugar daddy, or angel, who was footing the bill I was spokesperson for the group and as such I was front and center at the interrogation.

Remembering all my past encounters with hostile interrogators, I removed all negative thoughts from my mind and concentrated on the age-old wisdom, handed down from my forefathers, that you can catch more flies with honey than with vinegar. I was never sure why anyone would want to catch flies, but I thought that if this was considered wisdom of the ages, then it was good enough for me.

Patiently I answered all the officers questions regarding the theatrical contents of the truck and their concerns about the horde of people in the bus, who were by this time reacting to the delay and the long wait, by carrying on with typical stage-like tomfoolery.

The younger people were hanging out the bus windows, singing songs from the production, waving at other travelers and in general entertaining the onlookers. The older characters, Ratty, Mole, Badger, the judge, washerwoman, etc., managed to maintain their decorum and dignity, although periodically offering succinct comments on the state of the union.

Explaining our circumstances and the reason for being there at that particular time, and the fact that some of their own distinguished citizens had invited us there, and also that we were hoping to share our culture with the townspeople like good neighbours should, I confessed that I had once been part of the theatre scene in America, and had many wonderful memories of that great country and its cherished institutions. I added that it would be a pleasure and an honour if they would come to see our production the next night.

Within a period of time, actually it was almost their lunchtime, our charm and wit finally melted their resistance and resolve, and they were at last persuaded that our cause was just, and that in all likelihood we were not a serious threat to their national security, and therefore we were free to go.

Our production was held in the local high school auditorium, a theatre like venue with state of the art equipment and acoustics. Every whisper or word on stage was heard right to the very back of the hall, and at the final curtain the warm American audience gave us a standing ovation.

Our hosts arranged for our accommodation at a very nice motel close to town. Barb and I however, stayed at Biz and aunt Bea's house on the hill overlooking the town, and while the rest of the cast raised hell at the motel we, blissfully unaware of the ruckus going on at the other establishment, enjoyed quiet nights with our relatives.

The final morning we joined the others for breakfast and found the whole lot unusually quiet and subdued. Finally Tony filled us in. Evidently several of the cast members had let loose and played musical beds that last night, while

Tony and his wife did their best to track them down, hopefully to return them to their correct rooms. During this musical interlude one of the younger members of the cast tried her luck at eluding our director by bunking with Ratty who, by the way, was the least likely person in the group to carry on in this manner.

Tony had at last tracked this young lady to Ratty's lair, and after a lengthy discussion, persuaded Ratty to release his grip on her and allow her to return to her proper room. During this musical merry-go-round, Tony's wife was also on the prowl looking for others who had somehow become mixed up in this nocturnal soiree but, unlike Tony, she was very vocal with the miscreants, which caused a commotion that soon awoke the rest of the cast who then joined in the merriment.

The owners of the motel were a very nice couple and fortunately lived in a house a short distance from the site. They were not totally aware of the shenanigans that were going on at their motel, as the majority of the activity was carried out in near silence, rather like a Keystone cop episode on the silent screen. They did become fully aware of it, however, when a close neighbour happened to notice all the people that were running in and out of the building, and suspecting a fire, called the fire department.

It took some explaining as to what had happened that night and why there was such activity going on in and around the motel, but fortunately Tony was a master of communication, and after some eloquent dialogue persuaded everyone to go to bed including the Fire Chief and the Deputy Marshall.

This very interesting turn of events certainly influenced any thoughts that we might have had on any future stage tours, and convinced us that, in the unlikely event that we ever received another invitation to perform abroad, it would definitely be worthwhile to take armed chaperons with us. As for my part, I was very thankful to have been completely innocent of any wrongdoing in this episode, and able to hold my head up in the face of any criticism that fell upon our group, and particularly happy that I had the best alibi of anyone on the tour.

Whenever anyone asked us about our tour we always spoke of the friendship and camaraderie that had developed between the cast and the people of Port Angeles, and how they loved us and could hardly wait for our return.

After we returned to Victoria, and recovered from the rigors of the tour, we decided to stage *'Toad'* again, using the same sets, costumes and props as we had used before. The venue was a former nightclub known as the *Club Sirocco*, on View Street just below Cook.

The owner of the club was a delightful man. He allowed us to rent the large ballroom for our production, and permitted us to enlarge the stage area by building a stage apron that projected outward, and to also do other minor renovations to accommodate the play. We in turn agreed to give him a percentage of the ticket sales as rental for the facility.

We set the opening date for December twenty second, three days before Christmas, planning on running through the week to New Years, with the exception of Christmas Day. Unfortunately opening a play just before Christmas is very foolish, as we soon discovered, for most people are so busy in the days leading up to Christmas they will not take the time to go to a show; the week following Christmas however, is perfect for almost any theatrical production.

The advertising for *'Toad'* began in the middle of December, and we had good write-ups from the local papers, and every thing seemed to be just fine for a good run. But, the tickets did not sell at all, and by December twenty first there were very few tickets sold for any of the dates scheduled.

On December twenty second we opened to thirty people, most of them members of the cast's families. December twenty third and twenty fourth were even worse and we were very disappointed, but we hoped that Boxing Day would be much better and we continued hoping for the best. When Boxing Day arrived, we opened the doors hoping for a miracle, but fewer than fifty people showed up. After the night's performance, all the cast and technicians gathered for a heart to heart talk.

Everyone knew that I had financed the production, and that the lighting had been rented by the day, from *'Theatre Under the Stars'* in Vancouver, and that there was a minimum daily charge for the club, and that in all probability I would lose my shirt. So, they understood how I was feeling, not only about the loss of money, but the heartbreak and disappointment at spending so much time on the production only to have it fail.

After a long, agonizing talk, we all decided that it would be best if I cut my losses and closed the show. We immediately began dismantling the sets, packing up the lights in their cases, and getting them ready for delivery to Vancouver the next day. The following morning I arranged for the lights to be picked up and also the sets, props and costumes, and by twelve noon we were gone.

Several weeks later I dropped by the club to pay the owner the balance

'Die Fledermaus" directed by Cliff featuring fledgling tenor Richard Margison

of the rent. He had not called to ask for the rent, nor had I called him. When I walked into his office he hugged me, and told me that he was sorry that things had not worked out for us, and what a pity it was that we had not continued the show as we had advertised, because the very day that we packed up and left, the phone began to ring, people wanting tickets, some wanting to bring groups of kids, others wanting to bring relatives and friends, and that night over one hundred and fifty people arrived at the door to see the show. The owner said that he had never seen any thing like it, and that everyone he spoke to was broken hearted that we had not continued the run.

There are so many lessons to be learned in life, and this lesson was probably one of the most difficult ones I ever had to deal with. Not only did I lose money, but even worse, I let people down. For the rest of my working life I never forgot that disappointment and I resolved to finish anything and everything that I started, no matter the problems or losses or discouragement.

This resolve caused many problems throughout my life, because from that time on I found it very difficult to walk away from anything I started, even when it would have been the best thing to do. Even my dear wife was never able to completely convince me that there are certain things in life that are better dropped than continued, and so I kept plugging along, doing my level best to make everything that I did a success, and to a certain degree I succeeded. But now, many years later, I realize that some things would have been better left alone and perhaps that everything that I did was not necessarily a great success.

Cliff as 'Dame Twankey'

Dame Agnes and Madam Twankey

Dame 'Twankey

During those years life carried on satisfactorily, my four children were growing up, my construction company was doing fairly well, and I was enjoying the stage and acting in many plays and musicals. One day, my friend Tony asked me to play the role of 'Dame Agnes' in an English pantomime called *'Dick Whittington and his Cat'*.

Pantomime is an institution in England, and various *'Pantos'* are staged throughout the British Isles during each Christmas season. A male comic always plays the lead woman, and a beautiful girl always plays the lead boy.

My roles of Dame Agnes and Madam Twanky opened up a whole new theatrical venture for me, and I played the dear old souls many times over the following years, and never tired of the role.

Madame Twanky and Dame Agnes are lovable *'old broads'* who never hesitate to put their noses into other peoples business, but have hearts as big as all outdoors. They are extremely vain, and show it by the extravagant and seemingly endless supply of gowns and wigs that they showcase whenever possible. Although they border on vulgar, they manage to radiate a sense of well-being and oft times wisdom and charm.

All in all Dame Agnes' personality suited me to a tee and I was able to perform the role in *'Dick Whittington and His Cat'*, *'Aladdin'* and other Christmas *Pantos* for several years during the Christmas season.

There was never a time that I did not enjoy theatre to the full, and I probably would have been happy to be perpetually involved, however I did have a family to support and so I was always on the lookout for opportunities to make a little extra money.

Cast of 'Dick Whittington', Cliff as Dame 'Twankey'

Cliff on Stage

Madam Twankey in Aladdin

Romanoff and Juliet

Madam Twankey in Aladdin

Caine Mutiny Court Martial

An Appendectomy

My health has always been excellent and I seldom came down with anything other than the odd cold, but one day I began to have terrible pains in my side, which got worse as the day moved on. Finally I went to my doctor's office, in the building above the Owl Drug store at the corner of Fort and Douglas Street. I waited and waited to see him, but as fate will have it he was tied up with an appendectomy that had gone very wrong and he was not sure when he would return. After about a two hour wait, and unable to endure the pain any longer, I left his office and went into another doctor's office just down the hall, but that doctor was also unavailable, so I continued my two foot shuffle down the hall, going into and out of, every doctor's office that I came upon in the building. At last I found a doctor who had neither patients in the waiting room nor was he involved in any other case at the moment. I hesitated, wondering if perhaps I had stumbled on a quack's office by mistake. But, as I did not have any other options, and the fact that I was almost on my hands and knees with pain, I all but threw myself on the floor in supplication.

The doctor turned out to be a specialist from England, who just happened to be available at that moment. He did a rude thing with his finger and quickly announced that I needed to get to the hospital as fast as I possibly could, for my appendix was on the verge of bursting. After phoning Barb, I drove toward the Jubilee Hospital with all the speed at my disposal, suddenly realizing that I would have to leave my truck there for a day or so. Fortunately my mother lived two or three blocks from the hospital on Ash Street, and so I decided to leave my vehicle there

After parking at the side of the house, I tumbled from my truck like a wounded stag, hurried into my mother's house and asked my brother to take me to the hospital as fast as he could. Again, I encountered another difficulty: my brother's car was not working, and he also had to be down town within a few minutes. Obviously I had no more options, I would have to walk the last few blocks by myself. Cinching my belt up another notch or two, I began my walk toward the hospital, not completely confident that I would make it before the expected eruption took place, but determined to see the thing through to the very end if necessary. By the time I reached the hospital I was very close to being on my knees.

The people that saw me on that seemingly endless path may have come to the conclusion that I was a vagrant, watching me shuffle along, staring at the ground, obviously looking for cast off butts, or perhaps loose change. But I did not care what they thought, what the heck, I could have been taking my last steps.

When I finally staggered into the waiting room, and up to the registry desk I was on my last legs, but I had made it, and I was sure that all the staff in the hospital would no doubt rush to my aid. But I was wrong, the dear lady told me to take a seat over against the wall and wait my turn. After what seemed to be a very long time, I again approached the dear lady and explained that my doctor was probably waiting in the operating room for me at this very minute, and perhaps she should check into it before I was beyond the point of no return, and this whole nasty business came to a sorry end.

Somehow I was not making myself clear, for she asked me once again, to take a seat and said that she would get to me as quickly as possible. Drawing myself to an almost upright position, I looked into her watery eyes, although it may have been my own two watery eyes, I don't know for sure, and with all the authority that I could muster, I told her that if she did not get to me immediately I was going to ring the fire alarm. That must have rung a bell with her, because after a very short pause, possibly a minute or two, she asked me my name and then began writing on an admission form.

"What is your problem", she asked.

I replied that my appendix was about to burst and if she did not move a little faster I was going to die right there in front of her, perhaps even on her desk.

Immediately she made a call on her intercom, and within another minute or so, two orderlies hurried in with a stretcher and promptly laid me on it and then headed off toward what I thought would be either the operating room, or the morgue.

After an elevator ride and a short trip down the hall, they took me into a public ward and transferred me to a bed. They promptly removed my clothes, and then put me in one of those back-less, bottomless green nightgowns, that are so popular in hospitals.

Within a few minutes another orderly came into the room and told me that he was going to shave me. I told him that I had already shaved that morning. He said that he wasn't going to shave my face, indicating that the lower part of my body was his destination.

There was genuine concern on my part, and I informed him that they were taking out my appendix not my privates. After a good laugh which, by the way nearly did me in, he carried out his procedure as he called it and then left, probably back to the barber shop.

The doctor arrived and quickly did the rude thing again, which by this time was getting to be pretty routine, and suggested that we get a move on before the appendix ruptured.

The orderlies returned and rushed me up to the operating theatre on the next floor. The nurses made the necessary preparations, and the doctor filled the syringe with the anesthetic. As he injected the fluid in the needle he said that I would be out very quickly. The last words from me were,

"Remember doc, the appendix, not the privates."

When I awoke from the anesthetic I felt remarkably well, considering the four-inch scar on my abdomen, which I noted, was well above the other area of interest.

The next morning my doctor visited me and told me that everything went well with the operation and that fortunately the appendix had not burst, although it was very close to rupturing. My natural impulse was to hug him, but I quickly discovered that if I moved suddenly the pain in my mid section became unbearable, and so I merely thanked him for all his kindness and wished him the best for his efforts.

During my four-day stay in hospital I was in a four-bed ward with a French Canadian fellow by the name of Henri, whom I soon discovered was a near clone of Bob Hope. He had undergone a similar operation as myself, that is, on the abdomen, and suffered with excruciating pain whenever he moved too quickly or even jiggled his tummy in any way.

Owing to my natural desire to make people laugh, I soon discovered his abdominal weakness but at the same time he discovered that my incision was also susceptible to great pain if I jiggled or shook and so, without any mercy, we both went out of our way to make the other laugh, never hesitating to go to any length to out do the other. Our playful jokes were endless, for we found humour at every turn.

Nurses provided an untapped source of laughter as they traversed the hallways, bedpans in hand. Whenever they would pull the curtains surrounding our beds with the hope of privacy, the other comic would begin a never-ending line of patter, which often caused the poor nurses to scurry from the room with their bounty as quickly as they could, although there was always a nurse or two who could hold her own with these two rascals. Woe-betide the poor devil unlucky enough to require a needle in the bum.

There is no doubt in my mind that the non stop jiggling of our belly's over those laugh filled days, hastened the healing process in both of our bodies, and in my case I was able to return to work within ten days of having the operation.

Christmas Trees, a New Enterprise

During our stay in hospital my now close friend Henri, told me about an idea he had to make some fast money before Christmas. As my project was going to be finished by the end of November, and as always, I was in need of extra funds, I agreed to go partners with him in his little enterprise.

The business he had in mind, entailed purchasing Christmas trees from a fellow he knew in Princeton, who was in the habit of cutting trees from the surrounding mountains and then selling them to any one willing to pay one dollar per tree.

Henri was convinced that we could make a small fortune if we rented the site of a former car lot on Kingsway, and then stood the trees up in rows so all passersby would see them. He also intended to spray some of the trees silver, and sell them for double the amount we might receive for un-painted ones. All in all it was a great idea that couldn't fail, or so he thought.

After confirming an order of one thousand trees at fifty cents a piece, a price that seemed too good to be true, Henri and I made plans to go to Vancouver and arrange for a truck to carry the trees back to the car lot on Kingsway.

We first placed an ad in the Vancouver Province, advertising for a man with a truck who would be willing to drive up to Princeton and back again with the trees. After a one week run our ad netted us one lead, a young man who was in between jobs and pleased to be able to help us. The young man was willing to do the job for us for the very reasonable price of one hundred dollars, plus gas money.

Our Christmas tree business was off to a great start, five hundred dollars for the trees, one hundred and twenty five dollars, give or take a dollar or two, for the transportation, one hundred dollars for miscellaneous expenses, plus a reasonable fifty dollars for the lot.

A thousand trees delivered to our lot for well under one thousand dollars, by golly, this was one enterprise where I was going to make a killing, or so I thought.

On the first day of December that wet, windy winter, Henri and I started out on our expedition in great spirits and with high hopes, but neither of us was in any way prepared for the ordeal that lay just ahead of us.

The arrangements that we had agreed to were fairly simple; both Henri and I would have the necessary cash to pay all the bills, and then we would split whatever the profits might be. I managed to scrape up my half of the money by borrowing two hundred and fifty dollars from my sister Marie, and her husband Cecil. Even though Cec thought that this was a very chancy deal, with his usual generosity, he loaned me the money.

After the ferry set sail for Vancouver my partner informed me that he did not have the full amount of money for our project, as a matter of fact he was two hundred and fifty dollars short of the required amount. He had, however, brought his nearly new outboard motor with him, and was sure that his friend would accept the motor in lieu of his share of the money.

My first question to Henri, upon learning of his substantial shortfall, was why would this fellow who lived in the mountains, be interested in an outboard motor, and if he was not interested in the deal, what in hell were we going to do? Dear old Henri was sure that there would be no problem with his friend and, therefore, I should not concern myself in the least.

Several times in the preceding years, I had experienced similar scenarios, while engaged in some sure thing, money making enterprise, and I was never able to sit idly by and allow another person to screw things up for me; however, Henri was not only an accomplished comedian, he definitely had the gift of the gab. Trying my very best not to allow the bad news to upset me, I went along with his oratory and even convinced myself that every thing would turn out fine.

My feeling of impending doom abated somewhat, when we met the young fellow who was to be our transport agent. He was a charming fellow and was very happy to be working for us. Although his truck was near to being considered vintage, it seemed to be in reasonably good shape, and as he assured us, perfect for the job.

With a somewhat generous portion of trepidation and uncertainty I set out on this adventure with Henri in the driver's seat of his well-used panel truck. Our trucker followed at a distance, agreeing to meet us at a designated spot.

At that time of year the highway to Princeton is usually covered with snow, and this year was no exception. As a matter of interest it was even heavier than usual, but we managed to make it to the mountain village without problem, and happily met the driver who also made it without incident.

Finding our way to the mountain retreat of our Christmas tree friend was an entirely different proposal as most of the road encountered was knee deep in snow, and still awaiting the government snowplow.

After a long, hair raising trip, on a winding back road, we finally arrived at the man's well plowed driveway and cheerfully drove the remaining mile to his log cabin, and were overjoyed to see a large pile of mountain fir trees awaiting our arrival.

After a hearty hello and a near back-breaking bear hug from the mountain man, we got down to the business at hand, and without further ado put our cards on the table, telling him that we were a little short on money, but we did have a very expensive out-board motor that we were sure that he would love to accept instead of the full amount due him.

After a stunned silence on the part of the tree man, Henri overwhelmed him with his eloquence, finally convincing him that the motor was even better payment than a mere two hundred and fifty dollars, for he would be able to get at least that or more when the weather broke.

Within a short time we were hard at work loading the forest of trees, that were all but covered in the white stuff, onto the vintage truck. Eventually we had piled the trees to twelve feet above the truck bed. At this point, we discovered that our truck man had only brought three ropes with him, two of them too short to circumvent the load. Undaunted, we tied the two together and passed them under the truck and over the top of the pile, tying them at the top in a manner that we were sure would hold them until hell froze over, or at least till we got them to their final destination.

The long rope was sufficient to pass twice under and twice over the load, and went a long way to alleviating our concerns. At last we were finished and ready to start the long haul back down the Hope-Princeton highway.

The rain began as soon as we left the mountain man's home and started our trek toward the main highway, and within a short time turned the snow into a heavy wet sludge. After reaching the main highway without encountering any disaster, we gave thanks, and then turned our vehicles toward Vancouver. We followed our truck mate with the clear understanding that if for any reason we got separated we would meet at the car lot before midnight.

As soon as we began the trip on the main highway, trouble raised its ugly head, and what should have been a joyous trip quickly turned into our worst nightmare. The truck and friend, ahead of us was obviously trying to break all known speed records, and hoping to reach Vancouver before us. We, on the other hand, tried our best to keep up with him, but as fate often decrees, the best laid plans of mice and men quite often go sideways.

Before we had reached the half way point we noted that the load of trees on the truck, which was still in sight, had shifted toward the drivers side of the vehicle and appeared to be getting worse by the minute.

The driver didn't seem to notice this sideways movement and continued on his way, hell bent for leather. We did our best to attract his attention by flashing our lights and blowing the horn but to no avail, and he carried on seemingly oblivious of our efforts to get his attention.

At length we managed to overtake him, and signaled frantically, indicating that he should pull over right away. Again he seemed not to understand the message and continued on his merry way. Determined, we pulled in front of him, allowing the gap between us to narrow, and then deliberately slowed our van down, forcing him to either collide with us or to come to a stop. Fortunately, he came to his senses before hitting us and finally rolled to a stop.

Henri used a good deal of colorful French adjectives, while describing his feelings and concerns toward our hired man, and suggested that if he did that again we would take over the truck ourselves. This of course was highly unlikely, as our friend was younger and larger than either of us, and if we angered him he might well rearrange our butts instead.

After inspecting our load of trees, we all agreed that we needed more ropes to leverage the load back onto an even keel and to secure it so that we could safely continue our journey to Vancouver.

A passing motorist informed us that there was a Highway's work yard a mile or so down the road, so we set out to see if we could get some rope from them.

Luckily there was a road crew at the yard when we arrived and, after telling them of our dilemma, they loaned us enough rope to secure the load. I was relieved at this turn of events and promised them that I would see that they got the rope back, even if I had to drive back there myself. As it turned out, the next day we managed to find a Highway's department truck heading back up to Princeton and they took the rope back for us.

Once we had secured the trees, we continued our trip, with strict orders to the driver that he should never lose sight of us and that if we needed to stop him again, he had better heed our signals and stop right away.

By this time the rain had increased in intensity and the snow on the road was reduced to a slushy brown mess. Shortly after resuming the journey, the windshield wipers on our vehicle ceased functioning, and we were virtually blinded by the muddy residue left on the windshield. Thereafter, we had to stop every mile to remove the muck from the glass and meanwhile our driver disappeared from sight.

We arrived at the Kingsway lot at midnight exhausted by the harrowing trip, but there was not a sign of the truck or the trees. That night we slept in the car lot office in sleeping bags that we had brought along.

In the morning we phoned the truck driver, using the number that he had given us the day before, but there was no answer even though we let it ring at least a hundred times. We concluded that he was either on his way to our lot, or he was half way to Mexico. At any rate, we had no choice but to sit and wait for him.

By noon that day we were beside ourselves, not knowing what to do. We even considered phoning the police, but decided not to do that because we thought that we would look a little foolish, or even stupid. After all, how can one explain that a hired hand with a huge load of wet Christmas trees had absconded without a trace.

At twelve-thirty that afternoon, our man appeared and we rejoiced, in spite of the incredible tale he spun for us. According to him, he forgot the address of the lot, and supposedly drove up and down Kingsway half the night.

This of course was preposterous as we had watched for him till at least 2:00 that night. It was unreasonable to believe that he could have passed by without us having seen him, or even the likelihood that he did not see our mud covered vehicle parked at the front of the empty lot in plain view.

However, our joy at getting the trees back overcame our agitation and we forgave him and gave him the first twenty trees off the load as a bonus. Little did we know that he had already relieved us of one hundred trees and, as we eventually surmised, those trees were probably the only decent ones on the truck.

We spent the balance of that day nailing two-by-fours together to hold trees in an upright position. By the end of the day, we had approximately seventy trees standing in neat rows and looking absolutely wonderful. The rest of the trees stood in neat rows, supported by two-by-four railings that we had constructed, allowing customers the space to inspect and then hopefully purchase the tree of their choice.

We had fabricated a large a sandwich board with the price of the trees, spelling out that each tree would sell for one dollar per foot. The trees ranged in size from three feet right up to ten feet and we were convinced that we were going to make a small fortune.

Early the next morning, after spending another night in that cold office, we awoke to find that the wind had blown every tree all over the lot. Though somewhat dismayed, we stood all the trees up and prepared for our first day of selling. Within the hour the wind again scattered our flock. This happened several times that day.

On the third day we noticed a large truck stacked high with Christmas trees, being unloaded on a vacant lot two doors down from our site.

The trees were thrown in heaps along the front edge of the lot in an unkempt manner, which indicated to us that any prospective customer would in all likelihood choose our trees over theirs. What we did not take into consideration was the selling price of their trees.

Within an hour they had erected a sign, double the size of ours, stating that any and all trees could be purchased for the rock bottom price of two dollars a tree.

On the fourth day I returned to Victoria to perform at Langham Court Theatre, in a role that I had committed to several months before. I believed that my friend Henri would be able to handle things for a few days. What I did not take into account was human nature and the act of self-preservation.

When I returned to the lot on Kingsway, Henri informed me that sales had not been very good, as most prospective buyers had purchased their trees next door, paying only two dollars for the whole tree, rather than coming to us and paying one dollar per foot.

The long and short of the story, as related by my friend Henri, was that he hardly sold any trees, and he was sorry but there was not much money to share with me. Not completely believing his story, I carried out a secret tree count, and discovered that again, there were over one hundred trees missing. Not only did I note that large shortfall, I also found ten empty cans which recently held silver paint, hidden behind some lumber by the back fence. The silver paint was used to spray trees for special orders, and once painted, they fetched an extra dollar per foot.

My partner told me that he had only sold half a dozen painted trees, but I thought that perhaps that was not totally true, and putting two and two together I came to the conclusion that I was being shafted.

The two gentlemen from the lot next door had sold all their trees by that time, and quickly departed with their neat little profit. We on the other hand, ended up staying until the day before Christmas and even then we still had several hundred trees to dispose of.

When I discovered the trick that my partner had played on me, I did my best to greet every customer that set foot on that lot before he had a chance to get to them, and consequently sold enough trees to get my investment back, but without a nickel to spare.

Evidently, as I found out at a later date, Henri told anyone that would listen that I robbed him blind and made off with most of the profits. Somehow, this revelation cheered me, and I felt that perhaps good old Henri got his just reward in the end.

As time passed by, however, I began to realize that he also lost a bundle of money on the enterprise, plus his out-board motor which he loved dearly, and after all he was a pretty decent fellow and only did what he had to do, and really, it was only money.

Sometimes we tend to overlook the fact, that everyone on this planet has to make a dollar, and sometimes, when we find our backs against the wall, we may do things that appear immoral to others but, in the long run, self preservation being the powerful motivator that it is does its level best to win out, no matter the consequences. Certainly I did my level best to win without considering his welfare, but in spite of that wasted time and the loss of money, I came out of the deal a much stronger business man, and the experience taught me a whole lot about human nature. As fate again decreed, it allowed me another page in this book.

Thereafter, every Christmas, I rejoiced at the thought of someone other than myself selling trees from parking lots and street corners, and reveled in the joy of not being responsible for any trees still left on the lots the day after Christmas. But I never fail to feel the utmost compassion and sympathy for those poor devils left with a load of unsold trees, thinking, that there, but for the grace of God, go I.

Many times over the passing years when I looked back at that venture, I smiled, thinking how naïve I had been, perhaps even gullible having fallen for a fast line of patter and the chance of making a quick profit. But I also realize that it taught me a whole lot more in common sense than what it cost me in dollars. Fortunately, the experience I gained from that short venture, gave me the insight to effectively resist many other even more hair-brained schemes throughout my life. Although, if the truth be told, there were some business ventures that did indeed cost me a bundle plus a lot of wasted time, and when viewed with the twenty-twenty vision of hindsight, it is relatively easy to see that I should have had more sense.

My building career was going gangbusters and I was never without work. The philosophy that I developed over the years included the rationale that it is better to make a modest profit and keep working, than sit idle while waiting for the big score. Many jobs, while not bringing me great windfalls, certainly kept my income in a higher bracket than some tradesmen, and allowed me to invest in more real-estate, eventually giving me a certain amount of security.

Tenants Ghosts and Spirits

One of my real-estate ventures involved an old, run down, two story house close to Naden in Esquimalt. It was on a large lot and seemed to be a perfect candidate for renovation.

The real estate market in those days was very different from today. Very few small contractors purchased houses with the idea of tearing them down and rebuilding larger homes. They actually preferred buying old houses and then renovating them.

My specialty usually followed that line of action, and over the course of a few years I purchased several large homes and renovated them, creating small apartments which were relatively easy to rent, and quickly paid for.

In the case of the 'Naden' property I built an addition containing six apartments onto the side of the old house, and created three suites in the house itself. The total in all was nine apartments plus a full basement for storage and utilities including washers and dryers.

Most of the suites were unfurnished rentals, which I furnished when necessary. On one occasion, a young army couple requested furnishings, as they were going to be posted to a different base within a fairly short time and did not want to carry a lot of furniture with them.

When the time came for them to move on I inspected the apartment and also checked out the furniture, noting that one of the lamps that I had supplied was missing. When I brought the missing lamp to the attention of the tenant, a twenty five year old commando, he became very angry and suggested that I was accusing him of stealing the lamp, which of course was not the case. I only asked him where it might be, and in the nicest way I might add.

This young commando probably out weighed me by at least thirty pounds and by the look of the bulges in his T-shirt, that thirty pounds was all muscle. Naturally I did not wish to anger him further, and so I suggested that perhaps some one had broken into the apartment while they were out and stolen it.

For some reason this did not pacify him, and without a word he grabbed me by shirt and threw me against the wall. Not wanting to wreck the apartment by fighting inside, I made my second mistake. I invited him outside to settle the matter.

By the time we had walked down the outside stairway and across the lawn, I had grown tired of his abusive line of patter, most of which include the heavy use of four letter words, many of which questioned my legitimacy, but even worse also questioned my mother's morals.

As my blood pressure increased I too became agitated, and I began to believe that this boy needed a lesson in manners. Not wanting to engage in battle where neighbours might view us, I suggested that we should go to a wooded area just cross the street; there we could settle the matter without fear of interference. That of course was my third mistake.

Later, once I had time to reflect upon the seriousness of the situation,

I came to the conclusion that I was probably very lucky to be in one piece, as commandos are taught to overpower an adversary in as short a time as possible, inflicting as much damage as possible during the process.

As soon as we entered the wooded area, I began to suspect that I had made a grave error, and that I should have been anywhere but in that secluded place, and particularly with that demolition expert.

The first move was his. He grabbed me by the shirt, completely removing the garment with the exception of the collar and the cuffs. He then threw me to the ground and kicked me in the head. As I have pointed out in other chapters, my head is the strongest part of my body, and even when it comes in contact with an army boot, my head remains relatively unscathed. When the warrior threw me down and kicked me, which by the way goes against the Marquess of Queensbury Rules in boxing, I decided that enough was enough.

Jumping to my feet, and drawing upon all of my knowledge and experience in the boxing ring, I quickly launched myself into the most animated form of footwork one could ever imagine. Once engaged I was able to out-maneuver him and with all my strength, connect a flurry of blows to his body, inflicting significant damage, including black eyes, torn ear, and best of all, a direct blow to his mouth, which drove his teeth through his lip.

By that point, I was exhausted and my fists were in shock, as they had not been engaged in such activity for many years, so I decided that I would not push my luck any further, and I told him that I had enough, he was a dirty fighter, and I was not going to fight any longer. He, on the other hand was even madder than before and not only wanted to continue fighting but, I suspected, had every intention of killing me.

Not wanting to die so young, I told him that I was leaving and, without a backward look, I made haste to get the hell out of there. He followed close behind threatening me with every form of horror imaginable but I, with resolute determination, went straight to my vehicle and pulling a hammer from the trunk I suggested that he better get the hell away from me before I played a tattoo on his noggin.

A neighbour who had witnessed most of the contest called the police and as I opened the trunk to replace the hammer, they pulled into the driveway. One of the officers in the police car was very close friend of mine who had once been engaged to my sister Nellie. He was a former boxer and had at one time shown me a few fancy moves. He was grinning ear to ear when he saw that it was me.

The other constable accompanying my friend Bob asked what was going on. I said that the fellow who was a tenant, had assaulted me and ripped the shirt right off my body, and I wanted to press charges. Bob, barely containing himself, said that by the looks of it the other guy had gotten the worst of it, drawing my attention to the tooth that was sticking out of his upper lip, while I, apart from the remnants of a shirt still clinging to my body, didn't even have my hair mussed.

When Bob looked at me, a twinkle in his eyes and a barely suppressed grin on his face, I too broke into a smile. Bob suggested that I wait until the next day, and if I still wanted to lay charges then, I could come down to the Esquimalt police station and do so. However, he quietly mentioned that the tenant might even decide to lay charges himself, and with the obvious damage to his face, might be in a better position than myself.

Not wishing to prolong my association with the young warrior, I said that if he left the apartment right away I would not pursue it any further. Fortunately he did leave quickly and I never heard from him again. Of course I never saw the lamp again, but quite frankly, I never did miss it either.

Over the period of years that I owned the apartment building, I met some very interesting and colorful characters but during that period I also met some unfortunates who had experienced tragic incidents in their life.

On one occasion a particularly warm and gracious lady, along with her young son, rented one of the suites in the building. Shortly after they moved in, she told me about the tragedy that brought her to this point in her life. She and her husband, along with their young son, had spent several years building a large sailing vessel which they planned to sail around the world.

After years of hard work and patience, their project was completed, and the beautiful ship was launched on its maiden voyage. During their trial run just off the Washington coast they encountered stiff winds and heavy swells. She and her son stayed below while her husband worked above. Late that night she awoke with a start, sensing an unusual quietness above. She quickly made her way to the deck, but did not see her husband at the wheel where he should have been.

Frantic, she scanned the seas that surrounded the boat, and glimpsed a figure in a life jacket, bobbing on the surface of a swell a hundred yards astern. Screaming for her son, she wrestled with the boat's wheel, finally bringing the vessel about, but losing sight of the figure in the water. For most of that night she searched for her mate, but she never saw him again. In the morning she finally gave up the search and somehow managed to reach Port Angeles where she informed the authorities. They immediately launched a search, but were unable to find the missing man and eventually returned to port.

That poor woman must have suffered beyond comprehension, suffering not only from her loss, but also from her shattered dreams. Within a short time of meeting her she moved from my apartment building, and I never saw her again. That sad tale remained with me throughout my life, often reminding me of the blessings that my family and I shared for many years.

Another young family that had moved into the apartment, left a lasting impression on me, and many times over the course of my life I reflected upon that couple and their suffering and anguish, often reflecting on the vagaries of our existence. The young couple had a little daughter barely six months old. He worked on the Naden Graving dock, just a block or two from their apartment. One fateful day, a two-ton plate of steel fell on this young man, killing him. The poor wife was grief stricken but did her best to cope with the tragedy. A year later she and her daughter moved on, and I lost track of her.

Several years later, I decided to sell the building. A woman of about thirty-five made an offer, which I accepted. One of the conditions of the sale was that she might live in one of the suites for six months before completing the transaction. As I was in no hurry to sell the premises, I agreed to the condition, and she immediately moved into a vacant suite.

One day, about three months later while chatting with her, she told me a story that brought goose bumps to my neck. Apparently, she was a *Spiritualist,* and had wished to live in the building for a while to make sure that there were no evil spirits inhabiting the building. Once certain that all was well with the building, she would complete the transaction.

There had been many families living in the building over the years and the turnover of tenants was such that very few stayed more than a few months. Since the death of the young man there had been a constant turnover and absolutely no one would have known anything about the family or about his death.

Normally, any examples or discussion of *Spiritualism* would have left me unconvinced, but the tale she told me raised the hackles on my neck and also raised many questions about the after-life, and even partially convinced me that there is indeed proof of the existence of spirits.

During the months that this woman had lived in the apartment she had heard and seen things that convinced her that there was a ghost or spirit inhabiting the building. She had established that it was a friendly ghost, that meant no ill will or harm to the human inhabitants, and also, that he was a ghost who did not understand that he was dead. Therefore, he continued dwelling in the apartment even though his family had long since vacated.

Many times, the Spiritualist lady heard footsteps in the rooms above her, even though no one was at home. Often she heard doors opening and closing when no one was there. Even people who were living in that particular suite noticed peculiar things on a regular basis. Lights would go on by themselves, doors would open and close for no apparent reason, a mysterious figure was seen on occasion, and pots and pans would suddenly appear on the counter tops. Fortunately, the couple living there did not feel threatened or even frightened, but possibly even enjoyed the other tenant.

Finally one evening when the woman was upstairs visiting the couple, they all witnessed the appearance of a young man who stood quietly in the bedroom doorway. The Spiritualist assured him that it was okay if he continued living with them; however, the fact was that he was dead and should continue his journey into the next world where he belonged.

She knew that the ghost needed help to leave this world and to travel on to the next level of existence, and decided to help him by practicing a form of exorcism or friendly persuasion, as it was in this case, to help him on his way. For the next few weeks she spent her full time dealing with this phenomenon, and actually saw him several times, eventually persuading him to leave, not because she did not want him around, but rather to help him attain a better place.

When she told me of this unknown tenant and where she saw him, I was astounded, for that was the very apartment where the young man lived at the time of his death. The description included the clothes that he was wearing when she saw him. She described him as a youth of approximately twenty-two years, with long blonde hair and wearing a plaid work shirt and blue jeans. At that point the hair on the back of my neck rose up, and I felt as though I had seen a ghost myself, for her description was identical to the boy that had lived there those many years before.

A few short weeks later she informed me that the ghost had left the building, and that she was certain he had gone onto a much better world where he could live with other spirits like himself. She was delighted that she had been able to help him, and was convinced that the building had no evil spirits and therefore would suit her perfectly.

While the drama of ghosts and spirits was unfolding, my life too was changing dramatically; for without preliminary study, or even listening to advice, I committed myself to an entirely new enterprise that would ultimately change my entire life. I was going to open a restaurant.

My First Restaurant, "The Coach and Four"

I had absolutely no experience in the restaurant business. I had never even considered what operating a restaurant would entail, nor did I know of anyone who had ever experienced that form of insanity, or certainly never lived to tell about it. I was going in blind, as the saying goes, and mindless to boot.

The whole episode began innocently enough at a cocktail party thrown by an acquaintance of mine, who just happened to reside in an old mansion on Rockland Avenue. That area of the city often hosted artsy type parties, where one could hob-nob with upper class people and artists of all kinds and persuasions.

On that particular night I was introduced to a gentleman who, it turned out, was a renowned architect with offices in both Victoria and San Francisco. We got around to talking about renovations and restoration of old buildings, and soon began discussing our 'Old Town', a part of the city long neglected and rundown. Allan Edwards, the architect, had a passion for old buildings and had designed and built many restaurants in derelict buildings throughout the United States. Before I knew it, I was caught up in his enthusiasm with our 'Old Town', and began thinking that Bastion Square would be a great place to open a restaurant. My wife thought I was crazy, and insisted that I get that silly idea out of my head, not really thinking that I was serious, but I soon proved that I was indeed mad.

At that time Bastion Square was an open area roughly the size of a football field, and consisted of an assortment of derelict buildings, some built in the 1890's. One of the red brick buildings on the north side was used for furniture storage by a moving company, another housed a clothing manufacturer specializing in work clothes and the other building, once a hotel of ill-repute, was boarded-up and unused.

On the upper side stood the old courthouse, which was to become home to the Maritime Museum.

Facing the square on the south side were four large brick buildings. The centre building once home to the Peetz Fishing Supplies Company, was the building that I had chosen for my first restaurant. The building was for rent and seemed to be the right size.

The building to the east of it housed an engine shop which, unbeknownst to me, specialized in the rebuilding of diesel motors, and though I had not taken particular notice of the business while preparing for my venture, it soon became the centre of my attention, and almost ended my restaurant career before it had truly begun.

My architect friend thought that this would be an exciting and wonderful place to locate a restaurant, as there was a tremendous amount of free parking in the square itself and also on Wharf and Langley Street to the east and west of the site.

I was completely inexperienced and lacking any knowledge or history with the restaurant business, other than that year when I attended Central Junior High and asked to join the grade nine cooking class. They turned me down because boys were not allowed to take that particular course. That did not faze me at all, for I thought that I could overcome anything I put my mind to.

Little did I know that the best thing that I could have done at that time, would have been to have a sanity evaluation done or, better yet, been placed under strict protective supervision till the madness wore off.

Prior to the encounter with the architect, Barb and I had been searching for a larger motorboat so that we could spend more time together with the kids. We loved being on the water in our seventeen foot craft and almost every weekend we would cruise the waters of the Gulf Islands, stopping here and there for a picnic on some sandy beach, or walking the trails on one of the Islands, and enjoying the peace and quiet and sometimes solitude of those delightful shores.

Finally we found just the boat we were looking for. It was twenty-eight feet long and suitable for overnight excursions. We had enough money to purchase it, so there was nothing to stop us from taking the plunge. However, one fine night we attended the party that changed our lives for years to come.

Instead of investing in a beautiful yacht that could have given us years of pleasure, we sank our funds into a restaurant, which not only robbed us of the time together that we yearned for, but also took every cent that we could scrape together, and forced us further into debt than we had ever been in before.

Unfortunately, I always found it difficult to admit when I was wrong, instead believing that it would be a sign of weakness if I admitted failure or gave up or, heaven forbid, quit. So, once I had made the decision to open "The Coach and Four" restaurant in Bastion Square, I plunged ahead figuring that I could learn the business as I went along.

Alan Edwards created a beautiful artist's drawing of the restaurant dining room, designing every piece of furniture including chairs, tables, linens, light fixtures, bathrooms, carpets and drapes. The effect was stunning, as were the costs.

At the beginning of our discussions, I asked him if it would be possible to build the restaurant for twenty five thousand dollars. He thought that twenty five thousand would probably cover it nicely. What he did not mention was that the amount we discussed would only cover his work, the design and furniture. The cost of the kitchen and any other feature would be additional.

By the time I discovered that the amount I had would only cover half of the project, I was fully committed. The lease had been arranged, the plans drawn, and I was in too deep to get out. In hindsight, I realize that I would have been far better off to take my losses and drop the whole idea, but there was that old devil pride lurking in my inner self which meant that I was not going to be able to quit, no matter what.

As soon as I realized that I would need double the amount to complete this project, I approached the owner of Douglas Hawkes Realty, and asked if it would be possible to arrange a twenty five thousand dollar loan to finish my restaurant. After personally inspecting my various properties, he said that he would be delighted to arrange a loan for me. That was the beginning of a very successful and close relationship, for Doug and I became friends and over the years he helped me out on several occasions, one of the more notable transactions involving my property in Mill Bay.

The building in Bastion Square needed a whole lot of tender loving care before we were finished and ready to open. The former tenants had applied rough plaster to the interior walls and completely covered the original old brick walls. I decided to strip the plaster from the walls thinking that would be relatively easy, but as usual it proved to be a tougher job than I anticipated. The covering was an inch thick and adhered to the walls like solid glue making it very difficult to remove. After several days of chipping away with a chisel we resorted to using a grinding wheel hoping to uncover the brick walls.

One day when I walked into the area I could not see anything but thick dust, I knew that my helper was in there because I could hear the machine grinding away. I called to him to find out where he was so that I could get him out before he expired from the dust. When I called the grinder stopped, and a muffled voice that sounded like death itself, called hello. I shouted that he should get out of there right away. A minute or so later my helper stumbled out into the sunlight completely covered in red dust and almost unrecognizable. That poor fellow had been working in there with no protective mask for hours without complaint. I did not allow him in there for the rest of that day. The following day we once again attacked the walls with hammer and chisel, eventually baring beautiful red brick walls. After several weeks of construction, the interior was finished and ready for the furnishings and kitchen equipment.

The interior of 'The Coach and Four' resembled a Victorian era food emporium, the original old brick walls were magnificent and served as a perfect backdrop for a collection of antiques.

Included in the collection was an assortment of well-worn harness. Some of it still had some original horse manure on it. When the harness was hung on the walls and beams of the dining room, we were running out of time and the opening date was fast approaching, and unfortunately we hadn't had the time to clean and polish the leather or the brass fittings on the harness. The coating of manure was largely overlooked, until the day an avid horse type person indignantly brought it to my attention.

When faced with negative comments, I would usually take the offensive, and let the chips fall where they may; in this case they involved what was left of the horse chips. I patiently explained that we had been working for several months creating this gem of a place, and wanting to adhere to my original plan of authenticity, I personally had applied the horse droppings to the harness. Being very thorough in my research, I had made it my priority to search out only the best manure available, making sure that its texture was as near perfect as that substance would allow, and had only used the droppings from registered thoroughbred mares in foal. Furthermore, every piece of antiquity that adorned the 1890's circa, walls and beams, had been authenticated and had the stamp of approval from no less than the British Antiquarian Association, of which my great uncle was an officer and a gentleman.

Before my imagination got the better of me and I stretched the story beyond credibility, I thanked the lady and invited her to enjoy her meal and also thanked her for her astute observations, and invited her to drop by my farm, whenever she was in my area, so that she might see first hand my collection of antique horse brasses. The next day I had my staff wash all the damn harness.

Opening a restaurant entailed far more detail than I had ever experienced, but undaunted by the sheer volume of decisions I had to make while trying to get this enterprise up and running, I plowed my way through the mountain of problems encountered daily, eventually getting everything in place including staff.

The first member of my staff was a European chef who produced a pedigree as long as his arm. According to his resumé, he had cooked for every well-known restaurant in all of Europe, for heads of state, famous people, even members of Royalty. Not only was he a 'Chef Extraordinaire', he knew everything that was possible to know about wines and alcohol and the running of a restaurant as well.

There was no doubt in my mind that I had stumbled upon the perfect man for my restaurant. Not only did he plan and design my menu, he ordered all the china and cutlery, handled the advertising, ordered the kitchen equipment, the linens, contracted the food suppliers, hired staff; and as I found out at a later date, arranged for a kick back from some of the suppliers, and conveniently furnished his apartment with supplies from the restaurant, including liquor, food, utensils, linens, paper goods, and anything else that would save him the cost of purchasing his own furnishings.

One of the many details that had to be settled was the official name for the establishment. As the building had been built during the horse and buggy era of the 1890's, it was only natural to have a name that reflected it's historical significance. After a great deal of thought and consideration, Barb and I decided on, 'Coach and Four', a name that helped conjure up the image of a fine old English Inn.

The interior of the restaurant gave the impression that they were dining in a wonderful old Inn. The antiques, the hanging tapestries, the harness, the old English pictures, and the wooden coach wheels mounted on the walls helped create a warm and comfortable atmosphere. Many customers found their way to this quaint little eating-place in Bastion Square by word of mouth; of course being off the beaten path also helped bring many adventurous souls to our door.

Leather menu covers added to the ambience of the room, and also our selection of English style dishes helped to further our quest for authenticity. Steak and Kidney pie was a favorite dish, Roast beef and Yorkshire pudding, plus many other English favorites kept the customers coming back for more.

We were one of the first restaurants in Victoria to broil steaks on an open flame. Of course there were other establishments that opened during that year of 1964 that also used open flames for cooking steaks. However, I like to think that we were somehow instrumental in bringing charcoal broiled steaks to the attention of Victoria clientele and perhaps influenced other restaurateurs to follow suit.

As opening day drew closer, I became even more nervous than I had been before. We had scheduled the opening of "The Coach and Four", for the third week in June 1964, and were working as fast as we could to meet the deadline.

One of the main reasons that I wanted to open a restaurant was to promote entertainment and music and, as place of music and song, the waitresses were required to sing. Finding musical waitresses was not a difficult task, as it was close to summer and many talented students were looking for employment. Most of the girls we hired were either singers or pianists, and we were therefore able to provide both food and music for our clientele.

Whenever I felt that the girls had a spare minute, I would direct them to leave whatever they were doing and to gather around the piano and sing a song or two.

The biggest problem we encountered was that the girls were all as busy as could be and really didn't have the time to be doing anything but serve their customers, never mind gathering around a piano and singing.

Whenever I approached a waitress on the floor, a look of terror would often flash across her face, and she would move in the opposite direction as fast as she could. This game of hide and seek became more of a problem as the restaurant got busier, particularly when customers who were impatiently waiting for their food, noted that their waitress was standing by the piano singing, apparently ignoring them.

The idea of singing waitresses was a good one, but unfortunately, customers seemed to prefer having their meals on time rather than hearing a hurried rendition of *'Fly Me To The Moon'*, or an invitation to *'See The Pyramids Along The Nile'*. Quite often a hungry diner could be heard asking, *"Has Anybody Seen My Gal"*.

When we first opened our restaurant we did not have a liquor license, as the rules stated that a business could not apply for one until after six months of operation. I suppose the rationale was that if the restaurant managed to stay in business for six months, it had proved its worth, and was therefore worthy of recognition.

Unfortunately, six months without a liquor license was devastating for the business as most customers enjoyed having a drink or two with their dinner, and found it difficult to understand why they could not get at least a glass of wine.

During those long dry months, we sent our customers over to a licensed club just around the corner from Bastion Square. The club, no doubt, was very happy and likely made a tidy little profit, while we worked our buns off trying to make ends meet.

Meanwhile, an even worse problem arose, for after only a few weeks in business, we began to notice that there was an acrid smell of creosote in the dining room, and guests with sensitive noses were leaving the restaurant because of it. At first we tried different brands of deodorants to rid the room of the pungent acrid odor, but no matter what we tried, it still lingered.

Having customers leave because of the unavailability of liquor, or because of the creosote smells that hung around like a black cloud almost sent me to the mad house. After almost exhausting our resources, we began to notice that the odor appeared while the engine shop next door ran their rebuilt diesel motors, which unfortunately was most of the time, and so I paid them a visit and explained our problem and hoped that they could help me out of a very bad spot.

The owner of the shop next-door was a very agreeable fellow and promised not to run the engines during our working hours. Fortunately, this solution seemed to help tremendously, and after only a week or so the odor disappeared entirely.

Shortly after, I dropped by to see the motor shop owner, and he informed me that they had located the trouble; evidently an air duct in the engine room connected directly with our dining room, and had been exhausting right into our building. They bricked up the opening and our problem disappeared.

From the first day we opened we were very busy. Our chef actually did a fine job with all his special dishes and even invented a very unusual dessert, which he called, *'Deep Fried Ice-cream'*. He would cut ice cream into small blocks, wrap it in a layer of sponge cake, and then freeze it. When an order for this tasty treat came into the kitchen, he would take one from the freezer and drop it into a thick batter and deep-fry it until golden brown. It was then placed on a plate, drenched in over-proof Demerera rum and then set aflame. The taste was wonderful and every one who tried it raved about it. Often, visitors new to Victoria would ask taxi drivers where they could get the deep fried ice-cream that they had heard about.

When our probation period was finally over, we happily received our liquor license and quickly stocked our bar with some very fine wine and liquor. However, this new venture immediately presented more problems. The only person in the restaurant who knew anything about wines and mixed drinks was our chef, and so every time a drink was ordered, the chef would have to go to the bar and mix the concoction, and then go back to the kitchen and continue whatever he was doing before we interrupted him.

This raised even more problems because our chef, apart from being a very talented and knowledgeable individual, was also somewhat of a 'Prima Donna', He actually enjoyed his frequent trips to the dining room bar, where he would be in full view of the patrons, and where he could fully enjoy himself whilst putting on an elaborate display with flair and showmanship.

Often this bar extravaganza attracted as much attention as our singing waitresses did, and added greatly to the entertainment of the diners, who would often wave to him and frequently send him drinks. This again presented problems, because the last thing a restaurant needs is a tipsy chef.

There were many occasions when our chef became a little unsteady on his feet due to the amount of liquor he consumed. Finally, I was forced to pass a rule that any drinks that patrons would buy for him had to be non-alcoholic. This of course, presented more problems, for he had become used to the happy atmosphere each night, and did not want to drink Shirley Temples because they did nothing for him.

At that stage of the game I was almost beside myself. The waitresses didn't want to sing because it was difficult to give good service and their tips suffered because of it. Our chef was suffering from tantrums and my hair was rapidly disappearing from my head, Then my accountant informed me that expenses were too high, and I should try to lower them before I found myself in even hotter water than I was presently in.

When faced with prickly issues, I would sit down and make a list of everything that appeared problematic, and then decide which burr to deal with first. In this case, I decided to learn to tend bar, so I did a quick study on the art of mixed drinks and fine wines, and within a fairly short period of time, became quite proficient behind the bar. The chef decided that he was not going to lose his place in the spotlight and began visiting the customers in the dining room, usually laughing and joking with them while they attempted to eat their meal.

Quite often, the assistant chef would make signals from the kitchen where he was laboring, hoping to have the chef return and help with the orders.

All the while I would be quietly pulling at my rapidly thinning locks, and wondering what I could do to overcome this apparent mutiny. I knew of course that I was treading on thin ice, and that the chef was in charge of the rescue boat. One night the chef suffered what he described as a nervous breakdown, and decided that he needed a week off to recuperate. Not completely understanding what a nervous breakdown looked like, although I had wondered on several occasions if I was having one myself, I agreed to his prognosis and sent him home to rest. Evidently, he had for sometime been engaged in a full blown affair with one of my staff, and she was terribly upset by his condition and, as I found out much later, spent most of the week with him consoling him and also attending to his other needs as well. Meanwhile I was two people short in the restaurant and as busy as all get out.

After exactly seven days of recuperation, our man returned to the job of cooking and by all appearances, seemed to be fully recovered. However, the worst was yet to come.

The kitchen of our little restaurant was probably not much bigger than a kitchen of an average family home. The floor of the cooking area was two feet below the floor of the dining room and had three steps up to the main room.

An opening three feet high, and eight feet long in the wall separated the two areas. The serving counter formed the lower shelf of this opening and was approximately thirty inches above the dining room floor, which made it approximately four foot six inches above the kitchen floor. A person standing in the kitchen area would be in full view of the diners, at least, from the shoulders up, as would the cooking stove, the deep fryer, and one or two other pieces of equipment. The first tables in the dining area stood about eight feet from the serving counter, therefore guests in the dining room were often privy to any talk that went on in the kitchen itself.

On the backside of the cooking area, a narrow space contained the dishwasher and a small preparation table. The overall layout was appallingly cramped and made it extremely difficult to prepare even a minimum number of meals.

We installed a walk-in cooler and a large table in a room directly above the kitchen on the next floor, and did most of our preparation in that area, and also stored various supplies on open shelves there. Two vacant floors were above the prep room but were not used for anything and remained empty.

A creaky old freight elevator, installed in the early 1930's, served as transportation between floors. There was also a narrow flight of stairs accessible to the upper floors which were used much of the time as the elevator was very slow and shaky. The stairs led from the upper floors, down to a mezzanine area where the bathrooms were located and then down to the dining room itself. Some of the staff were very wary of the elevator and preferred the stairs; when the dining room was in use, however, they had no choice but to take the elevator.

Freight elevators were scary under the best of conditions, but this one was a classic horror movie candidate. Its ascent or descent could be controlled either by the person in it who would push the control button, or by another person on the lower floor, who not only could bring the cage up or down, as desired, but could also override the control on the elevator itself. This little known fact offered endless opportunities for the one wicked enough to take advantage of an unsuspecting occupant. It was open on all sides except for the upright, round wooden dowels surrounding the cage itself, which were the only things separating the operator from the spider webbed shaft and the hanging cables above.

Whenever we hired a new waitress or kitchen worker, I would introduce them to the elevator and show them how to operate it once they were inside. For some reason I never remembered to tell them that it could also be operated by someone else on the lower floor.

When giving them the operating instructions, I would also tell them the little tale about the ghost that had inhabited the upper floors since it's construction in the 1890's, and how it was referred to as *'The Hunchback'*. I assured them that there was absolutely no cause for concern, as long as they took the cage up to the second floor only. While I had no fears regarding the upper floors, it seems that some were petrified.

Looking back on the 'folklore' associated with my early days in the Coach and Four, I realize just how wicked I was at that time, and how I would stoop to the lowest level in my efforts to scare the hell out of someone.

My favorite trick, usually saved for a dark and stormy night, was to tell a new waitress to go up to the storage area on the second floor and bring back something or other that we needed for the bar. Often the dear soul would voice some reluctance and try to beg off, probably remembering my warning about the upper floors. I would go to great lengths to assure her that it would be quite safe for her to make the trip. After seeing her off, and giving more assurances of safety, I would call out to her, reminding her not to go beyond the second floor, while at the same time holding the control button that would send her on a non stop trip to the top of the shaft.

Awaiting on the uppermost floor was a white sheet, hung just beyond the edge of light cast by the elevator, and which appeared to be the stooped figure of an old man.

We never suffered any casualties during those fun days, but we did manage to scare the dickens out of a number of impressionable young serving staff who, much to their credit, never held a grudge, but would often go to great lengths to get even, by playing clever little tricks on the Squire himself.

Help, the Chef's gone Mad

One night when the dining room was full, our temperamental chef threw a tantrum. It was a night that I will never forget. A party of four happy people was celebrating an anniversary. They were sitting at one of the tables closest to the serving counter, and had ordered steaks.

One of the four bit down on a crusty roll and unfortunately his upper plate broke in half. I was never completely clear whether the roll was overly firm, or whether his plate was faulty but, whatever the cause, he called the waitress over and explained his problem and very nicely asked her to cancel his steak.

The waitress came over to me, and repeated the sad tale of the broken plate. I was very busy in the bar being very creative, mixing numerous cocktails and so I did not fully understand the gravity of the situation. At first I thought that she had told me that the gentleman had been eating the bun and the dinner plate broke, which in itself was not necessarily an unusual thing to happen. She repeated the tale and that he wanted to cancel his steak. Finally I understood the problem, and turned toward the kitchen to inform the maestro that he should cancel one of the steaks.

For some unfathomable reason, he took exception to my instructions, and completely ignored my request. When the steaks were ready, he prepared the platters and placed all four on the serving counter. The flustered waitress, not wanting to anger the chef, once again informed me that only three steaks were needed.

Thinking that possibly he had not heard me the first time, I again told him, in the nicest way possible under the circumstances, that only three plates were necessary. What followed was akin to a three-ring circus.

In hindsight, when reviewing the event, I decided that perhaps if the waitress had taken all four plates from the server and then brought one over to me, we would have avoided an incredibly volatile situation. However, Fate often takes charge of seemingly innocent proceedings, and turns what might have been a simple everyday blip into an episode worthy of Dante's Inferno. In this instance, Fate handled things in an entirely different way than we mere mortals might handle them, and subsequently revealed a highly humorous side that completely evaded the participants.

When the waitress suggested that she was only going to take three plates to the table, the agitated chef responded in a highly emotional way, unfortunately alerting the four diners, who were then privy to the chef's darker side.

It was never very clear to me what happened next, but evidently the chef snapped and let fly with all four steak platters, hurling them in the direction of the celebrants sitting nearby.

Hearing a loud clatter of breaking china, I turned and quickly became aware of four highly agitated guests rushing toward the front door. From all the evidence scattered at the scene, which mainly consisted of peas and carrots, baked potatoes, and four perfectly broiled steaks, I immediately assumed that the waitress had dropped the platters and that the guests were upset and leaving as quickly as they could.

The near hysterical server informed me that the chef had flipped, and thrown the plates at the four diners. Within a moment or so, I'm not sure just how long because everything was happening very fast, I hurried toward the escaping diners, doing my best to appear calm so that the other guests in the dining room would remain in their own seats, using every ounce of my compassion and concern in an effort to calm their anxiety, even resorting to my old habit of close contact, hugging and squeezing them, all the while, trying to explain the seemingly unexplainable to them.

Gradually, as the clues came together, and I began to understand the gravity of the situation, and exactly what had happened, I found myself begging forgiveness from the fleeing patrons, and unabashedly offering them a free meal should they ever return. The poor folk disappeared into the night with scarcely a backward glance and, as far as I remember, never returned.

The next hour I spent with the other diners engaged in damage control, as I visited every table explaining that the chef had suffered a major breakdown and that everything was under control and that the chef was under sedation, or soon would be. Within the hour the guests had settled down and laughter had once again returned to the room. I felt that even though we had a near disaster, all was not lost. And even though we had likely lost that unfortunate foursome, we would in all probability be the talk of the town before morning, and as the famous Barnum once said, "There is no such thing as bad publicity", or as someone even older once noted, "It's an ill wind that doesn't blow someone good", or words to that effect.

Once the dining room was in order, and the assistant chef had caught up on his orders, and the waitress recovered from the near calamity, I went looking for the maestro. He had departed the kitchen, entered the dining room without a word to any one, surveyed his handy work, and then disappeared up the back stairs heading toward my office.

As soon as the dining room was under control, I ran up the stairs, taking them two at a time, and found our man in my office stretched out on my settee, head thrown back, one leg on, one leg off. The back of his hand was pressed tightly to his forehead and peculiar sounds were issuing from what I assumed to be his throat.

For a moment I suspected that he had cut his damn throat himself, which seemed like a good thing for it would save me the trouble. However he was still alive, with no signs of any lacerations on his body. As I approached him, steak knife in hand, ready to finish him off, he let out a loud groan and sat bolt upright and said, "What happened?"

"What Happened?" I repeated. Let me tell you what happened! You have insulted my customers and they will probably never enter this building again. Ever since you came into my life I have treated you like a brother, suffered your tantrums, overlooked your drinking habits, furnished your apartment, shared the services of my staff, paid you handsomely, given you time off when you felt you needed it, and in short, been very nice to you. The only thing that is stopping me from throwing you through the window, is that I do not wish to damage the expensive chef's outfit you have on, as it cost me a pretty penny when it was tailored for you. Furthermore, I would like you to remove it this very instant and then put on your own clothes, and then give me your key and leave this building immediately, preferably by taking the elevator down and exiting from the back door."

Time will never erase that memory, as I stood transfixed, watching the chef carefully removing his neatly tailored whites, and slowly and deliberately drawing his trousers on over his tailored shorts. They interestingly enough were covered with bright red hearts, some skewered with cupids arrows, and I came close to asking him where he had found such delightful under garments, but caught myself in time and continued with my vigil.

His demeanor was remarkable. It was as if this whole episode had not taken place, as though he was preparing himself for an evening on the town; why, I almost held his jacket for him. At last, drawing his comb through his jet black hair, and without so much as a word or a glance at me, he casually turned and walked down the stairway and into the dining room, where he stood, wordlessly surveying his former kingdom. A hush fell over the crowd, waitresses moved as though in slow motion; it was a moment never to be forgotten. After what seemed an eternity he slowly moved toward the door, gently touching a shoulder here, an arm there. Finally drawing himself up ramrod straight, every eye in the room upon him, he threw open the front door and quickly vanished into the shadows of Bastion Square.

The next day the reality of my situation struck me like a thunderbolt. What had I done? Where was I going to get another chef? My first thoughts were obviously those of a desperate man. Thinking that I should call him and give him one more chance, or perhaps, I should give him the restaurant and leave the whole dang business and go back to my old job. I was doomed no matter what I did.

After advertising for several days and interviewing some unlikely prospects for the position, I finally hired a fellow who seemed to have a little more knowledge than any of the others that I had interviewed. He was a Frenchman and had spent years in France working under many prominent chefs, and even though he was not fully qualified, he at least knew how to make a casserole. This was a very important consideration, not that we had casseroles on the menu, but at least it showed that he had at least a rudimentary knowledge of cooking.

By that stage of my search, I had given up the idea of actually finding a trained chef, and had come to the conclusion that I would have to settle for an ordinary cook. My rationale was that if a person could at least cook, we could train him to handle our simple menu.

One of the most popular items on our menu was the steak and kidney pie, and we took great pride in creating and serving the best pie then available in Victoria. The first stage of preparing the dish was the most important. The kidney had to be boiled for a certain amount of time, which allowed all of its normal contents to be effectively removed. This step in the process was carefully laid out for anyone who might have a hand in the preparation, and this dear Frenchman was no exception. He assured me that he had vast knowledge in preparing this particular dish.

Several weeks passed by before I began to notice that steak and kidney pie was not selling as well as it had before this cook joined our staff. Without saying anything about the downturn, I started watching him at work and soon discovered the awful truth. He was not boiling the kidneys before mixing them with the stew meat.

When I observed the shortcut that he was taking, I stepped into the kitchen and in the nicest way possible informed him that boiling the piss out of the kidneys was imperative, and was probably the most important stage of the entire process, and furthermore, he had been made aware of this step when he first joined us, therefore he had no excuse for this breach of the rules.

He apologized and suggested that it had only happened this once. I then informed him that sales for this item on the menu had dropped dramatically in the past few weeks, and that he must be very careful each and every time he made it in the future. Assuring me that I had nothing to worry about, and that he would boil the kidneys until there was nothing left in the dang things but the memory, he returned the kidneys to their rightful place in a pot of boiling water.

For several days he religiously boiled the what-for out of the kidneys, but toward the end of the following week, I noticed that he was becoming less interested in the preparation and serving of the meals. Even the waitresses noticed the change and also noted that he had become noticeably sloppy and disinterested in his job.

Sensing that he was going through some emotional problem I invited him up to my office and asked him what his problem was, and why had he become so disinterested in his job. Though very reluctant to discuss his problems, he at last told me that he had received some very bad news from his home in France, and that he would have to return there very soon. It was a pity that he could not have remained with me a little longer, for I believed that he had potential and would have become a very fine chef in time. However, as fate often decrees, *'What will be will be'*

Again the search for a new cook began. Remembering past mistakes I carefully screened each prospective applicant, hoping that I might find a true gem amongst all the short-order cooks that applied for the job. Most of the would-be cooks had acquired their cooking experience in fast food joints or while incarcerated in some kind of institution, usually under the care of the state. Most of those unfortunates had not had the opportunity to learn more than the basics before their training ended, and therefore had very little to offer the higher-end restaurants.

Many applicants were screened before I found one who seemed to have the necessary training and was up to the job. This person seemed to have lots of energy and was willing to work hard, at least that is how it appeared for the first week.

One morning I arrived at my usual time, shortly before eleven in the morning. He was busy in the kitchen getting ready for the luncheon trade. I asked him how he was and if everything was okay, and he said "Yes". After a quick hello to the dishwasher I chatted briefly with the waitresses and then began preparing the bar for the usual luncheon crowd.

At five minutes to twelve I knelt down behind the bar to load the music tapes into the player. Five minutes later I stood up and found the dining room filled with hungry diners.

The waitresses were busy taking drink orders and I was kept busy mixing them. By twelve thirty I noticed that there were no food orders coming from the kitchen, and that the waitresses had gathered at the serving counter, and were looking very unhappy.

A feeling of imminent disaster overcame me, and I dashed into the kitchen to see what the trouble was. The cook was standing there, arms spread apart, and leaning on his worktable. In front of him, at eye level, was a line of luncheon orders, spread neatly across the entire face of the serving counter.

" My God", was the only thing that I could say; the cook was as drunk as a skunk. Evidently he had begun drinking the over proof rum intended for our famous 'deep fried ice-cream' as soon as he arrived that morning.

Not only was he plastered, it quickly became obvious that he had nothing prepared for lunch. The steak and pies were cold, sandwich fillers were unmade, the curry had a horrible colour that defied description, the ovens were unlit, the dishwasher had disappeared, the waitresses were as pale as ghosts, and I was livid.

Realizing that the ship was sinking, I immediately began filling the orders, with whatever was on hand. The poor waitresses, always the first on the firing line, did everything they could to calm the maddening crowd, but found it a near impossible task. By two o'clock the last order left the kitchen. The cook, who up until that time had not uttered a word, slowly dusted his hands, and said, "Well, we did it." After relieving him of his key, I threw him out into the alley, telling him never to show his face there again.

Clifford Becomes a Chef

The next decision I made was one that brought me more joy and satisfaction than I had experienced during that entire year. I was going to become the chef. From the moment I jumped into the kitchen and began preparing the meals, I felt a certain amount of satisfaction. Barb helped me most days, teaching me all about sauces and pastry and all the other things that I knew very little about, and I quickly learned the routine and managed to turn out a fairly good meal.

Presentation was fifty percent of a successful meal, and I enjoyed arranging the various types of food on the plate, in such a manner that the guests would spend the first few moments admiring the dish before taking a bite.

While cooking, I would quite often break out into song, which as far as I remember didn't offend too many customers. At that time I had a wonderful musician by the name of *Reginald Stone* playing in the dining room on weekends. Many times he would play songs that I was familiar with just so I could sing along with him. Reg and I became very good friends, and he remained with me for several years.

My mother-in-law, my sister, my cousin, and even my own mother, joined us at the restaurant and worked upstairs in the prep room during the year that I spent in the kitchen of the Coach and Four. They did all the preparation for the restaurant, and I was very happy that they were able to help me over that difficult time, and overjoyed at the great job they did.

After a year in the kitchen I began to feel the pressure of the daily routine, and wondered if I was really cut out to be a chef. Around that time I started feeling very down, and wishing that I could get out of the kitchen and back into the dining room where I belonged, so I decided to look for a man to replace me.

Happily I found a good replacement within a week or two. He was English, had a little family, happy marriage and willing to work hard. Just the kind of person I was looking for and, best of all, he was a great cook.

Getting back into the dining room was wonderful. Reg and I started performing together each weekend; he would accompany me on his Hammond Organ in a variety of Broadway tunes, and the hostess Irene Henderson, a wonderful English entertainer, would join in with her own fabulous Gracie Fields impersonations.

About that time I decided to add two balconies to the dining room, which would increase our seating capacity to ninety persons. The ceiling height was fourteen feet and I figured that if I built a balcony on each side of the room six feet wide and allowed six foot six inches underneath it, and six foot eight inches above it, I would be able to add several tables for dining, without losing any floor space. The main problem was that six foot six was probably contrary to the building code as was the six foot eight height on the balcony itself.

Undaunted, I drew up the plans for the balconies, and presented them to the building inspector at city hall.

He knew my work, and had always been very good to me in the past. He gave the plans a cursory once over, and then stamped them and told me to go ahead. Later, I found out that he had not taken a close look at the dimensions on the plan, particularly the figures which showed the upper and lower heights. This was a fortunate oversight, because he would not have approved them if he had realized that the height was not to code.

Not wanting to push my luck too far, I immediately got to work, and within a very short time installed the two balconies. Two weeks later, the chief engineer, and four other officials from the same department, came to The Coach and Four for lunch. Fate again took charge, and playfully decreed that they should sit under the not-to-code balconies.

This would not have been a problem had the engineer not been over six foot six inches tall, and had not bumped his head on the edge of the balcony. When he entered the restaurant I almost had a fainting spell, but recovering very quickly, I hurried over to them, intending to direct them to a table in the middle of the room where there was enough headroom for a giant. But as always, there is only one winner when dealing with fate.

When he knocked his head on the balcony, the entire engineering contingent, looked up at the offending molding and immediately began doing what they are programmed to do, calculations. Within a very short time, the five experts reached a unanimous conclusion, the balcony was too low. The following day the building inspector paid me a visit, and he too quickly reached the same conclusion.

Proclaiming my ignorance and the unfortunate oversight regarding the height restrictions of the balconies, I showed him the building permit, which mercifully I had close at hand, and pointed out that the height of the balconies had been approved by none other than himself, and that it would be impossible to make any changes at that point without losing my shirt, unless the building department would consider paying the shot themselves.

The building inspector had served with the British army in India for several years and was proficient in Hindi. During the next few minutes he began muttering to himself, speaking in a language that I suspected was Hindi. Having spent many years doing construction projects for East Indian gentlemen, I was familiar with the cadence and intonation of that particular dialect, and also sensitive to the hidden meaning behind negative comments.

When the first tear welled in his eyes my heart went out to him and I reached out, taking his hand and gently guiding him to the door, all the while cautioning myself that the next time I needed a building permit, I had better be prepared for intense scrutiny.

A View of Naughty Pictures

During the first year, following the completion of the Coach and Four, I helped my brother Frank finish some construction projects that we had on the go. One of the smaller jobs involved building a secret compartment in a closet of a large home off Rockland Avenue. As it was not too large or demanding, I did it myself.

An old acquaintance of mine was a landscape gardener, and he asked me to build the hidden space for him. I had no idea why he needed it or what he was going to put into it, and he never gave me any explanation. If I had taken a wild guess, I would have probably figured that he had two sets of books for his business or the even more likely explanation, that he had some valuables he did not want stolen. Either way, I completed the dividing wall creating the hidden space, and he was very happy with the results.

When the job was finished he paid me, then asked me if I was curious about the hidden chamber. I replied that it was not my business. He then revealed an enterprise that almost made my eyes pop out of their sockets. He was involved in pornography.

Strangely, I knew little about pornography at that time and the word was not really familiar to me, and other than a glance or two at naughty pictures over the years my experience was close to none.

When my acquaintance showed me his line of 'wares', I was more than a little surprised. The pictures were more explicit than I had ever seen. Not only explicit they were unbelievable.

After I recovered my senses, I managed to leaf through another stack or two of the contraband before giving up the struggle, and declaring that, I had not been initiated to that form of art, and as a matter of fact I did not know that it was even available here in jolly old Victoria.

The impresario informed me that it was not only available in the area, it was created right there in his own home, featuring his friends and acquaintances and, not only that, he was the creator of both the 'Stills', and the 'Films'. Evidently there was much more to his landscaping business than met the eye, and he was interested in much more than just laying sod or making flower beds.

When he invited me to attend his weekly gatherings, I declined, stating that I had always been interested in performing in films, but not this type of production. My talents, such as they were, would probably fall very short of the expectations and requirements of this particular medium. Furthermore, I had always been more interested in revealing my hidden talents rather than revealing my hidden attributes.

When I spoke to my buddies, and told them of the unbelievable goings-on at that mansion on the hill, they immediately said that they wanted to go there and see for themselves. I said there was no way that I would set foot in that house of horrors, unless I could wear a mask. Little did I know that they had a good selection to choose from.

At length I promised that I would phone the Impresario and make an appointment for them. When I made contact with him he said that he would be delighted to show them a special film, but only if I accompanied them. When I informed the friends that he would not show the film unless I was with them, they said that it would be fine with them if I came along.

After much arm twisting and cajoling, not to mention a good deal of begging, I relented and agreed to accompany them as long as they fully understood I would not stay for the finale. They agreed, and so I made the appointment with the erotic landscaper for the following night. Naturally I did not inform anyone of the arrangements other than my friends George and Rick

The movie mogul was alone when we arrived, and was all charm and charisma as he ushered us into his viewing room, a room surprisingly devoid of any furniture other than an over-sized bed, and subdued lighting.

It was evident from the moment the homemade movie began, that this was meant to set the mood for much more than I was willing to endure, friends or no friends. They however, were enthralled with the fare, and loudly applauded every move the dark haired lady made.

When the movie finally ended the director asked us if we would like to meet the star of the film. After a heated discussion, we agreed, and the dark haired lady entered the room. I instantly recognized her by the red, high-heeled boots she was wearing; come to think of it, that was all she was wearing.

For a short while there was pandemonium in the room, but after the initial shock wore off, and we had become accustomed to the presence of a nude lady in the room, we did manage to settle down, and within a very short time regained our voices and even ventured to ask the odd question of lady Godiva.

There were very few intelligent questions that came to mind at that moment, apart from the obvious, "What is a nice girl like you doing in a place like this", or "Haven't we met somewhere before? Do you have a regular job?" "Aren't you afraid of catching cold?" "Where did you leave your horse?" "Aren't you too old for this?" and even more completely inane comments that don't bear repeating.

Finally our host came to our rescue and formally introduced the lady as one of the regular patrons of his Friday night soirees, and suggested that perhaps we might be interested in a sample of the goings on that took place at those gatherings.

George and Rick, both single as a matter of interest, seemed overjoyed at the prospect of starring in a porno movie. For myself, I begged off with a headache, and excused myself from the proceedings.

The impresario was far more interested in my participating in the spectacle than he was with having my friends in it, even though they were both much more attractive than I was. Trying my best to remain calm, I explained to him that there was nothing about porno films that interested me, and also there was a very good chance that one day in the future I might consider running for a position on the city council, perhaps even the Mayor's seat, and it would never do to have a movie of that kind lurking in the background, just waiting for the right opportunity to spring out and wipe out any chance at public office. Furthermore, I loved my wife and would never consider putting myself in such a compromising position that would likely destroy our marriage.

The gentleman pointed out that his wife was an active participant in the weekly shenanigans in that room, and she quite enjoyed the whole affair. I said that this was a classic example of a horse of a different colour, so to speak, and she no doubt had her own reasons for her choice of Friday night entertainment. My wife on the other hand was a very private person and would never venture into such home entertainment.

Several months later an article in the Colonist told of a certain local businessman who had been charged with dealing in pornography. His home had been searched but very little evidence was uncovered, other than a small number of naughty pictures and several rolls of film which, when run through a police projector were seen to be naughty but did not constitute pornography in the true sense of the law.

Later that week I received a call from that gentleman who laughingly told me that even though the police had searched every room in his house, all they found were a few pieces of non-incriminating photographic art. The search included the closet where I had built the secret chamber, and though they spent an unusual amount of time in the closet, they had not discovered the hidden treasure. I was pleased that my workmanship had passed the test, but a little disappointed that his dark secrets had not been revealed.

A month later, a man and his wife had lunch in my restaurant. The gentleman introduced himself and his wife as friends of the infamous landscaper, and intimated that we all had something in common He then proffered me a large full-coloured book entitled *'Erotica'*, and suggested that I might enjoy the subject matter.

The hackles on the back of my neck began to rise and my cheeks turned a rosy colour. I refused the book, thanked him for the offer, but assured him that we had absolutely nothing in common, and would he please pass the word along to all his friends. That was the last time I had any contact with the Friday night moviemakers.

A Fast Way to Lose Money

Brother Frank continued in the construction business while I ran the restaurant. After one year in the business, my accountant informed me that I had lost twenty-five thousand dollars. I resolved to put the enterprise into the black or die in the attempt.

Sometimes having resolve alone is not enough to ensure success, and so I decided to sell a percentage of the enterprise to my cousin Cornelius. He worked in the far north for an American company helping to run a radar station on the 'Dew Line', and had spare cash to invest. He also had a good friend and fellow worker nicknamed *'Taffy'*, who was willing to put some money into the business as well.

Both Cornelius and Taffy put up some cash and several months later left the *'Dew Line'* and joined me at the Coach and Four. Signing them on as partners was very difficult for me. I had invested so much time and effort learning the business I was very reluctant to share it with anyone. However, they did keep their end of the bargain by putting up the money, so I signed them on as partners and immediately put them to work in the kitchen where they could learn the trade from the ground up, so to speak. They handled the dish washing when our regular girl was off, and also did some preparation whenever needed.

Gradually the two partners worked their way into the dining room, which allowed me some time off and gave me the opportunity to do some theatre. I divided my days up into slots, which I apportioned to both the restaurant and the theatre. My partners filled in for me when I was involved in the play.

Being single, the two of them spent as much time as possible looking for potential wives, and for the first year they actively courted girls. This at times was a problem because often they would be out entertaining their ladies while I was at work in the restaurant. After what seemed to be an endless process, they found wives and then began planning their wedding, finally departing on a month long honeymoon.

When the honeymoon was over my hope was that they would get back to helping me in the business and they did just that, until a week or so before Christmas when they decided to take a skiing holiday.

The Christmas season was particularly busy that year with many dinner parties and some outside catering. New Years was booked solid in the dining room as well as a private banquet elsewhere. My partners expected to be back before Christmas, so I was not too worried, at least not until the day that fate again dealt me the losing hand.

The boys had enjoyed several days on the slopes and where ready to return home, at least I think they were ready to return home. That day a phone call informed me that there had been a heavy snowfall in the mountains and they would not be able to get out of there until after Christmas. There was nothing I could do but dig in and cover all the shifts myself. This was not too much of a hardship as I was used to working all the shifts anyway, except for the few times that I was involved in a play.

The main problem was that we were extremely busy, and also shorthanded, so for several days we all worked full steam, dealing with a full restaurant and outside banquets as best we could. In the meantime I got daily reports of how the skiing was going on the mountain top, and the final report that it looked like they wouldn't get home until after New Years.

My partners were great guys and enjoyed the time they spent in the business, but it was getting a little crowded for all three of us in the little restaurant, so my cousin decided to go back to school. He worked very hard and eventually earned an Honors Degree in Law and moved to Prince George where he joined a well established firm and soon became a partner.

Once the restaurant started making money, I began looking around for more challenges, reasoning that if you could make money with one restaurant then surely you could make twice as much with another one. About that time the city of Victoria decided to renovate Bastion Square as a first step in the rejuvenation of Victoria's Old Town.

A well-known architect was enlisted to begin the process of rebuilding the old city. As Bastion Square was the oldest part of Victoria it was the natural choice to start with. Unfortunately the construction was destined to last for almost two years, and in the meantime the Coach and Four, cut-off from all but the most adventurous diners, and the mainstream traffic, suffered a substantial drop in business.

For almost a year the only access to the restaurant was by a shaky wooden bridge, which spanned a ten-foot ditch directly in front of our place of business. Even the bravest of customers crossed that bridge reluctantly, and little old ladies, the backbone of our business, were even more hesitant to venture across those shaky planks. Often we would stand on our side of the bridge encouraging the dear souls to take the last three or four steps to safety and our waiting arms. Getting them back over the ditch once they had finished dining was another story. On several occasions I had to go ahead of them and jump up and down on the planks to prove that they were safe to cross.

When the Bastion Square project was completed we faced yet another problem, for there was no more parking available on the street in front of our restaurant. The whole of the street had been raised and now formed a gigantic courtyard, not accessible to anything other than foot traffic.

While the Bastion project was admirable, it was a very difficult time for us financially; however we persevered and the square became popular, and home to several other restaurants, boutiques and offices. Many new customers found us, and our old customers, no longer facing the many obstacles, once again blessed us with their presence.

The Second Restaurant

After Bastion Square was completed, the city launched the Centennial Square project, another grand addition to our town. One of the new buildings to be constructed, was designed as a restaurant, and would be attached to the newly renovated McPherson Theatre by an enclosed walkway.

My search for a new enterprise seemed to lead directly to that second floor space in Centennial Square, and with scarcely a second thought, I embarked on my next venture, namely, another restaurant.

My partner was not overly thrilled with the idea of another restaurant, however the thought of having me out of his hair, was a strong incentive, so he agreed, providing that I would run the new establishment, while he would run the Coach and Four.

There were many items to negotiate with the city before an agreement could be reached, and I worked very hard to get a deal that was satisfactory to all parties. After months of negotiations the deed was signed and we became the proud lessees of The McPherson Seafood and Steakhouse.

The first problem that came to light was that there were many steps up to the restaurant, and older people shied away from steps like the plague and secondly, there was no parking close by, other than the city parkade on the far side of the square. Many people did not like leaving their car unattended in the multi storied parking garage, even though it was right next door to the police station, because of the many shady characters that made the square their headquarters. Some of those customers did not like the walk the short distance from the parkade to the restaurant, as there was the possibility of meeting an unsavory individual on the stroll across the square.

While I was in business there, I parked my car in the parkade and walked across the square every day, and I never encountered any bad characters; as a matter of fact I, often had very pleasant chats with the different individuals who frequented the square, many of whom became customers of the restaurant.

At one point we decided to provide valet parking on busy evenings, that is, until we discovered that one or two of our drivers enjoyed taking a quick tour around the town before parking the car in the parkade. After these nocturnal joy rides came to light, we decided that the folk who dined with us, would likely be happier parking their own car. At least they would then know exactly where the family limo was berthed.

When I was fifteen, the York Theatre, which was then used by a movie chain, became home to a professional group of actors. They were looking for acting talent and also staff to operate the theatre. I applied for the position of doorman, believing that I could somehow get the attention of the professionals, and perhaps land an acting job with the troupe. Unfortunately the group never managed to overcome the many hurdles associated with professional theatre and ultimately failed.

The disappointment that I experienced when I learned that this professional troupe was leaving Victoria, never really left me and I always felt that their failure was not only a terrible blow to me but, a blow to all of Victoria. After many years the theatre rose like a phoenix, and due to the generosity of the local businessman, Thomas Shanks McPherson, the theatre was refurbished and restored to its original elegance, and again became a home for live theatre.

When I became the lessee of the restaurant I was overjoyed. Being so closely associated with the McPherson Playhouse was wonderful. The manager of the theatre was most accommodating and welcomed my idea of promoting the concept of dinner and show packages.

Whenever there was a local production being produced for the McPherson, I would arrange with the group to hold a number of tickets for me, which I would then offer as a dinner and show package, or as we advertised, *'A Night on the Town'*. This package became very popular with theatergoers and most nights we had a full house for the shows.

Once the guests had finished their dinner they would proceed to the theatre through the overhead walkway from our restaurant, and to the second floor level of the theatre. There was a door between the restaurant and the upper lobby, which was closed when not in use. Being on the same level as the restaurant, it was very convenient and popular with our patrons.

When booking the *'Night on the Town'* packages, we tried our best to arrange the seating times so that the kitchen and dining room staff could keep up with the demand. This unfortunately was not always possible, as most guests requested the seven o'clock seating, which only allowed one hour dining before the show. Even guests that had booked an earlier time often arrived late, making it almost impossible to cook and serve a meal in time for the eight o'clock show. So there was always near pandemonium in the dining room on show nights.

Often we would get complaints from the diners who had waited too long for their meal, and therefore had to rush to get to the show on time. This was most frustrating for me as I was somewhat of a perfectionist, and did not like second best, particularly where customers were concerned. Whenever there was a problem I would do my best to fix it, but some times this was more easily said than done, and when customers were unreasonable, I would get hot under the collar, sometimes saying things that I later regretted.

On one occasion, the dining room was packed with diners going to the eight o'clock show and the kitchen staff was snowed under. This caused delays and some patrons became a little hostile.

The staff and I did everything we could to hurry up the kitchen but to no avail, and more than a few diners complained to me about the delay. One lady sidled up to me and in a low penetrating voice, began complaining about this and that. While listening to her subtle and increasingly negative comments, I noticed a little scar on her upper lip that became more and more noticeable as she rattled on.

There was something fascinating about that little scar, something familiar in the way it began to expand as her heavy make-up slowly melted, revealing more and more of her tortured lip. Suddenly I remembered a similar episode that occurred at the Coach and Four just after we had opened in 1964.

That incident also occurred on a very busy night, and I never forgot her hurtful manner as she ruthlessly went up one side of me and down the other. I also remembered the little scar, which slowly revealed itself as she ranted on. It occurred to me that she may have received the scar while engaged in a like conversation with some other poor unfortunate, and that he or she, unable to control their retaliatory reflex, whacked her on the lip.

The first time this verbal assault happened I was speechless, the second time was an entirely different story, and after carefully studying her scar to make certain that she was the same lady, I smiled sweetly, and suggested that she would be doing me a great favor, if she never darkened my door again.

The lady was thunderstruck at my remarks, and became even more agitated when I informed her that I was still suffering from the unfair attack that she had inflicted on me that night in 1964 at the Coach and Four and, furthermore, her husband had said that he had a great meal on each occasion.

Noting that her little scar was becoming even more visible by the minute, and her lip was quivering almost uncontrollably, I was immediately overcome with a deep sense of compassion for her, and without giving it another thought, I took her in my arms and gently pulled her little body close to mine.

Many times over the course of my life I have come to the realization that most humans are suffering from a lack of affection and love in their lives, and will almost always respond favorably to a hug and a kind word, and this lady was no exception. Her face lit up at this unexpected development, and she gave me a smile that I will never forget. Once again, I discovered that most everyone we come in contact with in our daily lives would respond favorably to kindness rather than harsh words.

Throughout my life I had generally responded to negative comments in an aggressive way, almost as a boxer would respond to a left hook. However, I was slowly beginning to realize that an aggressive response was usually more negative than the initial comment, and most often caused an even deeper rift.

Without being fully aware of this subtle change in my attitude, I gradually found myself stepping back from unkind or unfair comments, and allowing human kindness and compassion to speak for me. This subconscious act of compassion was a revelation for me and, as the years passed by, I found that turning a negative situation around and creating a positive outcome gave me a wonderful sense of accomplishment. Unfortunately, kindness does not always get the desired result with everyone, and occasionally I was disappointed by the outcome of a seemingly minor problem.

There was a hot line between our two restaurants that enabled Taffy and myself to keep each other informed about ongoing business and to also pass on any juicy gossip. This form of communication was great and we shared many interesting tit-bits throughout the day. Whenever the need or desire arose, one of us would pick up the red phone, which would automatically ring in the other restaurant, and we would exchange any interesting incidents.

On one occasion an older couple who had apparently enjoyed their dinner, discovered that the cost of their ice cream was more than they had bargained for. That particular dinner was on special but did not include dessert, so the couple ordered a scoop of vanilla to finish off the meal.

After eating everything that was served including dessert, they studied the bill for some time before approaching me in an agitated state. I had not noticed anything unusual in their behavior before that moment, and so I was unprepared for what seemed to be an aggressive manner as they stomped up to me with the bill clutched firmly in the extended hand of the husband.

The wife quickly informed me that they had not enjoyed the meal, the husband added to the tirade, announcing that they were never going to come back to this restaurant. After listening to the endless list of complaints, none of which really explained their concerns, I asked them to be a little more explicit so that I could fully understand what the exact problem was, and then I could do something about it.

Reading between the lines, I soon came to the conclusion that they felt that the ice cream should have been included in the meal. The easiest course would have been to include the dessert in the price of the meal and to alter the bill accordingly but, for some reason, my mood that day was one of love and benevolence and, instead of refunding them the two dollars for the ice-cream, I gave them a gift certificate entitling them to two free meals at our restaurant. Unfortunately, I forgot that our gift certificates stated that they could be used in either the McPherson or the Coach and Four.

Two days later, the hotline phone rang, and a highly agitated Taffy informed me that a couple had dined in the Coach and Four and presented a gift certificate to cover their meal. They had ordered an expensive meal, including dessert, and stated that they had enjoyed it very much. Taffy asked them where they had gotten the certificate. They said they received it from a man at the McPherson restaurant because they had been very unhappy with the meal they had there a day or so before. He asked them if they were fully satisfied, and they assured him that they were completely satisfied, but they would never return to that other restaurant.

That incident was very disappointing, because I had given the certificate to them in good faith, trusting that they would return and give us the chance to satisfy them. But they did not deem it necessary to give us another chance and went to our other restaurant.

It was incidents like this one that tended to blunt my ardor, and I always felt badly when I was unsuccessful in bringing about a happy ending in any dispute. From that day on I was extremely careful about giving anything away free, particularly to anyone without a legitimate complaint. When a customer was not happy with their meal I would alter the bill, but I would never again offer a full meal for free, unless it was eaten in my own restaurant and was of equal value to the rejected meal. Shortly after that experience, we had new gift certificates printed, specifically naming the restaurant where they would be honored.

Having a restaurant to run seemed to be a great way to meet people and enjoy life, but there was much more to it than met the eye. In later years I would often warn friends or acquaintances against the restaurant business, suggesting that there were many different ways to lose money with fewer headaches.

Operating the McPherson restaurant took much of my time and energy, but I thoroughly enjoyed the challenge and even managed to perform and direct several plays during that period.

While in the restaurant business I continued to manage my rental properties, collecting rents, carrying out repairs, looking for tenants and a host of other concerns. Anyone who has rented out properties will fully understand the reference I make to the 'host of other concerns'.

Nightmare Tenants

One of my properties was an up and down duplex. It was on the corner of Catherine and Henry Street in Vic West adjacent to several other properties I owned. It was across the street from brother Frank's house on Catherine.

Frank and I had previously renovated the duplex, which we rented out to a variety of interesting tenants, most of whom quickly became a royal pain in the butt. Over the years it received a lot of wear and tear from the tenants and finally required a complete overhaul. We replaced kitchen cabinets, carpets, tiles, and repainted every room making it look great. After interviewing several prospective tenants, I rented it to young couple and their brother. The trio appeared very reliable and gave good references, so I let them move in right away.

Before the month was up, brother Frank told me that it was a party house with dozens of people coming and going at all hours, every day of the week. The previous night there had been a party that spilled over onto the lawn and into the street itself. Frank tried to talk sense into the partygoers, but had no luck with them so he phoned the police. By the time the police arrived everyone was back in the house and seemingly under control. That lasted for a very short while and then went full steam from there.

Doing my best to keep a cool head, I visited the house to have a word or two with the tenants and found all three partygoers there. I explained that I had received complaints from the neighbours about the rowdy parties that had been occurring there on a fairly regular basis, and asked what did they have to say for themselves.

Butter would not have melted in their mouths, as they described how the few friends that they had invited over for soft drinks that night, had behaved themselves admirably, and how several other uninvited guests crashed the party creating all the noise and mayhem. Not wanting to come right out and call them liars, I asked them if the same party crashers had appeared each and every night or was it possible that perhaps some of their own guests were responsible for the nightly fireworks. They assured me that whatever had happened in the past was not going to happen again. Not wanting to belabour the point, I suggested that if the neighbours continued with their complaints, I would be forced to take drastic action.

Thinking that I had handled the situation quite well, and thrilled that I had used gentle words rather than threats, I descended the stairs. Before I reached the last step I could distinctly hear the trio berating my efforts, and comparing me to the rear end of a horse. I have been called worse so I did not feel too insulted, however they did not stop there but continued railing, questioning my legitimacy, suggesting that my mother was something other than a good housewife, and even commenting that the next time I set foot in that house they would kick me in the unmentionables. Resisting the urge to run back up the stairs, lest I become a fatality, I continued walking to my vehicle, pretending that I had not overheard their rough words, but contemplating my next move.

The tenant in the basement suite was a single man of fifty, and very likely took part in the ongoing shenanigans whenever possible. However, he had become tired of the activity and contacted me the following day, confirming all that I had overheard from the trio plus a few more choice suggestions that would have been very difficult for me to perform.

The following weekend the trio threw an even louder party. Upon hearing of the chaos that had occurred during that all night celebration, I blew my cork, and enlisting the help of my dear brother Frank, I did a very stupid thing.

On Sunday, the day after the noisy affair, brother Frank and I drove a large truck over to the duplex, parking it close to the front steps. We went up to the front door and knocked, no answer, we knocked again even louder than before, still no answer. I tried the door and found it unlocked, so we entered the house.

Calling very loudly to announce our presence, we went from room to room, finding several people who obviously were sleeping it off. During our walk about, we could not help but notice that the rooms were in terrible shape. Doors were damaged, from either being hit with a blunt object or more probably, by large fists. Some windows were broken; piles of sodden clothing were lying on the hardwood floors, which caused stains. There were smudges and dents in the plastered walls, and at least two doorjambs had been splintered, but even more mystifying, there were dirty footprints on the ceiling.

The whole scene reminded me of a similar incident that happened to me several years before. I had owned a fourteen-room house that had been built in the late 1800's on the corner of Oak Bay Avenue and McGregor Street in Victoria. Every room in the house was furnished with antique furniture, round oak tables and chairs, parlour tables, upholstered settees, beds, and a huge assortment of lamps and miscellaneous antiques.

That was the beginning of the 'Hippie' era, and several young people had passed themselves off as university students and rented the house from me.

Within a few months, the 'students' had completely destroyed the house and all the furnishings in it. Evidently they threw wild parties, sometimes with hundreds of other hippie types invading the premises breaking doors, windows, plumbing fixtures and even burning wood antiques in the many fireplaces in the house.

On one occasion I visited the house to see just how much damage had been done and was appalled at the amount of destruction that had occurred there. One of the few bedroom doors that were left intact in the house was locked from the inside, so I attacked the door just like the police do in movies, and knocked it off its hinges. There was a very startled couple laying on a mattress in the centre of the room, whom I informed had no right to be in the house, and suggested that they finish what they were doing and leave as quickly as possible, although I really didn't care if they did or not as the place was only fit for the wrecker anyway.

Shortly after filing an insurance claim, I had the whole building torn down and then sold the empty lot to a builder who soon constructed an apartment on the site. Funnily, the final payment for the property, due on the first day of June was not forthcoming because I had not signed the final papers, I technically became the owner of that apartment building. Without saying anything to my friend the realtor, I let the contractor proceed with the building until the roof was finished. Once the roof was installed, the contractor celebrated by mounting a Christmas tree on the top of the roof, a custom followed by some builders, which should have been a happy occasion for him and his crew. A day or so later, I phoned my friend the realtor, and told him that I was going to take over the building as legal owner, and that the contractor should be so informed.

My realtor friend was speechless, and quickly realized that he was in a particularly difficult position, as he had not informed his client that the balance of the sale was due on the first of June. How this oversight came about, was always a mystery to me, and I never completely understood where he had gone wrong. My friend was a true wheeler-dealer, and I was delighted to have caught him in this awkward situation. If ever he needed my love and compassion, it was now. The next day he arrived at my door, hat in hand, begging me to forgive him for this unfortunate oversight, and promising me that he would always be in my debt, and that he would make it up to me somehow. I suggested that he could start by making sure I was fully reimbursed for the strain and stress which this unfortunate incident had caused me.

He indicated that the builder was willing to pay me handsomely for this inconvenience and that he would have a cheque for me within a day or two at the outside. Friendship has always been more important to me than money, so I told my friend that all he owed me was the interest that I had missed by not having the funds invested for those few months, and also I expected that he should take me and Barb out for dinner in the very near future.

We did go for a wonderful dinner the following week, and remained good friends for many years and continued doing business together until he moved to the United States.

A Court Case

When brother Frank and I visited the duplex on Henry Street and discovered the damage inflicted by those young ruffians, I was livid. Remembering the destruction of the beautiful old house on Oak Bay Avenue by the same type of witless individuals, I forgot my resolve to settle things pleasantly, and proceeded to wake the sleeping beauties and inform them that this was moving day. I went from bed to bed cheerfully telling one and all that their hour had come and they were leaving immediately.

By law, tenants are entitled to quiet enjoyment of their rented premises, and also have the right to remain there until legal notice is served on them. I was well aware of law as I had many run-ins with unsatisfactory tenants and had been forced to take such action on numerous occasions. But somehow the knowledge and experience completely evaporated, leaving me in a witless state similar to that of my tenants. Without any consideration or concern for the law, I embarked on a deliberate course of retribution, shaking and terrorizing everyone I found in a bed or on the floor, and demanding that they get dressed and get out.

Not satisfied with waking every sleeper and throwing them out, I continued to dig the hole that was rapidly swallowing me ever deeper, and removed all the furniture and belongings that were in the house, and placed them in my truck. My reign of terror came to an abrupt end when I asked them where they would like me to take their belongings.

The tenant known as Joe, smiling like a Cheshire cat, said, "Take them where ever you like, they're yours now".

At that very moment the police arrived. The officers listened to the tenants as they described all the lurid details of the raid, and then demanded that the police should arrest me for carrying out this despicable attack.

Police are generally very sympathetic when landlords have altercations with unruly tenants, but they also understand the rules of the game, and the fact that tenants, though some are very undesirable, often hold the winning cards. Before the officers made any attempt to arrest me, they wanted to know exactly why I had carried out this highly unusual evacuation.

They accompanied me on a tour of the house where I pointed out the splintered doors, broken windows, foot prints on the ceiling, piles of refuse on the floors, and the beginning shoots of a pot growing operation. The officers noted the damage and also acknowledged that it was indeed pot growing in the bathtub, and agreed that I did have some justification for ejecting them. They did not arrest me but suggested that I should contact my lawyer as quickly as possible.

Even though it was Sunday, within an hour or two the tenants had written notice from their lawyer, describing the deep doo doo that I was now in, and informing me that I was going to have the full weight of the law on my case immediately. The lawyer, a well known civil rights proponent, spent much of his time in his little office, waiting for just such an opportunity to help this less fortunate segment of society.

One point informed me that I was now responsible for their immediate welfare, including accommodations, and as they now had no means of cooking, I was also responsible for their meals. Calculating the probable costs shocked me even further, and when faced with the facts the sensible side of my brain took over.

My most recent purchase had been an old relic of a house on the corner of Government and Hillside. At that point I had neither renovated nor decorated it, so I was suddenly struck with the thought that by letting them stay there, I might just be able to sort this whole mess out without losing my shirt.

When I informed them that I would allow them to move into the house, providing they treated it with a little respect, they reluctantly agreed to the arrangement. Of course I realized that I would probably never see another dollar of rent from them, but at that moment it seemed a very wise thing to do. At least I could always claim that I had treated them fairly, and might even get off with a lighter sentence.

Moving them into that relic of a house, however, did not get me off the hook, because they informed their lawyer that when I moved their belongings into the house, their fourteen hundred dollar stereo set was missing. Brother Frank and I had taken their load of stuff directly to the house without making any stops. They concocted the story that the stereo had been stored in the basement of the duplex and it had now disappeared. Amazed at their brazen antics, and bewildered by the lawyer's gullibility, I decided that enough was enough, and set about debunking their claim.

Within a very short period, their lawyer had me in front of a small claims judge. The lawyers writ included the entire gamut of legal gobbly-gook, and reasoned that nothing short of life at hard labour would make things right for his clients.

Prior to the court date, I had drawn up three different sets of plans for the basement of the duplex, reasoning that the made-up story of the missing stereo could easily be debunked if I could prove that they had never been in the basement, much less stored the set there. My theory was that if they could not identify the correct basement plan, they were obviously lying, and the judge could throw the whole case out of court, and get me off the hook.

Preparing for my day in court was of prime importance to me, and so I gathered as many witnesses as possible to give evidence in my behalf. The first witness for the defense was the painter who had decorated the suite the week before the trio had moved into the apartment. The second was the tenant living in the basement suite, who hopefully would describe the upper tenants rowdy behaviour during the first weeks. The only other witness that I could muster was the pizza pieman who had delivered an endless supply of pizzas to the parties, daily. Unfortunately I had to dispense with his assistance because he confessed to me that he had gotten along very well with the plaintiffs and actually thought that the whole group of desperados were great folk and besides, they gave big tips.

When my day in court finally arrived I was as prepared as was humanly possible, considering that I was actually as guilty as hell. Arriving at the court a half hour early, I studied my papers and readied my defense. The plaintiffs arrived en masse with their displaced entourage and, seating themselves directly behind me, immediately began sharpening their swords and daggers. When the Judge made his punctual entrance into the courtroom, the crowd hushed, and not a sound was heard, but the muffled thud of my heart.

The usual courtroom banter was exchanged between the Clerk and the Judge, and then his Worship cast his eyes on me, leaving me with the disquieting feeling that he was about to lower the boom on the moron before him who had taken the law into his own hands and bodily thrown these hapless tenants onto the street.

For several minutes he gazed about, first at me, and then at the tenants sitting very quietly, looking for all the world like misunderstood innocents. At last he asked the Clerk, who was appearing for the plaintiffs, and who for the defendant. The Clerk mentioned me by name as the defendant, and also naming Mr. Legal Aid himself, whom as yet had not appeared, as the plaintiff's representative.

It was raining, which explained the soggy condition of my legal opposition, when he hurried into court a full ten minutes late. The Judge, apparently accustomed to Mr. Legal Aid's tardiness, bid him good morning in a friendly manner, and asked him if he was representing the plaintiffs. The gentleman pulled a somewhat disheveled bundle of papers from his soggy briefcase, and laid them on the table in front of him, shuffled them two or three times, and finally admitted that he was indeed the man.

Immediately the Clerk read the list of wrong doings that I had inflicted on the plaintiffs, which made the charges sound even more reprehensible, particularly in the harsh glare of the court. My heart sank a little as I viewed the Judge's stern countenance as he listened to the brazen lawlessness on my part. Behind me, the hanging party had finished honing the knives, and were now preparing the rope.

His Worship asked me if I agreed with the charges, as presented.

"There were mitigating circumstances your Honor," I replied.

"I did not ask about the circumstances, I asked if the charges were correct," said his Worship.

" Yes, your Honor, they are indeed correct." I replied.

"Well then, have you anything to say regarding the circumstances?"

" Your Honor, the former tenants created such an uproar, with their partying and shenanigans, that many neighbours and the downstairs tenant, complained about the all night disturbance, both to me and my brother who lives two doors down from the duplex. I visited them and told them of the complaints that I had received, and insisted that they must stop immediately, or I would be forced to take drastic action. After removing their possessions from the duplex, I offered them accommodation in another house that I own, and they readily accepted my offer. My brother and I, then drove directly to the other house and moved the belongings into it. The following day their lawyer informed me that their expensive stereo set had disappeared. I informed him that we had driven straight to the other house and that there was no stereo among their possessions. They then informed me that they had stored the stereo in the basement and when they went back to retrieve the set, it was gone. I asked them how they had managed to get into the basement, and they said the door was open. This did not surprise me, as the door had never been locked, so that both the upstairs tenants and the basement tenant would have access to the washer and dryer.

Your Worship, may I introduce a set of plans showing the correct layout of the basement, along with two sets of incorrect plans, and ask the former tenants to identify the correct one?"

His Honor said that it was highly unusual, but if I thought that it would help my case, then it would be permissible. The plaintiff's lawyer leapt to his feet and objected.

His Honor said, " What are you objecting to? This is not a criminal case," .

The lawyer grumbled about the unnecessary waste of time. The Judge asked him to kindly sit down and allowed me to state my case.

On a roll, I presented the plans to the Judge, pointing out the correct one, and indicating the phonies. I then asked the tenant to come forward and view the plans. Looking very glum, the tenant approached the bench, and studied the plans for a few moments. I then asked him which plan showed the area where he supposedly stored the stereo set. He reluctantly admitted that he could not identify the correct plan, and then returned to his seat. His legal representative said that it was really unimportant whether he knew which was the correct plan and that the whole exercise was irrelevant.

" Your Worship', I said, " the tenants have suggested that I am responsible for the disappearance of their stereo set. I would like to point out to the court that, the likelihood of anyone storing such an expensive set in a basement that has always been left unlocked, would be very unlikely. Furthermore, there is absolutely no storage area available in the basement and, as you can see, there is barely room for the sink and washer and dryer. If I may ask my tenant who lives in the basement to take the stand, I will show that the upper tenants were extremely noisy, and totally unconcerned regarding the well being of neighbours and other tenants."

When this other tenant took the stand he agreed that they were noisy, but also admitted that they threw jolly good parties. Realizing that this fellow could very easily upset my defense, I thanked him and asked him to return to his seat, fully expecting the lawyer to cross examine him. To my surprise the legal beagle sat quietly, shuffling his papers but never saying a word.

My next witness was the painter who had decorated the apartment before the trio had moved in. He was marvelous, and corroborated my testimony regarding the broken doors and windows, and also mentioned the food that was splattered all over the walls which had ruined the paint job, and how disgusted he was when he saw the footprints on the ceiling. He even mentioned the cannabis that he saw growing in old coffee tins in different areas of the house.

The officers, who had seen the small pot growing operation, told me that I was fortunate to have discovered it in the early stages, because most problems develop when the pot has reached the harvesting stage. At that time the growers become very protective and sometimes will stop at nothing to protect their crop.

By this time the Judge seemed to be on my side, at least he no longer looked at me with the suspicion that was so evident at the beginning of the session.

When the lawyer stood up to rebut my evidence, the Judge said, "Really, Mr. Legal Aid, the evidence clearly shows that your clients were not ideal tenants, and Mr. Clarke acted in a perfectly normal way when he confronted them. Not only that, he provided them with alternate accommodation, even moving their belongings to the new location in spite of the evidence that they were highly undesirable tenants. The unfortunate fact is, that Mr. Clarke took the law into his own hands when he ejected them. The Tenants Act clearly defines the rights of tenants and the guidelines that landlords must follow when terminating their tenancy. Mr. Clarke negated his rights when he physically removed their possessions and all but threw them onto the street. However, the small claims court was primarily set up to see that justice was done in disputes of this kind, but not necessarily as defined by the letter of the law. This dispute between Mr. Clarke and your clients, is not of a common nature, and is far more complicated than is normal, therefore I will consider the case and render my judgement in due course."

Never one to gloat over another's misfortune, I shook Mr. Legal Aid's hand and thanked him for allowing his clients to put forward the idea that they had left the stereo set in the basement, rather than upstairs in one of the rooms; if they had done that, I would not have been able to refute their story nor defended my own. In later years, I met the same lawyer at various social functions, but for some reason or other this matter was never discussed.

Ten days later I received a four-page letter from the court, which covered all the details of the Judge's decision. After noting the different aspects of the case, he ruled that the tenants forfeited their claim by abusing their rights of tenancy, and by their behaviour, became the architects of their own defeat. Clarke on the other hand abrogated his rights as a landlord, by entering their home and ejecting them. Therefore, because neither party abided by the laws pertaining to tenancy, he declared that there would be no penalty assessed for either tenant or landlord.

One month later, the tenants moved away from the house that I had provided them and hopefully chastened by the previous experience, left the premises in exactly the same condition that they had found it. My brush with the law made me very cautious when dealing with future tenants. Whenever I was tempted to eject some ruffian from one of my rental properties, I remembered that episode, and tempered my actions accordingly.

The duplex on Henry Street was one of six properties on that block that Barb and I had purchased, and the one at 315 Henry was the very first house that we ever owned. My mother had loaned me five hundred dollars for a down payment. The full price was twenty-five hundred dollars, payable at fifty dollars a month.

It is hard to believe that a person could buy a house in those days for only twenty five hundred dollars, albeit shabby and run-down. However we did manage to purchase several houses for seven thousand dollars or less, and then fixed them up, and either sold them, or rented them. I often thought that I should have hung on instead of selling them, but dealing with some tenants was extremely stressful, and so I eventually sold all the properties and put the money into investments.

Our First Church

One of the properties on Henry was St. Paul's, a derelict church built in the 1890's. There was another church on Henry Street as well, St Saviors Anglican church built around the same time.

Barb and I were married in St. Saviors church in 1951. Strangely enough, we never attended church there, although we often discussed the possibility. Because of my work we never did manage to attend any church. That only occurred much later in my life and then it was under an entirely different set of circumstances.

St. Paul's Church was a large shingled building with a high bell tower on one side. Inside the church was sheeted with cedar tongue and groove and featured beautiful edge-grain fir floors, very well worn and faded by the time we purchased it. The building was typical West Coast construction and design, including the cedar pews and pulpit. It had been abandoned several years before my brother Frank and I purchased it. We had no thought of establishing a religious movement there, but rather intended to use it as a workshop for Frank's woodworking business.

Frank began a custom door business while there, and quickly became very busy supplying doors and jambs for many of Victoria's new apartment buildings. He was the first contractor in the area that specialized in doors and jambs and he kept very busy for several years.

There were many artifacts in the church when we took it over, including pews, pulpit, and an odd assortment of picture frames and miscellaneous decorations. An agent for the town of Barkerville visited us one day and offered to purchase the bell and pews plus any other bits and pieces that we had no use for Barkerville's original buildings were being restored, and the old church needed a bell and furnishings, so our collection of antiquities nicely filled the bill. Brother Frank and I both loved history and restoration and we were very pleased that our church furnishings would be put to such a worthwhile use.

Frank continued his door business in the old church, until it became too small to hold the amount of inventory he needed to carry, and eventually he moved and we sold the building. His own home was right next door to the church building and he continued to live there for several years and renovated and restored the home to its original beauty.

Horses

My love of horses throughout my childhood continued well into my adult life, and we as a family had many horses over the years. While living on Glanford Avenue we acquired three horses. My daughter Marlene absolutely loved the animals and began riding at an early age. Her first mount was a black Welsh pony that we named Dandy. This pony was not large, but was dynamite on four legs; we trained him to pull a cart and also used him for riding.

My horse, Happy Fella, was a powerful Quarter/Thoroughbred horse. He was a most wonderful mount and I enjoyed him for many years as a riding horse and eventually had him and myself trained for jumping.

When Marlene outgrew Dandy, we purchased a very nice horse Chico, who was also a trained jumper. Marlene took lessons and thoroughly enjoyed her years with Chico. Often Marlene, my son Michael and myself, would saddle

Cliff on Happy Fella

up our horses and pony and ride through the open fields adjoining our property. At that time there was mostly open space and fields in Royal Oak, and we could ride for miles through the area, enjoying wide-open spaces.

Our association with horses brought us into contact with other horse people, including Bob and Marjorie Shanks who ran a very well known tack shop in Victoria. Through our association with Bob, we met a number of enthusiastic horse lovers, and before long we embarked upon yet another enterprise that brought even more excitement into our lives.

Together with four other horse lovers we purchased forty-two acres on the west side of Elk Lake. It was part of a farm, owned by Frank Doyle, who subdivided the acreage, and sold it to us for a very reasonable price. We then created six one and a half acre lots for ourselves, planning on selling one of the lots to pay for the road that we built fronting our lots. We named it Doyle Road in honor of Frank. We had the remaining thirty acres rezoned for a riding academy and named it 'Elkwood Stables'. Our plan was to create a state of the art stable, which would accommodate one hundred horses.

The property had one thousand foot frontage on Elk Lake and accessed riding trails that encompassed both Elk and Beaver Lakes. We envisioned a world-class facility that would host many future horse events including fox hunts. The hunts would be done with the scent of a fox only and would not involve the live animal.

On two occasions I was involved in a foxhunt. The first one started on the Elkwood property and continued on the trails around Elk Lake and Beaver Lake Park. It was my first hunt and was one of the most exciting events that I have ever participated in.

The Hunt Master rode with the hounds that were following the scent of the fox laid over the course by another hunt official. The rules of the hunt forbade any other rider to pass the Master of the Hounds on any account.

My horse Happy Fella was as excited as I was and fully revved up for the event. On the starting signal Fella started out like a whirlwind, and I, likewise pumped, let him go full tilt after the hounds. In no time flat, we caught up with the Master of the Hounds, and probably would have passed him, which would have meant instant disqualification, had a group of riders not detoured and set off at a full gallop toward a fir tree that lay on the ground at the other end of a field.

Fella, not to be left behind, followed at a breakneck speed. I let him go full tilt hoping to tire him before we overtook the other riders ahead of us. This was wishful thinking as he was indefatigable.

When the other horsemen reached the fallen tree they began jumping, mostly at the smaller tapered end of the tree, although one or two jumped the middle section of the tree. From a distance, the tree looked very small, and I did not understand why everyone was jumping the narrow end, so I decided to jump the thick end.

When I checked my horse and shifted into jump mode, irrevocably committing both of us to the jump, I suddenly understood just why everyone had chosen the smallest part of the tree. Before me was the butt of a huge tree, possibly six feet thick. The first sound that escaped my mouth was a close cousin to the four-letter word that I had discovered when I was five and that block of wood fell on my head. My horse Fella had never jumped anything higher than three feet while I was on him, but now, I had unwittingly committed him to a jump that was in the neighborhood of six feet high.

There was no turning back, and with the eyes of all the other riders upon me and Fella, I stretched my self out along his neck, almost reaching his ears, and began praying. To my amazement, Happy Fella sailed over the tree, clearing it by another two feet. The view from that height was spectacular, but not knowing exactly what awaited us on the other side of the tree almost caused me heart failure.

Many times in my life I have felt the Lord's strength and guidance, and this was one of those times. Awaiting us on the other side of the tree was a jumble of twisted limbs and huge rocks, but the hand of God gently guided us to the only patch of grass within sight.

When the horsemen gathered for a glass of sherry at the end of the ride, there was little talk among them, and I felt that they must have been thinking that I was mad for taking that seemingly impossible jump. Finally, one of the older more experienced riders moved to my side, and quietly said, " That was quite a jump, well done."

Taking my horse over jumps was an exciting thing to do, and I continued with jumping lessons right up to the day that I made a shocking mistake. There was a riding ring in the back of my home on Doyle road, and I had set up a few practice jumps. One was very tight. It had been placed close to the north end of the ring, but was too close to the wooden fence to allow a horse to pass. This, as it turned out was definitely a mistake, as my steed was soon to prove.

Normally, 'Fella' was exceptionally trustworthy in the ring and would do his best on all jumps. However, he did have one flaw. That became very evident when he cantered toward a corner of the ring. The rider would have to be very alert, because 'Fella' loved to cut corners, and if you were not on guard he would not go deep into the corner, which was essential if there was a jump close to the end of the ring. I was well aware of this little trick that he would pull whenever he had a chance, but figured that I was in control, at least most of the time.

Jumping was part of my morning exercise. After cleaning the stalls in the barn, I would groom and saddle 'Fella', and then take him over a few jumps before getting ready to go to my restaurant. My steed was performing very well, taking all the jumps in a professional manner, and seemingly under control, at least right up to that last jump at the far end of the ring.

As I rode along the fence, I concentrated on taking him deep into the corner, so that I would have enough distance to set him up for the jump. As I approached the point of no return, I let my guard down for just a split second; my steed took advantage of that second and cut the corner, racing toward the jump fully intent on taking it. But, at the last moment, he decided that he was on too much of an angle to make the jump, so he dodged between the fence and the jump. That was the infamous jump that was so close to the fence that it did not allow enough room for my horse to pass through unscathed.

When my leg hit the fence post, I instantly knew that something was going to break, and I didn't think that it was going to be the post. As my leg connected with the fence post, my horse stumbled and fell to his knees. Not wanting to have a second encounter with the fence, I threw my affected leg over the horse's head and as gracefully as possible, fell to the ground, making sure that I did not land on the injured limb.

Landing on the ground with both legs straight out, in an almost perfect Angel pattern, I lay quietly until my daughter and wife who ran to my side. When they asked me if I was all right, I lifted the injured leg but noted that my foot remained on the ground. " I think it's broken," I said.

My dear wife said that she would call an ambulance. I told her that she should get my toupee first, and then call the ambulance. For some reason I felt that it was more important to have my manufactured hairpiece in place than it was to get to the damn hospital.

Our New Hair

Some years before, my two brothers and I, decided that our beautiful, God given, bare heads, needed to be covered. The three of us had begun losing our hair at an early age and all agreed that it was a terrible trick to play on young men. Without considering the consequences, we made an appointment with a 'Hair Restoration Clinic', intent only on getting an estimate on the cost of a hairpiece. The head guy was dressed in a neat white smock, and had what appeared to be a stethoscope hanging around his neck. It may have been a witch doctors charm for all the good it did.

He carefully examined our domes with a stainless, skewer-like probe, separating layers of the remaining hair with a surgeon's precision, and after a lot of squeezing and pinching, declared that most of the hairless follicles were useless. This did not come as a complete surprise to me because, even with my limited knowledge of hair follicles, I had already concluded that hair like grass does not grow on barren ground.

We obviously fell for the rug merchant's slick patter, for a few weeks later we set sail for Vancouver to pick up our handcrafted toupees at the company's 'Hair Restoration Salon'. The hairpieces were guaranteed human hair, but they did not tell us that the hair came from the Orient, and each individual hair was probably three times the diameter of our own fine hair.

When we tried them on, we were impressed by the image in the mirror, for the hairpiece blended very well. The only problem was that we hardly recognized the strangers staring back at us. The 'Technician' assured us that this was a common reaction and within a week or two we would become accustomed to the guy in the mirror.

Travelling back home on the ferry was a nightmare. It seemed that every person on the boat was staring at us, probably thinking they were in the presence of the three stooges. We were sure that they had guessed our little secret, for each one stared, with a look of disbelief in their eyes. When I arrived back home my beloved wife let out a shriek and ran from the room. The children reacted in much the same way.

Wearing a toupee became habit forming, and once the initial shock of friends and acquaintances wore off, the toupee and I became inseparable. For a while I even wore it in the shower. There was something mystifying about the hairy little thing. It was never comfortable to wear because it had to be glued to the scalp to keep it from blowing off, and it never completely matched the original hair because it gradually faded and would then have to be dyed, hopefully the same color of the real hair.

The first time I had it dyed, I insisted on wearing it. My barber thought that it would be much easier if I took it off, but I was adamant that the damn thing remained on my noggin. Needless to say, the whole effort was a disaster. The barber had never undertaken such a project before, and was only doing it as favor. The dye he used was many shades darker than my own hair, and when it dried it looked like something out of a horror movie. It was stiff and black and shone like the heavily pomaded hair of a Flamenco dancer. For three weeks I braved the stares and snickers of friends, finally washing it with a vengeance, which in turn removed most of the dye and restored it to the original color, two shades lighter than my own hair.

While lying on the ground, worrying more about the state of my head than the state of my leg, I began to realize just how stupid this hairpiece was, and vowed to get rid of it as soon as possible. This decision to throw the thing away was far more difficult than I imagined, and I continued wearing it for several years, before finally mustering the nerve to chuck it.

When the ambulance arrived I was ready for them, every hair in place, and then they took me to the hospital and, after a preliminary examination, confirmed that both the tibia and fibula were shattered. As one of the technicians so aptly put it, "Now that is what I call a break!"

For seven months I wore a cast on my right leg, which extended to the upper thigh, and caused no end of inconvenience. After using crutches for several months, I was fitted with a walking cast, and though it was difficult, I managed to climb the steps to my restaurant and conduct business as usual. Working with a full-length cast is not any fun, but with the help of my staff I was able to continue running the operation, albeit from a high stool behind the bar.

Elkwood Stables

A year before this encounter with the fence, Barb and I built a new home on our acre and a half at the Elk Lake property. Bob Shanks and one of the other partners also built their homes there, and we all looked forward to getting Elkwood Stables up and running. But, after a few short months, two of the partners decided that they did not want to go ahead with the riding stable, instead they wanted to sell the property, managing to persuade the others to go along with their idea.

To my mind, the idea of selling the acreage was crazy, because I knew that it would be worth a fortune one day, and all we had to do was to wait for the right opportunity and we would make a bundle. Unfortunately the majority wanted to get rid of the parcel right away rather than wait for values to change.

One of the partners, a real estate agent, offered to buy the thirty odd acres for eighty five thousand dollars. I immediately suspected that there was more to the story than met the eye, and asked the others to wait. But they still insisted that we sell, so I reluctantly agreed, warning them that we were making a big mistake. The partner quickly produced a sales agreement, which he obviously had prepared well before he presented the offer, and everyone signed it.

Within a month or two, the partner subdivided several acres off the acreage, which he kept for himself, and then sold the rest for more than he had paid for the whole package. When I heard about the transaction, I was not surprised for I had suspected it all along. He had pulled the wool over our eyes in a grand way, and all I could say to the others was, "Are you happy now?

Money was not the driving force in my life, although I will confess that I never was able to say no to a good deal. The idea did pass through my mind that we had a solid case to take to court but, as I said, money really was not that important to me.

Running the restaurant continued to be fun for me, and I still managed to do the occasional play or musical on stage.

Friends:
George, Cliff and Jack

Smockey Night

One of the more memorable events that I produced, was a fundraiser for the 'Mother's March of Dimes', sponsored by a service club in Victoria. The event was called 'Smockey Night', and was presented in the Memorial Arena.

For many months I planned the event, enlisting many fine musicians and singers to perform, who were then ably accompanied by the Naden Band, a wonderful group of talented musicians, including Paul Mascioli, who went on to become an agent for some of the top Country music artists in the country.

The 'Smockey' program included many well-known politicians and radio personalities. They played a game of hockey. At least it was supposed to be hockey. In reality it was a game of hilarious horseplay performed by the participants, and was always well received by the four thousand people that attended.

My part of the proceedings was to put together entertainment for the intermission and to highlight the fundraising effort for the 'Mother's March of Dimes,' which was officially launched on that night. The first year was a great success. The second year that I produced the event, was hopefully going to be the best 'Smockey Night' ever, as long as everything went according to my plan.

All of the performers were an integral part of the program, and each one contributed to the overall tone and theme. With the aid of local schools and music teachers, I assembled one thousand students, who were to sing three specially chosen songs. These songs were rehearsed for weeks before the event.

Every detail was carefully planned out with care and precision. The students would gather one hour before the event at the Glad Tidings Church on Quadra Street a block away. Exactly fifteen minutes before their appearance, they would march over to the arena and take their places at one of four entrances, on the four corners of the building. There, they would await their cue.

Key members of my crew were stationed at each corner of the arena and were inter- connected with me by earphones. The crew was to watch and direct the movement of the young singers, and supervise the staff supplied by the club.

My program was timed right down to the minute. The announcer, a well known radio personality, read a script describing the work of the mothers who had committed themselves to helping crippled children. At the start of the intermission, a thin wire was stretched across the ice at the centerline. It was attached to the front of a wheelchair, and held by one of my crew.
Another line was attached to the back of the chair and was held by another crewmember. At my signal it would be pulled across the ice.

From my position in the sound room, directly above the center line, I could watch and direct every move that I had scripted. I could also keep an eye on all four corners of the rink.

We had scheduled a rehearsal in a huge gymnasium at Work Point Barracks in Esquimalt, the day before the event. I made it very clear that it was vital that everyone in key positions be there for the rehearsal.

Every teacher and every student showed up at the appointed time. In all there were one thousand bodies. However, of the dozen key members expected, only one showed up. Unfortunately, the man who showed up, bless his heart, had a minor learning deficit.

The following day the arena was filled to capacity for the event. The skaters who performed in the Smockey segment were superb, and had the audience rocking in their seats.

At the intermission my crew began their preparations. The line was stretched across the ice, the wheelchair was in position, and the entertainers at the ready. Over at the Glad Tidings, one thousand young souls gathered with their choral directors and, for the last time, fine tuned their exodus and chartered their course.

Back at the arena everything was on schedule. Stanley Martin sang a powerful opening number, the Naden Band accompanied him with the flair and confidence of the Boston Philharmonic Orchestra, and one of Victoria's finest sopranos filled the arena with heartfelt warmth and compassion. The audience was ready for the message of hope.

Each member of the audience had been given a small box of matches when they entered the arena, and were now eagerly waiting for the signal to strike a match. Ron, the announcer, was in splendid voice and recited his lines, from the script, with resonance and conviction. At precisely the right moment I gave the signal to allow the children in through the corner doors. They filed in quietly and professionally and quickly got into position, ready to file out onto the ice as the wheelchair slowly crossed to the centre.

One of the most important features of this whole epic, were the sparklers that the children were to carry, lit, out onto the ice. Well aware of the potential danger of lit sparklers, we had arranged for the Victoria Fire Department to provide firemen for each corner of the rink where the children would begin their walk to center ice. These firemen placed a barrel of water in each corner entrance for emergency use.

Every move was well planned, and all four of my own personally chosen crewmembers well primed, the exception being the seven key members of the crew who had not shown up for rehearsal. Other than the man with the learning deficit, they had no idea what to do, and as I was to later discover, neither did he.

As the children filed into their corner positions, I frantically explained to whomever it was on the other end of my communication lines, to be very careful when they lit the sparklers. My instructions, which were also posted in each corner, specified that the sparklers should be lit ten at a time, and if there was a problem with any of them, they should be doused in the barrels of water.

From my perch in the sound booth high above the ice, I began the countdown. " In exactly two minutes the choral groups will enter and assume their positions. In exactly four minutes the lights of the arena will dim. In exactly four minutes and thirty seconds the announcer will begin his well-written and moving prologue. In exactly six minutes the announcer will ask the audience to light their matches. In exactly seven minutes the empty wheelchair will begin it's highly emotional journey across the ice. In exactly eight minutes all corners will light sparklers. As the sparklers burn for only two minutes and fourteen seconds, it is important to light them quickly. As soon as fifty sparklers have been lit and handed to the well-rehearsed children, they will slowly march onto the ice, preceded by their teachers. If the sparklers are lit quickly, the two hundred and fifty children that are in each corner will reach the centerline at the same time. "God speed."

Many times in my life I have had the opportunity of coming very close to attaining perfection but, in most of those brief moments, that perfection has slipped from my grasp, like liquid silver flowing through a sieve.

For months I planned the 'Smockey' event, calculating every move possible, going over every detail with my close friend Frank. He was one of the most important members of my own crew. His job was to make sure every other person was in his or her correct position. On that fateful night he arrived early, making sure that every person involved in our production was briefed and aware of his or her responsibilities.

When I began the countdown every last detail was in place, even the seven who did not show up at the rehearsal were briefed and in place. Every one was set and raring to go. Once the countdown began there was no turning back.

The choir, waiting outside was on time, and when I gave them their cue they filed in five abreast in perfect alignment. The lights dimmed, and thirty seconds later the announcer began the prologue. On command, four thousand matches flared and the arena was set aglow, as if by a magic wand. One and a half minutes later the wheelchair, bathed in light, moved slowly across the ice as though guided by a phantom hand. The only thing left to do, to complete this magical scene, was for the sparkler holding children, to march onto the ice and sing three songs.

Exactly two minutes and fourteen seconds before I gave the signal to light up, the unbelievable happened. That wonderful gentleman with the learning deficit, who was in charge of the southwest corner, began lighting his sparklers, managing to complete the feat within two and a half minutes, unfortunately 2 minutes fourteen seconds too early

Not wanting to be outdone, nor waiting for their cue, the group in the south-east corner, took the entire bundle of two hundred and fifty sparklers, and lit the whole lot with a blowtorch. Where they got the blowtorch remains a mystery to this very day.

The resulting mini-explosion frightened the fellow who was holding the bundle of sparklers, and in a state of panic, he overlooked the barrel of water at his side, and threw the sparklers onto the rubber matting, which covered all of the corner floors. Instantly the rubber matting flared, creating a cloud of thick black smoke. Along with a string of profanity, which included a generous serving of the 'F' word, I managed to give the northwest and the northeast corners their cue to light up.

Within two minutes, the southwest, the northwest and the northeast corners moved in unison toward the centerline. The southeast choir, hindered by the firemen fighting the fire, managed to reach the ice and begin their march, just as the other three groups reached the centerline. The sparklers held by the two northern most corners were fantastic. The southwest corners sparklers, which had been lit well before the cue, fizzled and sputtered for a few seconds and then went out. The stragglers from the southeast corner, moved as fast as they could on the slippery surface, trying to catch up to the other groups. Fortunately, only three or four of the stragglers fell before reaching the centerline.

For eight minutes the one thousand-voice choir treated the audience to the most beautiful songs and then an unscheduled intermission was called while the arena was cleared of the thick black smoke which had erupted from the southeast corner. My recollection of the remainder of that night remains a complete blank to me. Disappointment and anger had overwhelmed me as I watched this near masterpiece falling apart, and I swore that I would never do another production unless there was a guarantee that there would be enough rehearsal time available.

The following morning, the Victoria Fire Chief phoned me in what I can only describe as a highly emotional state. Obviously he had been informed of the fire and he was livid. There was something ominous in the manner that he kept addressing me by my surname rather than my Christian name. What he was not aware of, was the fact that I did not like or appreciate being addressed by the name Clarke, and that when it did happen, I always took it as a personal affront.

Normally I enjoyed talking with persons in high places, but unless they had the good manners to use my given name, I quickly lost interest in any thing that they had to say. After a verbal tongue-lashing and several offensive references to the previous nights production, and the near inferno that had occurred, I asked him his name. Probably one of the most effective ways of calming a madman down is by asking him his name. In most instances he or she will have to think deeply for a moment before coming up with the correct answer.

When they finally blurt out the right name, which in most instances is already known to you, it is fairly easy to adlib for several minutes, without having to respond to the matter under discussion. In this particular case I knew him very well, and as a matter of interest, had brushed shoulders with him at several social functions. At those events he had always impressed me as a very disciplined man and, though somewhat arrogant, seemed to be a person one could reason with.

The first thing I asked him, once he had settled down, was if he had ever worked with this particular club before. The answer was an affirmative. I then asked him if he had ever experienced any reluctance on their part to attend rehearsals. He could not remember any particular events where this had occurred, but allowed that it was possible. Without any further ado, I launched into my soliloquy regarding the Smockey Night production, explaining exactly what was required when directing such a large number of volunteers.

Recounting the effort and time that I had personally invested in this event at no charge, and also my dedication to making it a financial success for the Mother's March of Dimes fundraiser, I advised him that I was thoroughly ticked off at what had happened, and brought it to his attention that several of his own fire-fighters had been assigned to positions in the four corners of the arena, to avert just such an unlikely event.

The Fire Chief did not like being reminded that his fire fighters were in any way responsible for what had happened, and said that if he had anything to do with it, there would never be another event in any public building that used any form of pyrotechnics. Re-assuring him that I would never attempt such a feat again, and thanking him for his call, I commended him on his fine department and wished him great success in the future.

Surprisingly, the heated conversation mellowed out, and he thanked me for all the efforts that I had put into the event, and finished with, "Nice talking with you Cliff."

Evidently there was enough concern on the part of the service club to bring about a decision to scrap Smockey Night. Most of the audience thought that it was great fun, particularly the part where the smoke drifted upward creating a near ethereal effect in the upper realms of the arena. They thought that it had all been a part of the plan, and even the kids coming on in a slightly disorganized manner, was also very enjoyable as far as they were concerned.

Cliff, the story teller is taking a break

The decision by the group to scrap the event was a little disappointing, as it had always been a good way of raising funds for a worthy cause, and I enjoyed the challenge. Of course their decision was actually okay with me, as it allowed me time to get involved in other worthy projects.

Whenever I involved myself in any sort of production, I would totally commit myself to it with the resolve to make it a success. From the very beginning, I would make it very clear to everyone associated with the project that I expected them to dedicate themselves to it with as much fervor as I did. This did not always meet with unanimous approval, but it quickly sorted the wheat from the chaff.

Once everyone knew where they stood, the production would take on a life of its own, and each fully committed person would help bring it forward, successfully overcoming the problems that usually arise in stage productions.

Sometimes, unique problems arise, that don't fit the usual pattern, and ultimately require a whole new perspective.

Minstrel Shows

At one time, Black Minstrel shows were very popular with audiences and performers, and allowed talented entertainers a wonderful opportunity to perform on stage. Early in my theatrical career, the Junior Solarium League of Victoria invited me to produce a 'Black Face Minstrel Show'. This group was completely dedicated to the kids in the solarium, and worked as hard as they possibly could to raise funds for the cause.

There was an honorarium offered by the group, to help offset expenses incurred by the director. However, I was more than willing to forego the fee, because I knew and understood the tremendous effort that these people put into their fundraising events, to support the institution, and ultimately the unfortunate children themselves.

Recalling the films of my youth, about the life of plantation slaves in the

Minstrel Show at McPherson Playhouse

deep south, and remembering their beautiful songs and heart wrenching tales of slavery, I decided to learn as much a I possibly could about the history of black entertainment.

It quickly became obvious to me that 'Minstrel Shows' were an integral part in the life of slaves, and one of the few occasions that the black folk could get their own back with the plantation owners. On special occasions, the slaves would get together and put on a show, which always included the plantation owner in the role of 'Mr. Interlocutor.' He was strategically positioned on a chair in front of the black performers. His dialogue was scripted so the performers were able to poke fun at him without getting into serious trouble.

The black entertainers used wit and broad humour to entertain the assembled slaves and family members, taking special care to avoid upsetting the plantation owner. The musicians played tambourines, fiddles, banjos and animal bones, often using the jawbone of some farm animal, clacking and scraping the teeth, while accompanied by the instruments. These wonderful musical events were a source of joy and merriment for the unfortunate slaves, and provided a welcome break from the tedium of their labour.

The slaves' musical get-togethers proved so popular that by the beginning of the nineteenth century music entrepreneurs and impresarios, both white and black, organized travelling shows featuring black entertainers. The shows were so successful that white troupes began to emulate the original black shows, using white performers with blackened faces to portray the plantation slaves. One of the original troupes to tour a Minstrel Show, originated in Virginia and was billed as the 'Virginia Minstrel Show'. By 1846, Edwin Christy renamed the group ' The Christy Minstrels'. Their debut in New York was a smash success and the group continued touring for many years.

By the mid nineteenth century, these touring shows featured sentimental minstrel songs written and composed by Stephen Foster and other popular songwriters of the day. After the 1860's the shows increased in size, often having upward of one hundred performers. Inevitably the shows became flashier and grander, eventually introducing a greater variety of musical instruments and variety acts. The central character, Mr. Interlocutor, remained in white face while the remainder of the cast donned black faces as in the original style. These popular shows remained in the mainstream and influenced many famous performers including the great Al Jolson.

When I was asked to produce the 'Minstrel Show' I was delighted, for I had always admired the great talent of black entertainers, and believed that this medium was and remained a wonderful tribute to the original plantation gatherings.

The first year we presented it in the Oak Bay High School Auditorium, and enjoyed full houses. When we decided to repeat it the third year, we chose the McPherson Playhouse. We enlisted many fine entertainers and musicians and also a fifty-member choir. One of the choir members was a black man who insisted on wearing the same make-up as the white members, just so that he would look the same as every other performer.

One week before opening night we were informed that the National Association for the Advancement of Colored People, [NAACP] in Seattle, Washington had been informed of our show and did not like it at all, and suggested that we cancel it forthwith. When the Media got wind of it, CBC Radio interviewed me and asked if I was going to cancel the production, as the NAACP had requested.

Rising to the challenge, I suggested that if the NAACP wished to purchase all the tickets for the show I would be quite willing to do as they wished. If this was not possible, however, then I would be delighted to have their whole office as honored guests, so that they might see for themselves just what a terrific show it was, and the fact that it did not degrade the black man, but rather made fun of the white man, particularly Mr.Interlocutor.

The NAACP declined my offer; the media jumped on it, and the resulting publicity caused a rush at the box office and we quickly sold out all tickets. On opening night, the *NAACP* formed a picket line at the theatre, and passed out many information pamphlets, hoping that people would not enter the theatre.

Most patrons let it be known that they had no prejudice regarding other races and that they, like most Canadians, welcomed those of different colour and creed to this country. Therefore, their support of the production was also a gesture of support toward the black people of the world, and a display of their appreciation for music and talent in general.

The Junior Solarium League enjoyed the receipts, and the audience had a wonderful time. However, after much soul-searching and dialogue, the League decided that perhaps there would be better ways of raising funds without upsetting those sensitive to the black cause.

To the best of my knowledge, our Minstrel Show was probably the very last show of that type in North America. Though I was quite disappointed at the demise of this unique and historical form of entertainment, I was cheered that I had the wonderful opportunity of directing and producing this nostalgic bit of history.

Adding a Catering Hall and New Restaurant

Meanwhile, back at the restaurant, things were busy but rather ho-hum, and I was becoming a little bored with the everyday running of the enterprise. I decided that what I really needed was another project so I took over an existing catering business known as the Carlton Club, in Esquimalt, a few yards from Head Street.

My partner was not keen on the idea of adding another establishment to our mini-chain of two restaurants, and opted out of the deal. This left me with no alternative but to run it on my own, along with the McPherson. This, in theory was feasible but in practice it proved to be a great headache.

Taking over and operating this club, occupied my time and energies for a lengthy period. I moved the front wall outwards a full eight feet to include the surface of a large overhanging roof, at the front of the existing building, This added a considerable amount of space and allowed more room for patrons and also allowed a larger dance floor.

The club became very busy with weddings, parties, and other functions, including a terrific New Years Party. The catering needs were handled through the McPherson Restaurant.

This of course caused friction with my partner and the eventual break-up of our association. Not wanting to remain in a difficult situation, I turned both the Coach and Four and the McPherson over to Taffy, shook hands, and began planning my departure.

At that time, Peter Hartnell, owner of the Queen Victoria Inn, on Douglas Street, was opening a large restaurant on the main floor of his hotel. He heard, by the grapevine, that I was possibly looking for a new location, and called me with the thought that I might be interested in the location. Never one to look a gift horse in the mouth, I immediately said yes.

That enterprise was the beginning of one of the most interesting periods of my life. Though initially hitting it off with the well-known hotelier, I soon found that for energy and enterprise I had truly met my match, and so began a roller-coaster relationship. Anxious to open a restaurant as quickly as possible, so that I could continue catering at the Carlton Club, I entered into an agreement with the owner of the hotel and launched myself into yet another whirlwind operation.

Greeting Guests at 'King's Den'

The location of the hotel on Douglas Street, across from Thunderbird Park, was ideal. It was close to the Parliament Buildings, the Empress Hotel, and within comfortable walking distance of the Causeway on Government Street.

Peter Hartnell and I were very interested in completing the restaurant as soon as possible and also doing it as economically as possible. Through my contacts in the business, I was able to contact a person who had enough equipment to outfit an entire kitchen. It was stored in a barn in Delta, not far from the B.C. Ferry terminal. Both Hartnell and I visited the barn and inspected the equipment. We agreed that it would work very well for our restaurant. Strangely, we never actually met with the party that owned the equipment, but handled the entire transaction by phone.

We wondered if we might be buying hot items, so I contacted the local police, asking them if they were looking for any hot kitchen equipment. The officer in-charge said that they already had a full kitchen and did not need any thing else. Re-phrasing my question, I asked him if he had any reports of stolen restaurant equipment recently. After consulting another person nearby, he returned to the phone and told me that neither he nor the other officer in the detachment had any knowledge of heisted kitchen equipment, but if any restaurant had its kitchen equipment removed without prior approval, their department would surely have heard of it. That was good enough for me and the hotel owner, so we hired a large truck, loaded the heavy pieces, and returned to Victoria, elated at securing such a bargain and reasonably sure that it was all legit.

One day, while arranging for the suppliers and trades people to open the restaurant, one of the most important suppliers said that he had no desire to engage in any business with the owner. I assured him that I would personally take the responsibility to ensure that he was fully paid for any thing that he supplied. After much conversation, the man agreed to supply me with the necessary goods, but only because he knew that I would stand by my word.

Never one to keep my big mouth shut, I let slip this little bit of gossip regarding the reluctant supplier. My words quickly found their way to the gentleman in question, and he, feeling very much betrayed, let me know that he was no longer interested in doing business with me.

Because of the amount of time I had invested, not to mention the money, or my desperate need of an operational kitchen, I did my best to salve his wounds. Using my most persuasive powers, all of my acting ability, and a whole lot of whining and groveling, I managed to get back into his good graces, at least for the moment, back on track that is, working toward the completion of the restaurant. Little did I know then, the next four years of my life were going to be a tremendous challenge, and also, a formidable test of wills.

'The King's Den' restaurant opened with great fanfare, and at the same time I launched my twin project, 'The Black Prince Catering Company.' A banquet room on the top floor of the hotel was included in my lease. This beautiful and elegant room held ninety people and became a very popular place for banquets. My restaurant held ninety people as well, and the Carlton Club held an additional one hundred and fifty people. My life became very, very hectic.

There were two kitchens in the restaurant, one on the ground floor backing onto a parking lot, and one on the lower floor which opened onto the parking garage. Both kitchens had back doors, which allowed easy access both for things coming in, and things going out. However, this easy access was a two-pronged blessing, as I was soon to find out.

Anticipating a tremendous increase in new business, I stocked the restaurant with very nice silverware and china, and also purchased one thousand pieces of stainless steel cutlery, as well as a like amount of china for the catering business. This was stored in a small shed just outside the main kitchen near the backdoor. Whenever the catering place settings were required we would unlock the shed and retrieve whatever was necessary.

Within a short time I discovered that some china and cutlery was missing. Upon investigating, I discovered that the lock on the shed was often left with the key still in it, making it an easy target.

On the other side of Blanshard Street, in the front yard of St. Ann's Academy a few yards from our backdoor, was a colony of homeless people. I wondered if it was possible that these unfortunates had been helping themselves to our dishware, and perhaps also helping themselves to the left over food from the bin by the backdoor. After replacing the lock on the shed with a more secure type, namely one that did not permit the key to remain in it once clasped, I made sure that in future, left-over food was carefully placed in the bin in such a way that it could be retrieved easily by those in need.

Catering to the Carlton, the upstairs banquet room, the dining room, plus outside functions, was definitely a full time job and kept us all hopping. Fortunately I had managed to find Margaret Leeder, an incredible bookkeeper/manager, to watch over me and though it was the challenge of her life she managed to keep me on a straight and narrow during our four years in that location.

On the first New Year in our new location, we had one hundred and fifty guests at the Carlton Club for a banquet, ninety guests in the upstairs banquet room, one hundred reservations in the dining room, and one hundred and fifty guests at the Royal Victoria Yacht Club. My staff was incredible and somehow managed to get everything prepared and served on time, with the exception of the Yacht Club. Because of the terrific load on everyone, we were unable to serve the folk at the Yacht Club until one-thirty in the morning, even though we had been scheduled to feed them at midnight.

In the early hours that New Year's Eve at the Royal Victoria Yacht Club, I finally came to the conclusion that this was not the life for me, but rather punishment for past sins. A few weeks later, my accountants confirmed that the revelation that I had that night was probably very relevant for they had discovered that, in spite of the five-thousand dollar night we experienced on New Years Eve, we had once again lost a substantial amount of money during the past year.

Apart from the disappointment of losing money, my relationship with the owner of the hotel had become very strained and we seldom spoke to one-another. There is no doubt that life is a two way street and even though we tend to believe that we are always right, if we are honest with ourselves there are always two sides to every story.

In spite of the disappointments, and the stress of handling so many different functions, I continued taking part in theatre and also joining in the entertainment on the weekends in the restaurant.

Every Friday and Saturday we would have a musical evening in the King's Den, employing a variety of performers including myself. I was fortunate enough to meet many wonderful entertainers during those years, including pianists and singers, and often employed them for our musical soirees. Several of these very talented people went on to successful careers in Show Business. Eric Roberts, a very talented entertainer, remained with me at the Kings Den for several years becoming a very dear friend.

When I look back at those musical evenings, I wonder what the patrons really thought of having their host, bartender, owner, and sometime dishwasher singing to them. My songs were often sad and frequently rang of unrequited love, sometimes bringing tears to the eyes of the guests. After years of reflection I began to wonder if they were actually crying because my songs were touching and sentimental, or because their steaks were tough.

One of my most devoted fans was my mother. She would always join us for the show and a steak dinner and amazingly never wearied of listening to her son exercising his tonsils, and never complained of a tough steak.

She would appear early in the evening on a Friday and Saturday, frequently bringing a guest or two, firmly believing that they too would enjoy the musical artistry of her golden haired boy. I never disappointed her, and always dedicated my most sentimental numbers to her. 'O' Danny Boy', 'My Little Girl', 'Little Orphan Boy', 'Don't Cry Momma', and an endless repertoire of real tear-jerkers that never failed to bring my mom to her feet, and her guests near to throwing up.

Most of her guests never returned, but my dear mom never failed to show up on a weekend, and never failed to bring a new victim with her. On several occasions she even talked my mother-in-law into joining her for our musical evenings. My dear mother-in-law became a fairly regular customer along-side my mother, but being a rather non-committal sort of a person, never actually said she enjoyed the show and I always wondered if she was just being polite or merely sacrificing herself for the cause. At any rate, I truly appreciated her support, and often gave her a big hug to show my appreciation.

As time passed by, I came to realize that the restaurant business was not as gratifying to me as it had seemed to be in the early years, and I grew restless, and slowly began planning my next move, namely, my escape.

Red Barn Antique Store

There was a building close to my home in Royal Oak, at the corner of Wilkinson and West Saannich Rd. that had always interested me. It housed a stove store and repair shop. One day, with absolutely no reason in my mind, I stopped at the store and went in.

The charming gentleman who operated the stove store greeted me like a long lost cousin, and without any fanfare, told me all about the buildings that contained his business, and his home, and the fact that his landlord was going to sell it, and would I like to buy it.

Those words, “Buy it ”, were like waving a wiener in front of a starving dog, and I wondered how this fellow knew that I was an addicted buyer, and that I would succumb to almost anything short of another restaurant.

Within twenty-five minutes I had come to the conclusion that I should buy it. During that twenty-five minute discussion with the ‘Stove man’, an idea began to form in my mind, that this building would be a perfect location for an antique shop.

My interest in antiques started when I was very young and I actively engaged in the pursuit of anything of value that might be found in old buildings and garages. Whenever I came across anything that was old or interesting, I got very excited and felt a strong urge to add it to my collection, even though it might have technically belonged to someone else.

Throughout the years I did come across interesting old things, and did add many of them to my collection, legitimately of course. Over the years my collection grew larger and eventually filled my home with antiques and memorabilia.

That night I discussed the possibilities of opening an antique shop with Barb, but she was not all that sure that getting involved in yet another business

Red Barn Antiques 1977

venture was a wise thing to do. After all, my life was already so busy that there were not enough hours in the week to do anything but work as it was. However, I pointed out that if we purchased the stove store, I would sell the restaurant and catering hall, and get into a nine-to-five enterprise.

After discussing the idea and the merits of getting out of the restaurant business, my dear wife finally agreed, on the condition that I never even think of opening a restaurant again, no matter the temptations. I readily agreed to this condition of course, and never entertained the idea again.

When I contacted the owner of the building he was delighted, and so we were able to quickly reach an agreement on the price, and within two weeks, Barb and I became the proud owners of a run-down house and dilapidated stove store. The 'Stove Man' was overjoyed that he would be permitted to live in the house and be able to continue operating his business in the store; at least for a few more months until I could sell my businesses, and do some alterations and additions.

The next few months were very stressful as I went about the arduous task of finding a buyer for the restaurant and the catering business, as well as planning and carrying out changes to the new property, which included an addition that joined the two buildings together.

Selling the catering business was relatively easy, as George McDowell, one of my entertainment buddies, was looking for a place to open a nightclub, and the Carlton Club was a perfect venue for him. My friend was an extraordinary entertainer and soon established a home for his unique Scottish Pub-style show.

Selling the restaurant was an entirely different ball game, and almost caused me a nervous breakdown. Finding a potential buyer was not all that difficult. My good friend John, the realtor who sold that property on Oak Bay Avenue for me, who almost allowed me to reclaim it when the final payment went into limbo, had a client who was looking for a little restaurant where he could entertain his friends. And my restaurant was perfect.

Getting a fish on the hook does not guarantee a catch, and I spent several agonizing months reeling in this extremely cagey fish. Initially, the gentleman was very excited about owning a delightful little restaurant, and visited us almost every night for several months. The restaurant was very busy at that time, and it appeared that the enterprise was a dream come true.

Our discussions were always lively and seemingly positive, and I was on cloud nine. However, there was always the nagging feeling that this deal seemed too easy, and as close as I was to finalizing it or actually signing any papers, it still remained elusive.

Each time we sat down to draw up the agreement, this gentleman would set up even more hurdles. There were the normal financial aspects, such as dickering over the price that I wanted and the price that he was willing to pay, and also the equipment and bits and pieces that would be included in the price. It seemed that at each session, his demands increased dramatically, and my expectations plummeted drastically.

At the final showdown, he demanded that I include the electric organ and the piano in the final price. It would not be too difficult to explain my state of mind at that particular time, for I was in such a state, that I would have been willing to give up my firstborn, to get out of the restaurant business. When the gentleman suggested that the only stumbling block to reaching an agreement was the matter of the organ and piano, I drew on my extensive theatrical background, explaining how much that piano and organ meant to me, even managing to summon up a tear or two, before finally giving in to his demands, while my inner self was screaming, 'give him anything, anything, just get his signature on that paper'.

Finally the document was drawn up, the negotiations concluded, the signatures applied to the correct places on the papers, the witnesses content that they had done their duty, the transaction sealed and blessed by the Pope, and the deposit in trust. The closing date was approximately two months hence, during which time I had frequent nightmares about the possibilities of his backing out of the deal.

About this time, the owner of the hotel made it known by way of his intermediary, that he had no intention of giving his necessary approval to this arrangement. When I heard of his reluctance regarding this matter, I practically lost my mind. Not having a good relationship with the owner made things even more difficult and so, taking care not to blow my cover, I devised a simple plan of action.

Waiting for just the right moment, I approached him and stated my case. Firstly, I was adamant that I was going to sell my lease and, secondly, I was going to leave with his approval, no matter the odds. If he insisted that I remain to the end of my contract, I was going to ensure that his every waking moment would be as frustrating for him as mine would be for me and that our remaining time together would definitely be no picnic.

We had once been friends but, if this lack of acquiescence on his part jeopardized my business deal, his life was no longer going to be a bowl of cherries, but rather a bowl of pits. After this historic meeting took place, my 'good friend' the hotel owner, gave his reluctant blessings to the transaction, and once more all systems were go.

For two months I walked like a man in a minefield, being very careful to avoid any contact with the hotel owner, lest the whole thing self-destruct. Evidently he felt the same way, because he would poke his head out of his office and carefully look around before venturing forth. The new owner of my business was also strangely quiet, for he too seemed to be avoiding the restaurant like the plague. The whole establishment had a dark cloud hanging over it, as if it too was expecting a storm. Those two months were definitely the worst months of my life. I wanted out of the business more than anything, and every hour that dragged by, only heightened my feelings of imminent doom.

At last the day of my deliverance arrived. It was a bright sunny morning, the birds were hopping about in the trees and singing their joyful songs of freedom, but I didn't hear a sound. I thought that it was strange that things were so quiet, and I took it as a bad omen. When I mentioned my concerns to Barb, and that I was unable to hear anything, she suggested that I make an appointment with the ear specialist. Coincidentally, that was when I first discovered that my hearing was shot.

At the appointed time I arrived at the lawyers office in Victoria, and quietly took my seat in the waiting room, hoping against hope that my deal was still alive and well. Alone in the outer office, my heart barely beating, I awaited the buyer as one might await a triple root canal. After one hour of unimaginable suffering and angst, I came to the painful conclusion that he wasn't coming.

My first thought was suicide, but I managed to pull myself together, and as calmly as possible, under the circumstances, borrowed the receptionist's telephone and dialed the gentleman's home phone number. He answered the phone and I, fighting the urge to shout and rant, asked him if he had forgotten the meeting. He replied that he had not forgotten but that he, on advice of his lawyer, had changed his mind. On the verge of hysteria, I involuntarily laughed out loud. What was the problem I asked? He answered that his lawyer had told him the asking price was too high, and it really was not worth the investment.

My mind was definitely considering a complete breakdown at that point, and I would not have blamed it if it had. During those mind-altering moments I was asking myself why had my own lawyers never questioned my sanity, when I employed them to oversee my weird, or often questionable propositions. This question was never answered, and to this day I have often wondered about that particular lack of interest in my wellbeing.

When I finally recovered from my laughing fit, I informed him that this should not be an insurmountable hurdle, and we could still discuss the final price, but of course it would depend on just how much the final offer would be. Frankly, I was willing to pay him just to get rid of it. That very afternoon I paid him a visit, determined that this was going to be the final showdown.

My Colt 45's were loaded and ready when I went calling that day, and I was prepared for trouble, for this gentleman was either going to buy the restaurant or I was going to shoot myself in the foot. Drawing upon every ounce of my hard won acting experience, and in the highest spirits that I could muster, I asked him just what the problem was. His answer was as before: his lawyer had informed him that the price was too high, quickly adding 'by ten thousand dollars'. Not willing to let him and his illustrious lawyer weasel their way out of a deal. I asked him very gently if that was the only reason that he had to cancel the deal. He assured me that every thing was perfect with the deal, except for the price. Looking him squarely in the eye, and at the same time sub-consciously cocking the colt 44's, I quietly said, " I am going to lower the price by ten thousand dollars, on the condition that you and I, together, this very minute, drive down to my lawyer's office and complete the deal, final payment and all.

It will always be a mystery to me just why he agreed to take this last step, for I am sure that he had been fully prepared to bail out of our deal, and get away as quickly and as far as he possibly could from the whole affair. But, bless his little cotton socks, he did drive down to my lawyer's office with me, and did finalize the papers, and did pay me, and joy of all joys, did move in while I moved out.

Life took on a whole new meaning for Barb and me. I was home every evening, every holiday, every weekend, and we were able, for the first time in many years, to enjoy the simple things in life. While enjoying the simple things, I still carried on with the store renovations. By the time I was completely out of the restaurant business, the renovations were almost finished.

The original house was thirty or forty feet behind the store, which was close to the front property line on the corner of West Saanich Road and Wilkinson Road. My new tenant, the 'Stove Man', was still living in the house, and operating his stove store from there.

Prior to buying the property, I had casually suggested that I wouldn't mind if he stayed on in the house while I operated my antique business from the old store and the new addition. He could carry on his business from the house. This arrangement worked very well, for he was able to watch over my store as well as carry on his business from the house.

The new addition covered the ground between the house and the store and was connected by a doorway between the house and new store. Overall, the area for the antiques was just about perfect for my needs, and having my tenant close by was an added bonus.

A Buying Trip to England

Over the past months Barb and I had been collecting antiques and preparing inventory for the new store. One of the first things we did before opening the store was to book passage to England to shop for antiques.

Up to that time my association with antiques was at best casual. Although I had always been interested in them and had dabbled for many years, I had never fully immersed myself in the antique trade. But the time had come for just that venture so, with my usual 'Let the chips fall where they may attitude' Barb, my daughter Marlene, who was fifteen at the time, and I set our course for Jolly Old England, leaving on Boxing day, in one of the coldest years on record, and embarked upon one of the most fascinating enterprises that I could ever imagine.

The three of us spent five weeks in England, and made London our headquarters, so that we could see 'West End' shows and visit as many theatres as possible during our stay. Before embarking on that wonderful adventure, I contacted the brother of one of our very good friends, Arthur Budd, a well-known and fascinating entertainer. A large Theatre chain owned by Lord Grey employed the brother, Billy Budd. Billy was the stand-in manager of several West End theatres, including, 'Her Majesty's', 'Drury Lane', 'Queens', 'The Shaftsbury', and several others. Mr. Budd was gracious enough to provide tickets for us to shows in every one of the theatres and the tickets were always the choicest ones available.

He would always meet us at the door of the theatre and personally escort us to our seats. This was indeed an honour, inasmuch as he was also the manager who most frequently escorted the Queen to her private box, whenever she and her party visited any of the theatres.

The highlight of our visit occurred when we attended 'The Chorus Line' in 'Drury Lane Theatre. Mr. Budd escorted us to the Queens own private box, taking great pleasure in showing us the waiting room where the Royal Party spent time before the show and during intermission. His greatest pleasure was inviting us to sit on her private throne in the loo.

Of course I had always felt that my lineage was very close to the Royal Line, and I was delighted to have such an opportunity to get so close to the seat of power. Thereafter, when anyone suggested that I was a Royal Pain in the butt, I wholeheartedly concurred.

After one week of theatre going, we began our trek around England hoping to accomplish what we had actually come for, namely, to find antiques. In preparation, we made arrangements with an International Shipping Company in London to accept and pack all our purchases, and ship them by container to Canada.

Without any plan or consultation, we took to the road to see just what we could find that would be suitable for our new store. We would pull into every little village that we came upon, and immediately visit the local antique shops. There we would get as much information as the proprietors were willing to share with us about any antique sales or auctions happening in their town.

It is surprising just how much information one can glean by just talking to people and being honest about your intentions. Most everyone we talked with helped us unreservedly. This also taught us a very valuable lesson: namely that, when you are open and forthright, most people will go out of their way to assist you.

Many of those obliging dealers directed us to some wonderful buys and discoveries. These contacts in turn opened numerous doors for us, and helped us to find enough merchandise to fill a forty-foot container, and then some.

While driving down country roads, we would often come across 'Pickers', or 'Finders'. These people were similar to the garage-sale buffs. Many of these people were small or part-time dealers, but usually had a good selection of antique pieces that they had acquired from yard sales or old barns, or even estate sales. It was surprising that many antiques were considered to be junk by some pickers, which allowed us to make terrific buys from them.

At the time of our forays into the antique market in England, the English people did not especially value many types of antiques, and so it was fairly easy to pick up bargains there. The same items in Canada, particularly in Victoria, were highly prized and sought after and so we did very well over-all.

Probably the nearest thing to a boo-boo that we pulled was in the North Country near Leeds. We had discovered an old woollen mill, now home to a gentleman who collected, of all things, antique pianos. In the cavernous and tomb-like buildings of the former mill, he had accumulated and stored over five hundred pianos of every imaginable size and shape. Most of these pianos were absolutely beautiful and, to the untrained eye like mine, looked like a treasure trove of gigantic proportions.

The old mill had probably never seen heat of any kind, and was as damp as it could possibly be, a condition, not surprisingly, that wreaked havoc on the working parts of the pianos. Most had their ivory keys warped or missing, many of their wooden frames, which were covered in veneers, were either peeling or had already lost some of their veneers to the elements.

Being no stranger to the variables of wood construction, I did avoid choosing any pianos that appeared to be badly dealt with by the cold and damp. After several hours of opening, closing, peering in and around, and even up-ending some of the wooden beauties, we made our selection, all ten of them.

The owner of these relics was delighted to sell them to me for the grand sum of seventy-five pounds a piece. Had I known anything about pianos, I would not have selected any of them, because, each one had a wooden harp and what they call a birdcage movement. And, as I was to find out when I tried to sell them in Victoria, wooden harps do not hold a tuning for any length of time, oft-times not even until the piano-tuner had completed the job of tuning it. This of course proved to be a major stumbling block to selling them, for most people would consult a piano-tuner before committing themselves, only to have the tuner tell them not to touch them with a ten-foot pole.

It is always difficult to sell something that nobody wants, but I quickly came to the conclusion that these little beauties were just that, things of beauty and so, whenever someone asked about the pianos I would tell them that they didn't play worth a hoot, but they were practically priceless as a piece of art. Not everybody thought as I did, but there were enough connoisseurs who did appreciate true works of art, and I eventually managed to sell everyone of them, though making a very slim profit overall.

The saving grace to the whole piano escapade came about while I was dickering with the piano owner over the price of the musical instruments. I had noticed a narrow, shaky, and incredibly dusty mezzanine, that stood at the end of the old mill. Obviously it was an unused part of the building, but I did notice some wooden objects piled up on what remained of the floor.

Feeling a strange sense of adventure and excitement, an inner sense, that the seasoned antique dealer knows so well, I asked if I might look up there to see if there was anything that I could use. Obviously, feeling quite satisfied that he was dealing with a complete idiot, he gave me permission, and I eagerly climbed the remaining treads of an old stairway, which led to the dusty landing. There I found a number of old iron and wooden beds, piled up like cordwood and covered with layers of dust and plaster that had rained down on them, probably, over the course of a century or so.

Without appearing too elated, I returned to his end of the building and informed him that there was a pile of old beds up there, and would he like to get rid of them. Being a rather heavy man, it was obvious that he had never ventured up those precarious steps before, and therefore, probably didn't know what was up there. My gut feeling proved reliable.

Believing that I was definitely a seventy-five pound man, or as is known in the lingo of a seasoned wheeler-dealer, a bloke who would probably be willing to fork over another seventy-five quid for those old relics, he gave me a slap on the shoulder and asked if they would be worth another seventy-five'r to me. It would not be too hard to figure out that not only did I give him another seventy-five pounds, but I didn't even bother to ask him for a hand down with the beds.

One of the most amazing things about an excited dealer, when he gets a good deal, is the speed that he is capable of, while removing everything he has purchased from the premises. At times the speed seems almost supernatural.

That old stairway had never had such a shaking as the one it got while I removed the booty. As it was every second step was missing, and I am sure that I was going up and down four steps at a time, possibly even more in my haste to get every one of those beds into my van before an awakening took place. I didn't even stop to shake the dust off of them until we had traveled a long distance from there.

My beloved wife could not understand why I was so excited about a few old beds, and even suggested that we should take them back where we found them; why, they were nothing but dusty old junk. Sometimes it is best not to argue with the one you love, but this was not one of those times. I assured her and my little girl that we had just scored big time.

When I had the beds back in my shop, the 'Red Barn Antiques', I spent considerable time refinishing and restoring them. In all, most of the beds were hand-carved oak, possibly from the early 1800's.

The ten beautifully hand carved beds fetched several thousand dollars, and were true works of art. While I did not make much on the pianos, I more than made up for it on the beds, and there were many other wonderful treasures that we acquired on that trip as well, many of which still have a place of honour in my Mill Bay home.

The next five years in the antique business were probably the most productive and enjoyable times of my life. Each day I discovered more and more treasures, each discovery more exciting than the last had been.

There was a never-ending flow of beautiful 'Objects d'Art' that passed through my store. Hardly a day went by that I didn't receive a call inviting me over to a home, to evaluate or purchase a collectible or an antique. Often the callers were people who were on the Island for a short time, trying to settle an estate, and hoping to dispose of the items as quickly as possible. Of course I was not an expert in the antiques field and did not fully recognize the truly valuable pieces that were offered me, but I did recognize the beauty of most of the memorabilia that I discovered and assumed that if I liked it then it must be worth handling.

Antique Restoration

Many pieces of furniture that I acquired were in very poor shape and badly in need of restoration, so I would take them to one of several people whom I knew refinished furniture. Most of the time the refinisher did a credible job of restoration, but there were a number of occasions when I thought that I could do just as well, so I decided to learn the art of refinishing myself. Fortunately, my experience as a carpenter held me in good stead and I quickly learned to repair and refinish wooden furniture, learning many tricks along the way, and eventually becoming quite proficient in the process.

During my years in the antique business I was continually on the lookout for derelict furniture that could be restored, and was rewarded with a never-ending flow of wonderful pieces of solid wood treasures, often at tremendous savings. Some of my most prized pieces were almost unrecognizable when I first looked at them and I almost passed them by, but somehow I was able to see potential in them and much to my joy they often turned out to be fabulous collector items.

Over the years, while I operated my antique store, I collected a tremendous number of antiques which I restored, thinking that one day I would have a place large enough to display them. About that time I invested in a large property in Dolphin Bay, close to Nanaimo on Vancouver Island. The land was owned by my friend Doug Hawkes, and was in the preliminary stages of development. The plan was to subdivide the land and sell off the lots for housing.

Within two years of making this investment, I became nervous of the whole enterprise, and asked Doug if he had any parcels of land closer to Victoria that I might build on myself. He had a twenty-eight acre parcel in Mill Bay that he had been trying to sub-divide for some time, but had not made much progress to date. If I would like to exchange my shares in Dolphin Bay for the land in Mill Bay, he would draw up the necessary papers right away. Within a short period of time the legal documents were drawn up, and with the exchange of one dollar, the Mill Bay property became ours. Two years later there was a drastic downturn in the economy, and my friend Doug, subsequently lost many properties including the Dolphin Estates.

Clearing the Forest

The Mill Bay property was completely covered with trees, and one could see nothing but forest from one end of the property to the other. When I took my Barbara on a tour of the property, she rebelled. She was not going to move up to this God forsaken piece of land under any circumstances.

I, on the other hand, considered the land to be a terrific challenge, and I sweet talked my dear Barbara, using every trick that I had learned in the past thirty years of marriage, to win her over to this latest bit of madness.

My plan was to clear the land and build an antique village of sorts, using as many old things as I could lay my hands on. The first challenge however, was to clear the property of as many of the trees as necessary.

Never having cut trees or cleared property before might well have been an obstacle for a sane person. But once again I charged into the project with a minimum of thought or preparation, hired a man with a D6 Bulldozer to start clearing the land, bought chain-saws, axes, and a whole lot of logging implements that I figured I would need to finish the job, and moved into the woods, intent on clearing the land within a week or two.

The twenty-eight acre property sloped downward in an easterly direction toward the ocean half a mile away. This, of course, was conjecture on my part as at that point I couldn't see anything but the damn trees, most of which stood over seventy feet high, all of which were surrounded by thick salal and other native plants and bushes. Undaunted by this dense vegetation, the D6 and I started our journey toward the sea.

Shortly before we started our land-clearing venture, a man phoned me to see if I would be interested in some old furniture that he wanted to dispose of. The furniture was on his farm out on East Saanich Road, not too far from my antique shop. I drove to the location right away, only to find that the furniture was not suitable for me. The man suggested that I might be interested in other things he had around the farm and continued to show me the odd items that he wished to unload, none of which interested me.

One of the items he showed me was a #930 Bob Cat, the largest Bob Cat made, and it included a backhoe attachment. He had used it in his swimming pool business, excavating for the pools and grading the land around them once they were completed. The replacement cost of such a piece of heavy equipment, would have been in the range of $120,000. He offered it to me for $20,000, including an impressive assortment of attachments.

Initially I said that I was not interested in the machine, but after a short period of reflection, I told him that I would pay him $18,000 for it, if he included the heavy-duty trailer. He readily agreed to my offer and even delivered it to my property in Mill Bay the next day.

Within a few months we began clearing the land. I spent two days a week on the site and employed a young man to help me. This young fellow knew how to operate heavy machinery including the Bob Cat, and proved to be a Godsend. He could make that Cat do anything, including standing itself on end,

Cliff hauling logs with Babe on Pine Lodge Farm 1986

which proved to be a decided advantage when we needed to carry out repairs or change a flat tire. Unfortunately the young buck inflicted more damage to the machine than I considered reasonable, and so I took the reins again, and learned to operate it myself. Within a very short period I could do everything the young man could do with it, with considerably less damage to the machine. Over the years that it took to prepare the land for development that wonderful Cat paid for itself over and over again.

Like everything that I have tackled in my life, clearing the twenty-eight acres took a whole lot more time than I could ever have imagined. In the first place, falling trees is only the beginning of the process. The timber has to be limbed and cut into specific lengths, particularly if you wish to have it milled into lumber, which I chose to do with much of it. In this case I employed a young fellow with a portable sawmill to cut the trees into lumber for some out buildings. The rest I cut into firewood, which I stacked all over the property, eventually constructing a large shed and filling it with all the cut wood. Ultimately I created a wood lot similar in size and volume to those I enjoyed visiting many years earlier on Market Street in Victoria.

Many of the cedar trees were small and not suitable for lumber. These were cut into posts and used to construct a fence around my twenty-eight acres. I spent a tremendous amount of time drilling holes in the rocky ground, and building a five foot high fence around the property, as well as cross fencing much of the pasture which had been wrested from the forest. The multi-railed fence would have been substantial enough to contain a herd of elephants, rather than the herd of Black Angus or, later on, the Hereford cattle that I ran on my farm.

For several years, my workweek included two days in the forest, and five days in the store. Much of the time that I spent in the forest entailed back breaking labour. I won every square foot of pasture only by sweat, tears, and endless patience.

One never to be forgotten hot July day, during my second year on the job, I was sitting on a stump looking at the tangle of trees which the D6 had pushed over the previous day, wondering why on God's earth I had ever started this project. After two years I still couldn't see anything but trees and bush. Although there were many cleared areas, some already planted with grass, I still had no view and I was beginning to despair, believing that all I would ever accomplish would be the creation of a picturesque farm surrounded by dense forest.

The burning desire and hope that kept me going was that somewhere beyond those trees was an open expanse of sea and sky, a dream which was becoming dimmer as each day passed. But finally, a short time after I sat on the tree stump wondering if I would have to spend the rest of my life searching for that elusive view, I saw the outline of Mount Tuam, on Salt Spring Island.

Normally, a glimpse of a large mountain would not be an exciting event, but when I caught sight of Mt. Tuam that wonderful summer day I rejoiced and thanked God for such a wondrous gift. From that moment on I knew that there was indeed something special awaiting me just beyond those trees, and I worked as never before to reveal God's plan for me.

Within a very short time, after falling many, many trees, a small opening appeared, and glory, glory, there before my very eyes was the sight that I had been dreaming of for so long, the sparkling blue ocean.

To say that it was the happiest day of my life would not be an exaggeration, for I had been working for over two years toward this day, and now it had arrived. I knew that my efforts and dreams would be rewarded even beyond my wildest imagination.

Once the Mountain and the ocean were in view, we spent much more time cleaning up the site, taking down many more trees and improving the pastures and clearing trails throughout the property. Eventually the whole twenty-eight acres were crisscrossed with trails suitable for vehicle traffic and included over a mile of 'elephant fences', with huge gates at the main entrance.

These gates were hung on a framework of logs that might have equaled the fortified entry to Fort Victoria in the early days of the colony.

My two-day workweek continued for quite some time, while I built outbuildings and a small, rustic 20' X 20' cabin, which I used as a place to sleep, whenever I felt the urge to 'rough it'.

One day, while visiting the site of the Bamberton cement works on the Malahat, I was taken with an old school house. Evidently it was slated for demolition along with most of the original Bamberton Village. The manager was delighted to hear of my interest and allowed me to arrange for the removal of the school house from the property, and also gave me permission to remove as many doors and windows as I wished from the old houses, before they were demolished.

A house moving company arranged to transport the schoolhouse from Bamberton within the following two weeks. Meanwhile I contacted the telephone company and the hydro authorities to inform them of the move. The plan was to move the building, which was forty five feet long and thirty six feet wide, along the highway to Kilmalu, north on Telegraph to Meredith and lastly up Mutter to its final resting place.

As I drove the proposed route the following day, I noted that there seemed to be enough width on the main roads to accommodate the school; however, a section of Meredith Road seemed a little too narrow because several hydro poles were very close to the road. When I measured the space between the large trees on the south side, and the hydro poles on the north side, I discovered that the width was less than the required thirty-six feet so I contacted the Hydro company and explained my dilemma, and asked what my next step was.

The Hydro boss was a very nice fellow, and suggested that their poles would probably be better located away from the road itself, and agreed to do the work immediately, if I would share the cost. The actual cost to me was a thousand dollars, which I felt was very reasonable as I had acquired the school for nothing and the moving company was only charging me four thousand

our first cabin 1980

1982 Bamberton School House, before and after..

dollars to move it and lower it onto its foundation, once in place.

Moving the monstrous structure took place at two a.m. one morning. The early hour was planned to avoid any unnecessary traffic, and things moved along very well, that is, until we reached the intersection of Kilmalu and the Island Highway. At that point we discovered that the maze of overhead electrical wires, were far too low to allow passage of the building. We then decided that the only other possibility would be Hutchinson Road, further north. Fortunately there was no problem passing along Hutchinson as there was plenty of room on either side. For the most part there was also sufficient room along Telegraph as well, until it reached the point where several telephone poles blocked its passage. The three telephone poles were very close to the road itself, and would have touched the roof of the school as it passed by, with the danger of tearing the lines down. So the school was parked in a field until a solution was found. The problem was quickly overcome when a crew from the Cobble Hill Telephone department arrived and leaned the poles over, just far enough to allow safe passage for the school. Best of all they did it with no charge. Finally, the school was in place, the foundation constructed, and the building gently lowered onto the footings. The moving equipment removed from under the structure, and the building was finished and ready for whatever I was going to use it for.

During the previous five years I had accumulated many historical artifacts, including stained glass windows, doors, light fixtures, and a beautiful wooden balcony that had been a very prominent feature in the Capital Theatre in Victoria. This particular balcony was the very one where I stood with my feet between the spindles, looking down upon the movie-goers in the foyer, those many years ago. It was destined to become the central feature in my home.

Those were very busy years for me, as I was not only collecting pieces to build into the house, I was also collecting antique furniture to furnish it. Somehow, the more I collected, the more I became inspired with grand ideas, eventually drawing up plans for a lodge which included nine bedrooms, eleven bathrooms, kitchen, dining room, den and a large baronial hall or living room.

Front entrance to Pine Lodge Farm

Naming Pine Lodge

Once I realized what I was about to do, and the cost of it all, I suggested to Barb that perhaps we should consider doing bed and breakfast to help cover expenses. Barb, bless her heart, once again went along with another of my wild adventures, and together we laid the foundation for what would become the Pine Lodge Farm B&B. Barb suggested the name Pine Lodge because I had ordered sixty thousand feet of white pine from a small mill on Sylvester road. The pine trees had come from a stand of timber near Youbou, in Cowichan Lake, and seemed perfect for the project. When the pine lumber was delivered, all sixty thousand feet of it, we proceeded to stack it in piles around the field just below where the house now stands. For six months the lumber lay about while we prepared everything to begin construction.

At long last everything was ready to go. My dear brother Frank took charge of the project and, with the help of two other young men, began the six-month building project. For the next few months the rain fell continually, making a difficult job even more difficult. The lodge was designed to replicate an early style of architecture, using as many antiques or near antique artifacts as possible. The wood flooring had been milled from trees on the property and when finally installed was absolutely perfect. Every light fixture, stained glass window, and wooden door was refinished and carefully restored to its original lustre. The restoration of furniture and building items had taken several years to accomplish and, though adding tremendous challenges along the way, had all come together to make this home one in a million.

While brother Frank laboured on the Pine Lodge, I spent my time preparing all the artifacts for installation. This was a time consuming job as every window, door and light fixture was a different size or thickness, necessitating a unique framework for each piece.

Many of the artifacts were stored in the Bamberton Schoolhouse which by that time was filled to capacity making it very difficult to find the room to manufacture the framework or, for that matter, even make the decision where each article should be installed. Often the item in question would have the hinges or locking devise on the wrong side or edge, making it impossible to use in a particular room or closet. Often I would have to reset hinges or door locks to make the item usable in the place I had intended them.

All my light fixtures had been rewired and approved for use by my good friends at Water Glass Studios in Victoria, a shop that specialized in light fixture restoration and Art Glass Replication, an art which they had perfected, and applied to my own collection with care and attention. The balconies that became the centerpiece of the grand hall and upper staircase required several months to refinish, as there were many coats of paint covering each section. The paint removal took weeks of painstaking labour followed by countless hours sanding, repairing broken spindles, and restructuring each section in order to fit them into their designated spaces. Happily, the thirty foot section covering the full length of the upper balcony fit perfectly when finally placed in position as did each section used on the staircase and at both ends of the balcony. Gradually the lodge took shape, the roof framing was completed, the cedar shakes hand-cut by my good friend Eric Roberts were fastened into place, the rooms and trim were freshly painted by my dear brother Harold, and the pine boards and battens left in their natural state. Finally every nail was set, the hemlock and fir flooring sanded and lacquered, windows, doors, and lighting installed, drapes hung, antique furniture in place, and a large house for Lady, my Dalmation-Black Lab cross dog placed on the outdoor porch.

Capital Theatre railings in front room of the lodge

Lady Adopts our Family

Lady was the smartest animal that I ever encountered. Considering that my mother was a devout animal lover her entire life, we always had stray dogs and cats dropping by for a meal or two, plus the many forms of rodents that I harboured over the years; and considering Prince, that very special Border Collie that used to accompany me on my paper route each morning (until he decided that running several miles every morning was not what it was cracked up to be, and finally reached the point that no amount of persuasion or cussing for that matter could get him out of my bed in the early morning). That gives you an idea of just what I mean when I say, "Lady was the smartest darn dog that I ever owned."

About the time I began clearing my land in Mill Bay, Lady made her appearance in my life. Early one morning, while we were still living on Doyle Road in Saanich, I discovered a snarling, teeth bared, skinny black dog on our lawn. I told it, in no uncertain terms, to remove itself from my lawn. The vicious black object flatly refused to budge, so I threw a missile of some size at her. Still she refused to leave, so I went into the house and told Barb and daughter Marlene not to go near it, as it was probably rabid.

That night, despite my request to phone the city pound and have it removed, the black dog was still lying on our lawn in exactly the same spot as it had been before I left for work that morning. Marlene had poured a bowl of water for it to drink, and said that the poor thing was starving and we should feed it.

I laid down the law saying, "No way, if we feed it, we will never get rid of it".

After Marlene fed the dog, she looked at us, licked her chops once or twice and then grinned at us.

The next morning the dog was still in the same spot but, just as I was about to leave for work, the pound keeper drove into the driveway, stepped out of his truck, walked over to my vehicle, looked toward our canine visitor, and said, " Is that the dog?'

My answer was affirmative, but the keeper made no move toward the animal, he merely stood quietly looking at it. For some mysterious reason, I also stood gazing at the beast, without making an effort to hasten her departure, in fact I found myself looking directly into her deep brown eyes, thinking that she didn't look too vicious, and observing that she appeared quite content just where she was.

After quietly studying the animal for a few minutes, the pound man turned to me and said, " What do you think?"

I was about to say, " Go get em", but the object of interest looked directly into my eyes, and, I swear on my mothers grave, spoke to me with as much clarity and passion as in any communication that I had ever experienced with a dog, and said, "Don't send me away, I'll make it up to you."

Well, what could I do? The message was clear; if I didn't keep her I would pay for it for the rest of my life. To save face, and to avoid looking like a sap, I told the pound man that I would keep her for a couple of days, decide what to do with her, and call him once I made my decision. Before the man disappeared from view, the black beast got up and walked over to me and nuzzled my leg. Marlene was ecstatic, Barb was wonderful, and I was caught, hook, line and sinker.

Each day Lady, as she was now known, did everything within her power to ingratiate herself into our family, and succeeded, probably beyond her wildest dreams. Guided by some mysterious instinct, she focused her undivided attention on me, quickly overcoming any resistance I might have entertained.

Within several weeks she presented us with a magnificent gift of ten gorgeous puppies, five spotted black Labs, and five Rottweiler pups. It would appear that sometime before finding her way to our home she had tarried with a handsome, ne'er-do-well Rottweiler and perhaps even a handsome black Lab. When we first discovered her new family, she looked directly at me, grinned from ear to ear, and distinctly said, "I told you I would make it up to you."

From that time on, Lady and I spent as much time together as possible. She always accompanied me when I worked on the farm in Mill Bay, and we enjoyed many interesting conversations during our countless trips up to the property. While I never was able to teach her to speak English, she certainly understood everything that I discussed with her, often making truly intelligent observations of her own.

When requiring her presence, all I would have to do was whistle once, and she would come running no matter what she was engaged in at the moment, which was very unusual, as most dogs I ever owned usually ignored my calls unless it was to their advantage to come when called.

One night, soon after Lady made her appearance, I had a butcher over to cut and wrap a steer that had been hanging for twenty one days. I had picked up the carcass that day, and it was still resting in my truck awaiting the hand of the butcher.

Lady stood watching as the two sides of beef were cut and wrapped, occasionally enjoying scraps of meat that came her way. We were very busy and weren't watching her too closely, other than when we threw her scraps from the cutting table, and so we never noticed that she periodically disappeared for short periods of time.

When all the beef was cut and wrapped, I went to the truck to retrieve the liver, the tongue and the heart but, unbeknownst to us, Lady had already made frequent trips to the truck, and had completely devoured everything in sight. This, considering the fact that we had been quite generous in feeding her scraps, was unbelievable. Lady offered no apologies or explanations for her amazing feat, rather she looked as pleased as punch, no doubt reasoning that she had ten extra mouths to feed, and what the heck, we shouldn't expect her to starve herself.

One of Lady's greatest pleasures was running. She would race around fields whenever possible, stretched out like a racehorse, her tongue hanging out a mile, and grinning from ear to ear. The farm presented the best opportunity for running, because the lower field was longer than a racetrack, and obviously presented a challenge to this faster-than-a-speeding bullet canine. She would take off from the house site, and would run full speed to the very end of the field, run a circle or two, and return at an even faster pace, and then quietly sit down at her favorite spot and serenely gaze over her domain.

Whenever I prepared to cut down a tree, I would tell her just where I thought the thing would fall and just where she should stand. Once I approached a large tree, much larger than I would normally tackle, and pointed out to her that even though it was on a downward slope, I was going to defy gravity and fall it uphill.

My experience with tree falling was not fully developed, and I did not know that it would take a very skilled logger to manage such a fete. So I positioned her in a spot downhill, then set my chainsaw in motion and cut a large wedge from the upper side of the tree, figuring that once I cut through the tree on the lower side it would miraculously fall upward.

As soon as I had cut half way through, on the down side of the tree, it gently leaned backward binding the saw in such a way as to make it almost impossible to remove. Undaunted, I fetched my other saw and proceeded to cut a thin wedge from the tree just above where the first saw was pinched in what proved to be, a death grip.

Lady eyed my handiwork, and immediately moved to a different spot, well away from the tree itself. Completely unaware of the danger I was in, I continued with the saw-cut. Within a few short moments the tree suddenly lurched downward, snapping off the remaining bit of wood still attached to the stump, and came crashing down, ending up on the ground, precisely where I had been standing moments before. Fortunately my reflexes propelled me away from the tree with the velocity of a man shot out of a cannon, and the only thing, belonging to me that ended up under the tree was my cotton hat.

After a short discussion with Lady concerning that particular incident, I decided to leave the larger trees to those who knew more about them than I did. From that time on I engaged professionals to drop the big ones, while I concentrated on the smaller sized ones that I felt comfortable with and, as there were hundreds more to come down I never ran short of work to do, and also Lady didn't have to continually worry about my welfare.

My dog continued her long runs, usually resting afterwards on her favorite spot on the lawn near the backdoor of the lodge.

One very cold day, shortly after we moved into the house, while awaiting my return from my antique store, Lady went on one of her runs around the lower racetrack and returned to her favorite place on the lawn for a rest. Barb happened to be looking out the window at that moment and noticed that when Lady sat down she suddenly became aware that the ground was frozen, and it obviously was more than her tushie could stand. She raised up onto her haunches, but her nether regions still refused to remain so close to the ground, So she went over to the porch and retrieved a pillow from a chair that was still outside, returned to her spot on the lawn, and laid the pillow over the offending area, then assumed her normal position, completely satisfied that she had done the right thing. Barb knew that no one would ever believe it, and took a picture as proof.

Gradually my dear Barb was becoming accustomed to the Pine Lodge Farm and all the chores that went with it. Actually life was better than it had ever been.

Convincing Barb to sell our house on Doyle Road had been extremely difficult, because she did not want to move away from the city and into the wilderness, but I finally smooth talked her into selling the house and putting the money that we would receive into the Pine Lodge.

For six months, while the For Sale sign was up on our front lawn, Barb was quietly praying that it wouldn't sell, and that I would come to my senses before it was too late, and before our house with its beautiful view overlooking Elk Lake and the distant ocean was gone forever.

There is no doubt that I had asked myself the same question many, many times, "Why would one want to move from an absolute paradise, to the far reaches of Mill Bay?" But my stubborn nature wouldn't allow me to admit defeat and so I pressed on. I did promise Barb that if the house did not sell by the time the listing expired I would give the whole thing a second look.

Once again fate dealt us a hand that appeared to be a winner. On the last day of the listing, a young couple from Prince George made us a cash offer with no strings attached. They had just won over a million dollars on the 6/49, and had fallen in love with our place and were prepared to buy it at once. When I look back to that moment I wonder if our life would have ended up differently if we had not moved.

Driving back and forth from Mill Bay to my shop in Royal Oak was beginning to wear on me. I began to begrudge the time away from Barb and the farm, and decided to sell the Red Barn Antique store. I reasoned that I could continue on with the antique business from my home or, better yet, build a bigger and better store in Mill Bay. That was not to be, however.

Lady sitting on pillow

Building a Museum

After selling the property in Victoria I held a going out of business sale, hoping to off-load the contents of the store. Many items sold, but I was left with the major portion of my antiques and collectibles which I moved up to the farm, storing them in every available space. The main space used for the collection was my beautiful barn that my son-in-law Bernie and I had just finished building, which also housed my three horses in a lean-to attached to the back of the main structure. By storing all the remnants of my antique store plus my own personal collection in that building, I created a very fine museum type showroom. The collection included several horse drawn wagons, every conceivable kitchen gadget ever invented, blacksmith tools, carpenters implements, show harness, sleds, a collection of stoneware jugs including some original ginger beer bottles identical to the ones I used to collect when I was six, plus a large assortments of ginger beers from every corner of B.C.

When Rose's Jewelry in Victoria closed down I purchased six enormous glass display cases, all of which had been constructed just after the turn of the century, and had been installed in the jewelry store by the builder himself. They were moved directly to my 'Museum', and promptly filled with a vast assortment of ancient memorabilia, including the ginger beers, and every other type of collectible imaginable.

While all this activity was going on Barb and I began our bed and breakfast business at the Pine Lodge. Considering the fact that we were far off the beaten track and completely unknown, things began to happen very quickly. A new acquaintance suggested that I write to as many B&B guidebook publications as possible, which I did. He just happened to be involved in the travel industry himself, and was able to help us in many ways. He even arranged for the American publication 'Country Living' to visit the farm for an interview and a write-up.

One fine day a helicopter landed in the field closest to the lodge and dropped off a couple from the magazine. The couple included the magazine's publisher herself, and her photographer, an award winning professional. They stayed overnight in our Lodge, and enjoyed the experience and graciously included us in a Vancouver Island cover story. The story included several pictures and featured the ginger beer collection as well as other items of interest on the farm. When the article appeared in their magazine we had a number of inquiries for lodging, and also requests for more information on the various collections. This led to yet another interesting opportunity for us: the possibility of renting antiques to movie-makers.

We placed an ad in the magazine, 'Hollywood North', and soon developed a modest rental business, catering to both movie companies and theatrical productions. While we never made a fortune, we did meet some very interesting movie people including the cast of the highly successful "Little Women", which was being shot on location in Cobble Hill.

Several of the cast were housed here during the filming, including Kirsten Dunst and Claire Danes, both delightful and well-mannered young ladies. Their mothers and their personal tutor accompanied the two starlets, and during their stay we shared many pleasant moments, including a wonderful farewell party on their last night.

During their stay here at the Pine Lodge, Claire Danes invited us over to the movie set and introduced us to Winona Ryder, the show's star. For some reason I had no idea who Winona Ryder was, and when she was introduced, all I could say was, "What did you say your name is"? Claire quickly set me straight, " This is the star of Little Women." Winona smiled graciously at me, and said that it was a pleasure to meet me. Much later I kicked myself. Heck, if I had played my cards right, she might have given me a role in the movie.

There were several movies that used our antiques in their productions and usually we were invited to the sets to see how things were done. Quite often we would get to meet the actors, which was always a thrill, of sorts.

Joining the Chamber of Commerce

Once Barb and I had things under control on the farm, I began to look for other things to get involved in. For some insane reason I thought that it would be fun to get involved in the local Chamber of Commerce. The Chamber was not large, that is, it had very few members but the people involved were just great.

Before long I was elected vice-president, which wasn't necessarily because of my abilities or talent, but rather that there was no one else to take the position, and I didn't know how to say no.

When the president refused to run again, much against my protestations I was unanimously elected to fill his place. I'm not even sure there was a quorum in attendance that night, but it didn't seem to make any difference. They passed the resolution anyway, and from that moment on, I didn't look back; of course there wasn't much to look back on in any case.

From the moment that I was catapulted into the president's seat, I did as much as possible to make the rest of group sorry for their foolishness. Certainly I knew as little about Roberts Rules as I did about anything else I ever tackled, but it didn't seem to matter to the others, as long as I turned up to all the meetings.

When I first began attending the meetings there were only four or five members who showed up regularly, but gradually a few more folk became interested and before long our ranks swelled and included seven dedicated followers, who were subsequently referred to as the 'Group of Seven'. They were local businessmen who believed most of what I told them. Their names were Grant Garnett, Klaus Seibring, Wayne Allen, Jim Dakin, Morris Simard, Fred Little, and myself. What was most remarkable about the group was their willingness to go along with my crackpot ideas.

At that time Mill Bay was still regarded a Sleepy Hollow by most travelers. The highway was still two lanes at the widest point with only one traffic signal to slow the light traffic down. The village did boast two gas stations, two restaurants and a coffee shop. It definitely had the feel of a place of peace and tranquility for the weary travelers.

The Birth of Mill Bay Jack

The 'Group of Seven', however, had other ideas about how the village should be viewed, and set about getting Mill Bay put on the map, figuratively speaking, and so, began a crusade to make it a destination point. One of the first brilliant ideas I put forward was that the place needed a central figure that would spark interest in the area. I, of course, had a plan. We would invent an imaginary figure to represent Mill Bay.

A very close friend of mine, Guy Randall, affectionately known as 'The Old Timer', spent his entire life glorifying the lives of the explorers who opened up Canada. He and his wife Nora would dress in clothes reminiscent of our early day trappers, and travel all over the province, visiting schools and relating tales of the 'Old Days', to the fortunate students lucky enough to be able to sit in on their lectures.

Guy was six foot four and as strong as an ox, and a very impressive figure dressed in his buckskins, sporting a long rifle with a powder horn slung about his chest while Nora, equally impressive in her own deerskin leathers, would regale the kids with their stories of early day pioneers.

History was of great importance to me, and I thoroughly enjoyed hearing my friend spin tales of early Canada, while Nora would delight the audience with poems written by well-known authors. Sitting around with the group of Seven one day, I threw out the idea that we could create our own mythical character patterned after Guy Randall to represent our town. This character would be called Mill Bay Jack. I further proposed that we carve a twelve-foot figure of Jack and display him in the town square, or wherever he would attract the most pigeons. Mill Bay Jack would be depicted as a logger rather than a buckskin clad frontiersman; in this way we could build on the rich logging history of the area.

Mill Bay Jack in Pioneer Square, Mill Bay 1985

In the 1800's, well before the Island Highway, there was a mill just where Shawnigan Creek entered the bay. Logs cut from lands above the bay were skidded down a specially constructed flume to the mill and then cut into lumber. To this day there are old pilings and mill slabs at the former site. According to some sources, the pilings supporting the Empress Hotel were logged from the same land and barged down to the inner harbour.

One of the group of Seven, Maurice Simard, a former logger himself, felled a large cedar tree and supplied the twelve foot section for the statue of Mill Bay Jack. The chamber employed a young carver, Julien Oullet. He set about the task admirably, first carving a small figure which would become the replica of the finished statue using pictures we had taken of Guy Randall as an example. I was so taken by this carving that I purchased it for my own collection, and still have it to this day.

Carving a twelve-foot statue from a twelve-inch model was certainly a challenge to the young carver, but he did very well. The project took quite some time and after some minor problems, he completed it and then applied the many coats of paint that were necessary to cover the highly porous cedar.

At long last Mill Bay Jack was ready to be placed on the concrete pad we had prepared at the front of the Pioneer Square shopping mall. This building was built on property owned by Grant Garnett, a founding member of our group, and designed and built by another member our select group of seven, Wayne Allen.

Once positioned in the square, it attracted a lot of attention from tourists, passing travelers, flocks of pigeons, and the somewhat bewildered resident folk of the area, who were often heard to ask the question, "What the hell is it for?"

Meanwhile, I was busy writing 'The Legend of Mill Bay Jack', a mythological story of a man of gigantic stature, born in the wilds of Shawnigan many, many years ago to a happily married Sasquatch couple. Jack became the first Sasquatch logger in the area and, to the best of my knowledge, probably the last. However improbable this tale seemed, it was my story and I was sticking to it.

The character, Mill Bay Jack, grew up in the hills around Shawnigan, and being a restless youngster he took to knocking trees down just for the fun of it. His handiwork was noticed by an old logger who took him under his wing and taught him the trade, beginning with concept of sawing a tree, and falling it rather than merely knocking it down.

Jack, though a slow learner, eventually mastered the craft and made quite a name for himself in the district, displaying his unique talents harvesting logs from the forest. He was famed for ability to fall a tree, and then drag it through the woods to the mill without any mechanized equipment.

While dwelling in the fantasy world of this mythical being, I told the incredible story at every opportunity. Many times I brought an audience to their feet, though sometimes they remained seated and stayed for the whole tale, which certainly pleased me a whole lot.

The Beginning of the Mill Bay Country Music Festival

Inventing the story of Mill Bay Jack did not end there; rather it was the beginning of a great adventure. My buddies in the Chamber were not completely satisfied that this large statue was really doing anything toward advancing our plan of putting Mill Bay on the map so, with much more study and thought, we came up with the concept of the Mill Bay Country Music Festival and Jamboree.

In 1986 the group of seven decided to finance a Festival featuring Country music. An acquaintance of mine was an agent who happened to specialize in Country music, and at that time had an office in Victoria. When approached with the idea of producing the Festival, he was delighted. He had many Country entertainers on his roster, and thought that the timing was just right to mount a yearly event.

Having no experience, or even the knowledge of mounting such an affair, I turned the hiring of entertainers over to him. Within a very short time he had a very good line-up of professionals ready and willing to get it off the ground. The last Friday, Saturday and Sunday of May 1987 was decided on for the event, and once the project was in motion we enthusiastically forged ahead, and with total commitment we began working out the myriad of details necessary for such a production. Our very special Mill Bay Jack became the official presenter of the Festival, and each and every bit of advertising we employed carried a caricature of good old Jack with his trusty axe, prominently displayed on the front cover.

By this time, the local villagers were fully convinced that the Chamber was definitely driven by something bordering on insanity. Who would ever think that such a crazy idea would fly? Who would ever drive all the way up to Mill Bay to see a bunch of country crooners? My goodness we must have gone off the deep end.

The Mill Bay Country Music Festival was a huge hit, providing great music and gaining a loyal following over the course of it existence. The first event, though successful, was not without problems. Fortunately our agent, Paul Mascioli, had arranged a great program of entertainers, including Canada's great Lady of Country music, Carol Baker, plus a line-up of many fine performers.

As Barb and I were running a Bed and Breakfast, we provided accommodation for the headliners, while all the others musicians were placed at other local B&Bs. My good friends Vicki and Gordon Simpson provided space for a number of them in their own home.

Gordon was my vice-president and right hand man, and truly amazed me with his expertise and ability while assisting with all the details to make the production fly. He quickly caught on to my style of, 'fly by the seat of my pants' operation, and managed to pinpoint many details that I often overlooked in my race to get things done.

He would describe his job, when asked, as a person who had to follow in the path of a cyclone, straightening out and picking up any and all fallout, and re-organizing it into a workable form. Such was his dedication to our projects, we became and remain fast friends. During the course of the Festival business, we branched off into yet another enterprise. We both threw ourselves into negotiating a deal with a small Victoria newspaper to produce a weekly column promoting the Cowichan Valley to Victoria. This column would allow us to pass on special events information for our area and hopefully tap into the larger Victoria market, and bring more and more cash laden patrons to our part of the world.

The weekly newspaper at that time was distributed to several locations around Victoria and the outlying districts, and was striving to increase its readership. My proposal to introduce an up-Island column interested the owner and he offered me the centre two pages. Filling two pages with both editorial and advertising weekly proved to be quite a challenge, but we tackled it with both verve and naivete. I would write the editorial and solicit the advertisers while Gordon would unscramble the information I supplied him and create the advertising copy. This arrangement worked perfectly, and made us a few extra bucks in the process.

While my writing skills were not great works of art, they did allow me to promote the Mill Bay Country Festival and other local events. The length of the editorial depended very much on the amount of advertising Gordon and I were able to generate each week, for the editorial had to fill whatever space was left.

As the months passed I found that the more advertising I could sell, the less writing I would have to do, and so I worked as hard as I could selling space to businesses around the valley and as far afield as Cowichan Lake. Whether our efforts ever increased business for the loyal clientele will never be known,

Mill Bay Festival in Kerry Park, Mill Bay

Cliff at Mill Bay Festival

although I must admit that when we decided that we would cease our weekly offering, no one seemed at all disappointed, or for that matter even mentioned it.

Promoting the Mill Bay Country Music Festival was a labour of love for me, and I spent every possible moment getting the word out that the festival was definitely a 'must see' for any country music lover, and the Kerry Park Arena was definitely 'the place to be'

For six months prior to the event I would travel up and down the Island, distributing fliers and posters, arranging advertising, signing up additional entertainers that I felt would add to the value of our production, and in general doing everything possible to promote it.

Each year the festival grew larger, attracting crowds of enthusiastic supporters, and each year we would have to enlarge our campground to accommodate the increasing number of fans who brought their motor homes and tents to stay for the whole three days.

Many of the mobile traveling fans were musicians themselves, and usually there was as much entertainment in the campground as there was in the arena itself. On any given night the impromptu merriment would continue until the early hours, often bringing a spate of calls from close neighbours who went to bed with the intentions of pursuing a night of restful sleep. However, over the course of the event, those very same neighbours were magnificent in their generosity, and continued to support the festival in spite of the late-night country troubadours.

There are always problems and pitfalls connected with an event such as ours, and often I would find myself in a very difficult situation where I would close my eyes in utter dismay, and ask myself that eternal question, 'What on earth is a nice man like me, doing in a place like this'?.

Our First Festival Blackout

The first year almost proved to be our last. During the Saturday afternoon performance, the lights in the entire Kerry Park complex went out. The audience sat still, patiently waiting. But as the minutes of darkness slipped by, some of the audience began to leave the arena. Without any hesitation, a number of the entertainers took their non-electrical instruments and proceeded to entertain the audience in the open areas of the building unaffected by the blackout and, to their everlasting glory, managed to keep the majority of them from leaving. Finally, one and a half hours later, the power was restored and the show continued. Evidently, a motor vehicle had crashed into a power pole on the highway, resulting in the blackout.

The following year, several months before the event, I paid a visit to the Hydro authority in Duncan, and had a chat with the gentleman in charge. I explained my concerns about power outages, and the resulting chaos resulting from the last year's incident, and asked if there were any safeguards that might spare us a repeat of the previous years near disaster.

After studying the map of the power grid in our district, he said that they could re-route the power supply by switching it to a different station, and this would lessen the chances of another power outage. A few days before the event, the Hydro Company did indeed switch the feeder lines through another power source in order to supply the Kerry Park Arena, and our show was able to operate for the three days without any power troubles.

The second year event was a great success and even more country music fans paid for three-day tickets than they had the previous year, which helped put us over the top and allowed us to pay off the small shortage of the prior year. This was a wonderful vote of confidence for our festival, and so we made plans for a third annual show.

The seven original organizers of the festival, including me, were delighted that our faith had paid off, and once again tackled the enormous job of producing the Mill Bay Country Music Festival. Paul Mascioli again provided us with a winning number of entertainers for the event and we produced an even better show than we had before, boosting our sales even further, and bringing in an even higher number of trailers and tents.

One of the biggest problems with the trailer business was that we needed to supply shower facilities for the campers. This was accomplished by opening up the washrooms and the showers in the Kerry Park Arena itself. We charged these campers two dollars for a shower. This worked very well, until the manager of the arena figured out that we were making the dollars and he was supplying the showers. So he informed us that from then on he would collect the fee for the showers from the campers himself. We really didn't mind as we had so many other pressing details to attend to, plus the fact that we were always having a problem finding some member of the Chamber to get up early enough to catch these bathers before they found the showers themselves. So we happily turned the shower contract over to the arena, gaining even more co-operation from the arena boss himself in return for this gesture.

Looking back on the festivals always brought back happy memories for Barb and me, for we met many great people and also developed an appreciation for country music.

As I became more involved with the country events, I decided that I needed some professional instruction on the best ways to manage festivals so, in the second and third year I attended seminars in Whistler that specifically dealt with festivals similar to ours. The seminars were fun and were also a great source for the type of information I felt I needed. There was a variety of instructors who were invited to speak at the daily meetings, and I learned many interesting things which helped me along the way.

One morning we attended a breakfast meeting that featured Catherine Wellner, a storyteller. She was a professional teller from Seattle, who traveled extensively throughout the country performing and instructing at Story Telling Festivals, both in the United States and in Canada.

Cliff and Barb

Country dancing

On one particular morning Catherine entertained the group with a magical story about a seal and her young pup. I was completely enthralled with this form of entertainment, and invited her to visit my home in Mill Bay, and to take part in a yet to be organized storytelling event. A month or so later Catherine visited my home, and took part in a storytelling event that I had organized with a number of close friends, and subsequently initiated me into the world of storytelling magic, a magical world that I enjoy to this very day.

That year I introduced Cowboy Poets to the festivals program, and enjoyed the stories of these tellers. There was a band of cowboy tellers that specialized in tales and folklore of the west. Unfortunately we were only able to find enough of these tellers for that one year, and so I reluctantly shelved the Cowboy Poets Corner, hoping to try it again another year.

Our Second Festival Blackout

The sales for the fourth year of our event were even greater than before. The parking area was sold out, the tickets were at a premium and the advertising had attracted fans from as far away as California and Saskatchewan, and things were looking very good.

Thursday was the final day to get everything prepared and ready for the expected crowds. Decorations were being hung, booths for the vendors were in position, stages were being completed, electricians were installing the heavy-duty cables that would power all the stages and vending booths, everything was unfolding exactly as we had planned. At 4:00 p.m. I was standing in the middle of the arena, my hands extended toward Heaven, savoring the moment and feeling that my world was complete and perfect, and thanking the Lord for his Grace and guidance. Precisely at 4:10, I heard an explosion, that seemed to emanate from somewhere in the arena.

Shocked back to reality by the noise of the explosion, I whirled about like an out of control Flamenco dancer, looking for the source of that ominous sound. I slowly became aware that my as yet unfocused eyes were being drawn toward the electrical room in the north east corner of the arena

For several seconds I stared in mute horror at that little room as smoke began billowing from it, staring, yet not fully permitting my mind to contemplate the possibility that a disaster of cataclysmic proportion had just occurred there, and if the truth were to be known, not really wishing to know.

Within minutes, the arena staff invaded the electrical room with fire extinguishers and fire hoses, an assault which actually helped to create even more smoke. All I could do was stand in the center of the arena, speechless, baffled, and slightly giddy as I watched the whole episode unfold.

There are events in everyone's life that never completely fade or disappear from memory, no matter how much time passes or how much water flows under the bridge, and this was one of those times.

Evidently, one of the two highly proficient and professional electrical tradesmen, who were handling the electrical hook-up, had inadvertently dropped a wrench into the main service panel that supplied the power to the entire arena complex. The wrench had landed in such a way that an arch of electrical current set off an enormous explosion and engulfed the whole panel in flame and black acrid smoke. Unfortunately, the electrician closest to the panel took the full force of the explosion and was seriously injured; his helper thank God, though shaken up and in shock, was not injured.

Needless to say, neither of the two gentlemen was able to continue working on the power supply, which of course was crucial to lighting our event, and the likelihood of getting replacements to complete the job, was virtually zero, for a large section of the electrical panel had melted with the heat of the explosion.

While all this drama played out, I stood rooted to the spot, not able to move, not able to speak, and barely able to comprehend exactly what had happened. One of the arena staff, being more than candid, informed me that it looked like the event would not be able to go on, as there was no power available and not likely to be available for some time.

Prayer had always been a part of my life, I prayed each night before I went to sleep, I prayed when I bought lotto tickets, and I prayed when I was in deep trouble. The prayer that sprang from my mouth when I realized that the show was likely doomed may have sounded to an innocent bystander like a strong dose of blasphemy but, as God is my witness, it was a deafening plea for help. The cry heard throughout the arena, which evidently came from me, though more of a lament than a song of praise, clearly begged His guidance and Grace. And God did help us!

The manager of the complex got onto the phone immediately, and was able to contact the senior engineer of the Westinghouse company, the maker of the now defunct panel, who just happened to be in Victoria at the time, and somehow communicated the urgency of the situation to him. He was able to persuade him to come up to the Kerry Park Arena and spend the entire night rebuilding the all but destroyed panel, and, glory be, he had it temporarily repaired and functioning by eleven Friday morning.

At that particular time, I was still not completely aware that the Lord was the sole director of my life, and though impressed and extremely thankful with the outcome, I never gave full credit where the credit was due. That awakening, and blessed enlightenment, was yet to come.

By 4:00 p.m. Friday, everything was complete and ready to roll. Food concessions were up and running, stages fully operational, a full staff of volunteers, including Barb and my daughter Marlene, were at their posts, and I was on cloud nine.

Introducing Country Dancing at the Festival

As soon as the doors opened for business, crowds of country music fans began pouring into the building and we were off to one of our best festivals. That year I invited Joe Archer, a local instructor, who was a country-dance expert, to set up a dance competition for the festival. Hundreds of dancers from clubs throughout B.C. and Washington State attended our event and competed in both country ballroom, and line dance competitions.

This dancing competition, became known as 'Cowichan Goes Country', a great addition to the festival, and eventually became a sell-out event. It was conceived and perfected by Jim and Daphne Anderson, members of one of my dance classes.

When we were first introduced to country line dancing, Barb and I joined a club and became avid dancers ourselves, eventually getting a group of beginners together and teaching them everything that we knew, or at least what we thought we knew. Within a short time we had organized several small dance groups, and instructed line dancing classes two or three times each week. We used several halls for these classes and had the time of our life, all the while learning new dances, and attending seminars, hosted by professional instructors.

Our line dance career was not only fun, it was also tremendous exercise. During our classes we made sure that everyone worked as hard as possible, dancing for a minimum of two hours without a break. Though it was an extremely demanding form of leisure activity, our classes grew larger each week, and we became known as line dance fanatics. Our students credited us for our ability to help them lose weight, as well as our ability to teach them new dances. Fitting all these activities into our already busy life was more fun than a barrel full of monkeys, or so the saying goes.

Keeping Busy on the Farm

Our bed and breakfast was going full steam. The farm chores were endless for I was raising meat birds, pigs, turkeys, and laying chickens, and doing my best to keep the raccoons from eating all of my chickens plus trying to keep the Scottish broom from overrunning our twenty eight acres.

The Scottish broom was a constant problem, but I was able to keep it under control by pulling every damn plant I came across. This did take a fair amount of time each year, but I managed and not only that, experienced a great deal of pleasure ripping them out, roots and all, and casting them aside where they lay until they shriveled into nothingness. There was a time that I became intent on finding the name and location of the hair-brained Scot who brought this noxious weed over to this country, wanting to burn his effigy at a stake surrounded by a flaming pile of the stuff. However, I had other more urgent priorities, and I was never able to satisfy that desire, although, I will confess that I still harbour ill feelings when it comes to Scottish broom.

Raccoons were, and still are, "a horse of a different colour", or something along that line. We tried everything to keep them out of the hen house; the first line of defense was locking the chicken coop door at night. This worked well when we remembered to set the latch, but there were always the nights that we forgot. But the raccoon patrols never forgot to check the coop each night. Evidently they train their offspring to religiously check coop doors at least once each night, twice if possible.

The major flaw in the strategy of locking the chicken coop each night is that the brainless chickens themselves take every opportunity to stay out after curfew, even though they will be invited out to dinner by a raccoon, with the

Bell Dan Babe

obvious intent of making them the main course.

Chickens sometimes fly into trees to avoid being chased back into the coop at night by the diligent farmer, and when they do manage to escape his vigilance they will happily sit on a branch and contentedly cluck away until Mr. Raccoon, who just happens to be a master tree climber, strolls by and displays his tree climbing prowess to the dumb cluck. Apart from showing a raccoon the business end of a shotgun, there are very few ways of discouraging them from using your prize hens for their own consumption.

Once, after reading somewhere that raccoons don't like the smell of human pee, I announced to my beloved wife that from that moment on we were going save every drop of that precious by-product we could spare, and then spread it around the chicken coop, and wait to see what happened. Needless to say, it did not stop the pilferage and, not only that, I began to suspect that it actually attracted even more of the no good bandits.

To this day we have to be very alert to keep these little black-eyed rascals from inviting our chickens out to dinner, and I do believe that we have discovered the perfect way to keep them out of the hen house. Two years ago I had a worker friend of mine install an electric fence around the perimeter of both chicken runs, and it appears to work very well. Evidently raccoons climb the fence posts that surround the enclosure, and then test the electric wire with their noses to see if it's safe. The electric jolt that they receive from the wire doesn't hurt them, but gives them enough of a jolt to make them think twice about going any farther. Hopefully they have spread the word to their family and friends that the chickens are surrounded by a wire that is not at all friendly and should be avoided at all costs.

Each year the Country Music Festival became more and more popular, and I and my committee continually thought up new ideas to keep it interesting and entertaining. The service clubs ran the parking lots and the trailer park and kept improving their operations and managed to keep the public happy. They also earned a nice little profit for their organizations. The Chamber too managed to build up a substantial bank account, which helped fund the event the following years.

Unfortunately, there were folk who believed that the Chamber should not have retained the profits from the events, but should have spent it as quickly as possible. My concern was that there should always be funds available for the continuation of the festival, and to provide for the eventuality of a disaster, or a sudden down turn in the fortunes of the Chamber.

The sixth yearly festival did not do as well as previous years, and there was a concern that perhaps a different approach would be necessary to avoid a complete disaster, and it was decided that a professional agency in Vancouver should be invited to handle the production of Seventh Annual Festival.

The Demise of the Mill Bay Country Festival

Meanwhile, my life was extremely busy with other projects, which included a small store that I had built in 1990, in the Cobble Hill village. That, plus many other factors, contributed to the fact that I was not able to carry on with the festival, although I did put in a one page proposal offering to manage the Seventh Annual for a percentage of the profits as my fee. The agency on the other hand required that their fee be paid up front. After studying the agency's colorful and lengthy proposal, the members of the Chamber decided to give the Vancouver professionals a chance to prove their worth and allow them to produce the Seventh Annual Mill Bay Country Music Festival.

In an effort to save costs, the event was scaled down with fewer acts. Other measures were taken to lower expenses as well, unfortunately the cost cutting also lessened the appeal of the event and the festival lost a considerable amount of money. The following year the festival was pared even further, and due to a severe cash flow shortage, the event was discontinued shortly afterwards.

Building Cobble Hill Country Furniture

In the meantime, I had acquired a double lot across the street from my Cobble Hill store, with the idea of building another, even larger store to promote business in the little village. What I did not realize was that I was once again opening my life to even more work and challenges.

When I built the original store in 1990, I leased it out to a couple that opened and operated a country craft business. The craft store did quite well, but the general feeling was that it would be better if there were more retailers in the area, and so I considered the possibility of opening another retail outlet. Of course the vacant lots on the opposite corner were not for sale at that time, and therefore the idea of constructing another building was merely an observation on my part. But one day for sale signs suddenly appeared on both the lots, and naturally I spotted them right away. Evidently a real estate agent realized the potential of the site and persuaded the two owners to sell.

When I rushed home and told Barb that the lots were for sale, she was completely underwhelmed, and told me that I was out of my mind and that I should get help as soon as possible. In my own mind I was convinced that this was a sign from a higher power and that I should buy them as quickly as I could, before anyone else saw the signs.

Within a very short time, after overcoming Barb's resistance to this new venture, I made an offer for both the lots, which was immediately accepted by the owners. I then made arrangements for a surveyor to consolidate the lots into one large lot, and then proceeded to have the lot approved as a building site.

Once the lots were consolidated, I calculated the maximum size building that we could build. This turned out to be twenty five hundred square feet, not very large, but by using the basement we could double the size. There again it was not a huge building, but it would be sufficient to house three small businesses.

I placed an ad for tenants in local papers and I soon had three people interested in renting the spaces, and so we began constructing almost immediately. The construction went very well and before long we were close to completion. That was when I received the news that all three people had changed their minds and would not be taking any space in the building after all.

Barb suggested that we sell the building then and there, but I was not so easily swayed, and I began making plans to open an antique store. My son Mike offered to help me with the store and I was overjoyed at the prospect of having my son working with me. So with Mike at my side, we forged ahead and completed the store very quickly.

There were many antiques at my home that could be sold in the store, but not enough to fill it adequately, so we decided that we would need to sell some new furniture as well as the antiques to make it a viable business.

My son-in-law Bernie was an experienced furniture salesman, and he recommended that I go on a buying trip to Highpoint, North Carolina, the home of the largest furniture and gift show in North America. There I would find every type of furniture available, including reproduction antiques and country furniture, plus any other style that might interest me.

Highpoint was absolutely incredible. There was over seven million square feet of display space in the small town, and almost every major

Cobble Hill Country Furnishings 1993

manufacturer in the United States, Canada, England, and Italy were represented there.

Trying to decide just where I should look for the style of furniture that I was interested in was an incredibly difficult task, as there were endless showrooms to see, and thousands of stairs to climb. But, like a schoolboy in heat, I ran myself ragged, rushing in and out of showrooms like a wild man, eventually finding enough items to fill my store.

The amount of merchandise that was available in that little town was absolutely unbelievable. I had never seen anything like it in my life, and trying to make a final decision seemed like an impossible task, but somehow I managed to choose a number of manufacturers and types of furniture, and overall, was very happy with the results.

My years of experience in the antique business was invaluable and I was able to find a variety of solid wood furniture for our store, and in the process, set a standard that proved to be very hard to beat.

Once the selection of unique furniture pieces was in the store, along with the terrific variety of antiques that came from our warehouse, we were able to open the Cobble Hill Country Furnishings to a warm welcome, and over a period of five years many happy clients often returned, helping to make the store a profitable and happy experience.

Probably the most difficult part of the furniture business was selecting the right products for the right customers. So I was most fortunate to connect with several of the top-notch manufacturers while in High Point, who happily provided me with high quality solid wood products, and first class upholstered furniture.

There were many one-of-a -kind products to choose from, and I was like a kid in a candy store, who wanted one of everything, but of course my little store just wouldn't allow a huge inventory, so it was necessary to control the overwhelming urge to buy everything in sight. Of course there was the money factor as well, and restraint was the order of the day. Otherwise I would have quickly found myself in deep water. As it was, I needed a lot of extra cash to defray all the expenses that it cost for the building, land and merchandise.

At that time we had a museum full of interesting and collectible items on the farm. My intentions were to keep all these artifacts intact and continue displaying them in the barn. We needed space for the inventory from High Point, however, and of course we needed extra money to pay for everything that was on order. Reaching a decision to sell the collectible items in the museum was an extremely difficult thing to do; after all, we had been collecting those artifacts for over thirty years and were very fond of them all. But it was a decision that was necessary if we were to carry on with the furniture store.

Once the word got out that I was selling my museum stock, we were kept very busy with dealers and other interested parties who lined up for the opportunity of picking up the highly collectible merchandise. Within a short time the barn was empty of all the items that we had spent years collecting.

Thinking back on the course of events, with a great deal of nostalgia and perhaps even regret, I realized that I had changed the course of our life in a very drastic way. Certainly the past twenty years had been absolutely wonderful, and the time that I had shared with Barb, working the farm, was priceless.

Now we were on to yet another adventure that would have us working seven days a week. My dear, long-suffering Barb, could not understand why we should get tangled up in another time consuming venture, when we had been so happy on the farm. She wanted to sell the building and truly retire, after all we were nearing sixty and it was time to settle down. But, with the same old rhetoric that had been used all our married life, I made a promise to her that I would give this new business exactly five years and then we would sell everything and enjoy the rest of our life together, travelling, doing all the things that we never had time to do before. But, once again fate stepped in, and dealt us a hand that we could never have anticipated or imagined, even in our worst nightmare.

Strangely, the hand we were dealt didn't look half bad on the surface, and so we continued to forge ahead, building up stock, increasing sales, doing our best to get the store running smoothly, efficiently and profitably. Making the store profitable entailed a lot of hard work and perseverance. My part of the operation included selling furniture during the day, restocking the store before opening each morning, and delivering the sold product at night.

Many customers were more than a little surprised to see me selling them the furniture during store hours and then delivering it to them at night. My excuse was that I was getting old and needed the exercise. Actually, delivering the items to their homes allowed me a great opportunity to see just what other pieces might fit into their living space, and also gave me another chance to sell them even more merchandise.

Delivering furniture was fun, and a very happy experience for me, and in the process my body received a complete exercise program free of charge. It was also very convenient, for my muscles were getting toned while the rest of me was doing profitable business

Fitting a Square Peg into a Round Hole

Delivering furniture did have its own unique set of problems. Firstly, you always had to take the correct measurements of the piece that you were delivering, so that you could successfully get it into the house and up or down narrow hallways.

There were many occasions when we would arrive at a customer's home, only to discover that the piece we were delivering wouldn't go through the front door, or down the hallway, or worse yet, wouldn't go around a sharp corner in the hallway leading to the bedroom. Most of the problems were solvable, if one were ready to use a healthy dollop of ingenuity and imagination, and be willing to take a chance. This was where my experience in carpentry and furniture restoration came in handy.

Whenever we were faced with such an obstacle as a narrow hallway, I would often remove the widest part of the piece of furniture, usually the top of it, and then manage to inch it down the narrow passage without doing any harm to the walls or the piece itself. Sometimes the removal of the legs as well as the top was necessary in order to get the damn thing into place. There were even times when I would have to totally dismantle the infernal thing in order to get it into its designated space.

Handling the customer, while trying at the same time to dismantle their beautiful piece of furniture, was an entirely different matter. In most cases I would ask the customer to look the other way or go have a coffee while I carried out the dismantling process. Sometimes the customer would insist on staying put for the whole ordeal, and in order to keep their mind off the project at hand, I would entertain them with stories and anecdotes, hoping that my humour was sufficient to keep them distracted till the deed was done.

This usually worked well, however, there was the time that we delivered a magnificent King size, mahogany bed and dressers to a home in Sooke, only to find that the bed would not fit up the stairway leading to the bedroom. The owner of the piece eyed me suspiciously when I informed her that I had to take the bed apart.

Her husband seemed entirely at ease with the dismantling process. She on the other hand was appalled at the thought of seeing her beautiful and expensive Lexington bed, made of the finest Honduras mahogany available, pulled apart in her own living room. While examining this one of a kind bed, it occurred to me that I was in deep trouble, for there did not seem to be any way to get the thing apart. Obviously, my next remark to my helper did not help the situation at all, for I told him to go and get the chain saw.

There was total silence at this suggestion, both from the husband and the wife, although there was a definite twinkle in his eye when he excused himself from the room. Realizing the hole I had dug for myself, I tried my level best to repair the damage my loose tongue had caused, and immediately set to work calming her fears. There has never been any doubt that my special talents have always included the ability to smooth talk most ladies along with the best of them. What I had not comprehended was the fact that this lady lacked even the most rudimentary sense of humour.

Pulling every bit of jocular material possible out of my ever-present bag of laughs, I gave the performance of my life, and when the bag was emptied of everything but the trick nose, I tried my tap dancing routine, hoping that it might thaw the frigid temperature that had settled on the room. But to no avail, my lady remained colder than a Witch's mammary glands.

Finally, casting all pretense of humour aside, I leveled with the lady, assuring her that this bed had been designed by master craftsmen, and built by people that had been in the business of furniture design and construction for countless ages, perhaps even reaching back as far as Noah's Ark, and that it was possible that one of them actually had been married to one of Noah's daughter and had even been included on the voyage, when they set sail as the storms came. It was my humble opinion that this bed would come apart very easily, all I had to do was find the hidden key and we would be in business.

After studying the back of the bed for some time, I let out a whoop, for I had discovered the screws that secured one end of the bed to the other end. All that was necessary was to remove the screws and then slide it apart.

The Lady had other ideas and told me that it would not fit in the room, and that I should take the whole bedroom suite back to the store. Now, returning furniture to the store, or refunding money, was not in my operations manual. When I delivered a piece of furniture, it stayed delivered. Trying my best to ignore the ravings of the now red-faced lady, wc sct about dismantling the bed. The whole time the lady kept up a steady stream of objections, assuring me that it would not fit into her bedroom and I was wasting my time.

Once the screws were removed, we were able to take it up the stairs, place it in the huge bedroom, fasten it together, rub a little furniture oil on the joint, which completely removed all the evidence that it had been taken apart. The suite looked absolutely fabulous in the room, but when I turned my eyes toward her, hoping for some form of confirmation, I was faced with a very agitated lady. She said that I had ruined her bed, and that she did not like it anymore.

Rapidly losing patience, I mentioned that it had taken us one hour to drive from my store to her home. We had laboured two hours doing our best to get the bed and the dressers into her bedroom, and had succeeded in spite of the difficulties of a steep stairway and a low ceiling. The relevant fact, that I was a professional furniture finisher and restorer, a carpenter of forty years experience, an entertainer of some note, a sixty year old law abiding citizen and taxpayer, the apple of my mothers eye, and one of the best lovers that had ever walked this earth and finally, the clinching argument on my part, the inescapable fact that her cheque had been cashed and that there was no way I was going to give any of the money back. At this point the husband entered the room, remarked that the suite looked absolutely fabulous and thanked me for all our hard work and patience.

The lady was not amused but she did not say a word, she merely gave her husband a look that conveyed a message that is timeless and recognizable to any red blooded husband, and that is also sufficient to reduce most lovers into incoherent babbling idiots. My heart went out to him immediately, for I knew that this magnificent bed was not going to favour him with anything more than a fitful nights sleep for some time to come.

Money was not, and had never been, the driving force in my life. My only desire had been to enjoy everything that came my way whether it was easy or difficult, and, if it was not enjoyable, then it was not worthwhile and I would quickly lose interest, and move onto other more interesting and enjoyable enterprises.

When I mentioned that my own personal working manual did not allow the return of justly earned goods or monies, it should also have been stated that my pride in doing a good job was the thing that truly propelled me and encouraged me to work long hours, even when there was faint hope of making an honest profit. So when the job, whatever it happened to be, was completed, I fully expected and even demanded that the bill be paid in full.

That character trait guided me through my entire life, and particularly when I was involved in the sales field. If there was time and effort invested and a product delivered, there was only one satisfactory conclusion for me, and that was, 'payment in full'.

Of course there were many times that the delivered product had some flaw in its makeup, and I would do everything within my power to make it right or, failing that, replace it. On many occasions the imperfections would require a lot of effort and time to correct, but they would be corrected and the piece finally delivered, and paid for.

It was noted by most retailers that there would always be a certain percentage of returns in any business, in most businesses at least seven percent, in some up to fifteen percent. At the end of my five years in the furniture business my son-in-law Bernie, now the proud owner of Lazy Boy Galleries in Victoria and Nanaimo, declared that he had never seen or heard of a business that was able to operate with close to a zero return rate.

Within a very short time, our store was handling and displaying many interesting lines of furniture and accessories, and we subsequently managed to develop an extensive number of clients from all over Vancouver Island. As sales improved so did the quality of our merchandise, and gradually we took on many well known lines of both antique reproduction and top line contemporary furniture, which gained us even more clients, and kept our cash register ringing its merry bell.

Opening a Second Hand Store

In the second year of business at Cobble Hill Country Furnishings, our friend and tenant who occupied the little store across the way moved out, leaving us with a vacant store. The idea came to me that we could start a second hand furniture store there, stocking it with items that I came across while delivering furniture to our own customers. These pieces could be purchased at a very reasonable price and also sold at bargain prices.

One of our sales-girls who went by the name of "Cat" loved the idea of a second hand store and offered to run it for us. She was little dynamo, and took charge of the store, applying all her energies to the task at hand, and kept the merchandise turning over quickly and profitably. At her suggestion, we built a coffee counter, installed coffee urns, a Latte machine, and all the necessary equipment to run a small coffee operation, and then opened for business.

We never did make any money on the operation, but we did have our share of fun during our few short months of business. Eventually Cat moved on to another job, and we decided to sell the building, rather than trying to operate it ourselves.

Within a few months, a young couple purchased the store, set up a music business, established a youth choir, gave music lessons, developed a Jazz club, and sold coffee. The owner led the Jazz bands himself, and also gave piano lessons in his spare time. Their operation was very successful and continues to be successful to this day.

When we sold the little store, we were relieved and very thankful at having that stress removed from our life. It was at that time that I finally realized that we could indeed cut down on our workload and begin reaping the benefits of our years of hard work without seriously disturbing the world economy. From that moment, we began the countdown toward our long awaited, day of retirement.

An Omen of Things Ahead

One day in 1997, while Barb and I were sitting at our dining room table enjoying a cup of coffee with two other friends, I was suddenly aware of a disturbance in the sky to the east. Out of the corner of my eye I became aware of a shaft of dazzling white light on the horizon, moving toward us. Within a moment, the shaft traveled from the horizon to our home, slicing through the sky, our porch, our window, the dining table, and finally right through Barb herself. Barb jumped up as though struck by lightning, and said, " What was that?"

In near shock, I described what I had seen; our friends had not seen the shaft of light, but did see Barb's reaction, and were astounded at what they had witnessed. My concern for Barb left me feeling ill and, though I later joked about the incident, I felt something very profound and unusual had occurred, and wondered just what it was and what meaning it held for us. The feeling of unease stayed with me for some time, but strangely Barb and I never discussed it privately, and only mentioned the event to a few friends afterwards.

Sometimes momentous events occur in our lives that defy explanation, and that bolt of light was just such an event. It did puzzle us for a long time, but we never explored the phenomenon or asked anyone who dabbled in the supernatural to research it for us, However, my daughter Maureen did mention it to one of her friends who had a keen interest in the spirit world, who warned her that it was a very bad omen. Maureen did not wish to upset us and never mentioned it again.

After that episode both Barb and I decided that we would sell our bed and breakfast, the store, and anything else that caused us stress, and live the life that we always dreamed of.

Life for Barb and me continued moving along in a fairly orderly way. Our B&B was still as busy as ever, and we enjoyed meeting many interesting people from all walks of life, and from many parts of the country. One nice couple invited us to visit them in New York, even offering us the use of an apartment they owned on 76th Street, several doors down from Broadway. We had previously made plans to attend a trade fair in High Point, North Carolina the following month, and decided that a stop over would work very well for us.

After spending a few days at High Point, we headed for 'The Big Apple' and took up residence in the couple's spare apartment. Evidently they had just joined forces and were in the process of painting the apartment before selling it. This was indeed fortunate for us for we had a nice place to stay, which was comfortable and conveniently located.

Our week in New York was spectacular. The couple had arranged for tickets to several of the best shows in the city, and also took us out for dinner on the first night there.

During the day we toured many attractions including the Trade Towers. Riding the elevators all the way to the top of the towers was quite an experience for a couple of country folk, and of course the view from the top was terrific. Strangely, while we were on top of the building, I commented to Barb that I would not want to be up there if there was an emergency, for it would be a horrendous feat to get out of there quickly. I suppose most people would think the same thing on their first visit there for it was an incredibly high building and, for a first timer, kind of scary.

Cliff and Barb on a Caribbean Cruise

Our Visit to New Orleans

In October, the following year, we made a trip to the High Point Market, and included a quick side trip to New Orleans. For many years we had wanted to visit that fascinating city, but never quite got around to doing it, but once there, we had a ball.

The apartment was located in the heart of the Latin Quarter, and at the back of the building were the original slave quarters, that were built in the early days of the seaport town. Our apartment was on the second floor of the building and overlooked the front yard of an old mansion across the narrow street. My imagination went wild at the thought of life in those early days, and Barb and I explored every nook and cranny, reveling in the nostalgia associated with the city.

We dined in every old town restaurant possible, delighting in the wonderful Louisiana cuisine that abounds in that part of the world. We went to outdoor markets, we enjoyed delicious praline treats and other mouth watering sweets, found only in that delightful place, we took carriage rides through the narrow streets of the Latin Quarter, we sipped beers while strolling along Bourbon Street, we enjoyed the finest Nor'leans Jazz, we visited historic homes and buildings, we rode the trolley that traveled along St. Charles Ave., past the world famous above- ground cemetery, and into the heart of the Garden District, and finally, we took a dinner cruise on an old paddle wheeler that travels up the Mississippi River.

By that time we were completely bewitched by the magic of New Orleans, and though we should have known better, we decided to buy a time-share in an old hotel on St. Charles Ave, a time-share that was being vigorously promoted on that particular voyage. Little did we know that we would never share the pleasures of New Orleans again.

Barb and Cliff.
New Orleans 1997

A Fatal Decision

When we returned to Victoria the following week we immediately returned to our busy schedule, but each day we would enthusiastically discuss the idea of total retirement. Later in the year I decided that we should go to Toronto to a gift show, scheduled for late January, 1998. Barb did not want to go, and asked me why I would want to go there. My quick reply was that I didn't really know, but once again I reasoned that it would be a good thing for the store, and we could get some new ideas for gifts and accessories as well.

To make the idea of a trip to the Toronto gift show as attractive and appealing as possible, I made arrangements to stop in Vancouver on the way back, to see the show, 'Lord of The Dance.' We had always wanted to see that particular group, and so Barb went along with my idea, although somewhat reluctantly. For some reason, I too felt strangely reluctant to make the trip. I wasn't quite sure why I felt that way but I did, and made a mental note that if any other message or warning came my way, I would cancel the trip.

Two days before our flight, I awoke early, turned to Barb and without any hesitation or reason said, " Take Marlene to the bank today and give her signing authority for all of our accounts."

Barb never questioned me, or even asked why, and later that day she took Marlene to the bank and made all the arrangements. During our married life we took many trips to different parts of the world, but never before had I suggested such a thing. Never before had I ever considered that we would not be in a position to continue looking after our own businesses. But, for some strange reason, neither Barb nor I questioned it.

That evening I asked Barb if she had signed Marlene onto the accounts. Barbara simply said, "Yes", but then, as though asking a question as an after thought, she asked me what I would like to have done if anything happened.

I took that question to mean; what would I like done if we were to die. I immediately answered that I would like to have side-by-side graves in Royal Oak Cemetery, where so many of my relatives, including my parents, had been interred so that we could be together forever. Barb looked at me for a moment, and then turned away. I continued on toward the bedroom, where I had been heading before asking that prophetic question, and that was the last time we discussed that topic.

The weeks leading up to our journey to Toronto had been very busy as we arranged all the necessary details prior to our departure. One of the troubling questions that continually dogged me, was why were we going to Toronto anyway. We certainly didn't need any more stock for the store, and it was probably very cold back east. The logical place to go at that time of the year would have been somewhere warm, like New Orleans, the place that so intrigued Barb and me, and the place where we had experienced one of the most enjoyable times of our lives.

The day before leaving for Toronto, while talking with Barb, I made a comment that our life was going to change drastically, and that after this trip we were going start living life to the fullest. We were going to do everything that we had ever wanted to do, and that was a promise.

One of the holiday trips that we had booked and looked forward to was an ocean cruise beginning in Fort Lauderdale and continuing through the Panama canal. Barb's sister Marion and her husband Arthur had made arrangements to go with us on that voyage scheduled for February 25, 1998. The four of us were looking forward to that time together, and had been talking about the trip for several years, without actually booking it.

Life should have been wonderful, for Barb and I were finally going to realize our dream of being together and enjoying our remaining years, far removed from the seven day work weeks that had always controlled our lives. But for some reason I still felt that something was not right.

Every night, over the course of many years, I made a point of praying for good health and the blessings of a long life for both of us. My prayers always included the request that I might always be allowed to look after Barb, and that I would be able to make up for all the years of sacrifice that she had patiently endured, while supporting my countless enterprises and escapades.

All my life I considered that I was a Christian, and that the Lord had always watched over me, protecting me from my endless missteps and follies, and hopefully would grant me a long and fulfilled lifetime of happiness with Barb. Even though I seldom attended church, read the bible, or supported the Lord's work, I always felt that God knew my heart, and was satisfied with me in spite of my shortcomings.

But now, looking back on my past life, I realize that my heart and mind was completely centered on my own interests and successes and that my drive and ambition depended solely on my own strengths and determination rather than on the Lord's love, will and blessings.

My credo throughout life had been, 'Don't explain, don't complain,' and I fully believed that I alone could bring about success for myself, and that I really didn't need the help of anyone else. If I worked toward a goal with determination and grit, there was nothing that I could not attain for myself.

This of course, was as far from the truth as I could get, for even though I attained a certain degree of success I never fully reached the heights that I aimed for. Every success that I realized always fell short of my expectations, and, due to my self-driven confidence, I never understood why I was continually falling short of my goals. It was only in the years following our trip to Toronto that I discovered the sad truth.

Our Last Trip Together

On the morning of January 23, 1998 Barb and I boarded our flight to Vancouver and then continued on to Toronto. During our time on the aircraft I felt very strange, but it was difficult to say just what the problem was, just that something definitely was not right. Normally we both enjoyed traveling by air, and usually spent the hours happily reading a good book, or perhaps even napping, but this trip was different.

All I could think about throughout the trip was that there was a possibility that the plane might crash, and my mind was never completely at rest, worrying about how my children would fare if something happened to us. What would happen to our store? Who would run it if we were gone? Altogether a lot of dumb thoughts kept running through my head, and no matter how hard I tried to rid myself of such absurd thoughts, they would not leave.

When the plane finally landed in Toronto I breathed a sigh of relief, and quietly thanked the Lord for watching over us, and keeping the plane in the air until we reached our destination. Of course there was still the air trip back home to think about, but I had resolved to wait until we were back in our seats before I started worrying.

In Toronto, we took a cab to our hotel, the Wyndam Bristol, which was very close to the International Gift Show Centre and was also fairly close to the airport itself. After checking into our hotel room, we unpacked and then went to the hotel restaurant for dinner. The meal was excellent and certainly lived up to its five star rating. However I did not enjoy the evening, although we both agreed that the meal was superb.

Prior to dinner we had our usual two olive martinis, and also enjoyed a bottle of fine wine during the main course. But still, I was unable to fully enjoy myself, and once again, I failed to mention the strange feelings that I was experiencing to Barb.

While we were dining I found myself looking about, and observing other people. A fellow about our age was seated at the next table with an attractive lady, whom I assumed was his wife. The couple were enjoying themselves and were engaged in an animated conversation and also drinking the same vintage wine as we were. Casually glancing their way, I noted that they were having a good time, yet at the same time, noting that I wasn't. Barb too, was very quiet throughout the meal, but strangely she never said a word about anything that might be troubling her.

While preparing for bed that night, I realized that I hadn't adjusted my watch to Toronto time yet, so I attempted to do it by moving the hands on the watch, but for some unexplainable reason, I could not figure out the time differential. Normally this was not any problem, no matter where we were or the time zone we were in; after all, it was a simple task to move the hands forward, or reverse them. But on this occasion my mind seemed befuddled, and I could not figure out the simple three-hour difference, so I asked Barb to do it for me.

The following morning we had breakfast in the hotel coffee shop.

Breakfast had always been the most important meal of the day for us, and we usually enjoyed it as much as we would any fine dinner. However, on that particular morning, our breakfast was merely a repeat of the previous night's dinner, and not at all enjoyable.

After finishing breakfast, we caught a cab to the trade show site, and immediately began making the rounds of the gift show displays. The show was very large and impressive, but it seemed that something was not quite right. Everything seemed out of focus to me, and slightly surrealistic. I felt light headed, not my usual enthusiastic self, and as the day progressed my mood continued to darken, and nothing seemed to lift me from that peculiar state.

Finally, at three in the afternoon, Barb said, "Let' go back to the hotel."

For some reason her request annoyed me, and I suggested that we wait another hour before returning to the hotel; after all, we only had three days here and we needed to keep going, but Barb explained that she was tired and would like to have a lie down before dinner. Reluctantly, I agreed to leave the show, reasoning that it would be easier to leave than argue about it. So we began looking about for a taxi to take us back to the hotel.

The complex that we were in covered several acres, and the closest cab was at the front of the building, at the opposite end of the show rooms where we were, and really a long walk for Barb as tired as she was.

As we were not familiar with the floor layout, we exited through a side door and found ourselves in an enormous parking lot with not a cab in sight. As we wandered about on the parking lot, a small passenger bus stopped close by, and the driver inquired if we would like a ride to the front of the Centre, we agreed and happily boarded the little carrier, thankful for the lift.

When we arrived at the front entrance there were several cabs waiting for fares. The area itself was very busy, and there was a constant movement of vehicles coming and going, creating a mini traffic jam. We jumped into the first cab available and gave the driver the name of our hotel. Obviously he was a little miffed that our trip was going to be a very short one, and immediately turned on the meter, well before the front door had time to swing shut. To make matters worse, the cab stood still for what seemed to be a very long time before it finally began moving.

Whenever traveling on holiday or on business the price of taxi fares was of no importance to us. We had learned to ignore the ticking sound of those little contraptions, and to enjoy the trip wherever we happened to be. But on this particular occasion, my mind was not where it should have been. I was unsettled, and somewhat befuddled, and everything that was happening had an ominous feel about it. Even the minor aggravation of a slow taxi ride was more than I could stand, and inwardly, I became upset with the driver, and by the time that we arrived at the hotel, I was in a near frenzy.

The tab was only nine dollars, but in my state it may as well have been one hundred. I pulled a ten-dollar bill from my wallet, and gave it to him in a rather thankless fashion. He muttered something that sounded discourteous, although in all likelihood it was probably my own demons that were causing me the upset and concern I felt.

After a short nap, and feeling a little better, we dressed for dinner. There was a dining guide on the side table in the room and I glanced through it, looking for a nice place to dine. There were two restaurants that caught my eye, one was a steak house called 'El Zorros,' the other was 'The Outback.' I asked Barb which one she fancied,

"Which one is closer to our hotel," she asked.

'The Outback,' I replied, it is three or four blocks down the street, and we can walk there."

"Lets go there then, I really don't feel like going too far tonight," she answered. "

"Okay," I said, " We can go to 'El Zorros' tomorrow night."

The temperature outside the hotel was quite cold, and we noticed as we walked along Dixon Road to the restaurant three blocks away that there were three or four inches of snow lying on the grassy areas along the way. The Outback Restaurant was on a flat area of land at the top of a sloping bank of snow. We stopped and looked at the bank of snow, and were tempted to climb it instead of walking a further distance to the driveway.

Normally I would have taken Barb's hand and pulled her up the slope as a lark, but this time I thought that we might look a little foolish, even though there was no traffic on either the road or the sidewalk, and so we continued walking to the parking lot entrance, and then up to the restaurant itself.

My introduction to 'The Outback' restaurant chain was in High Point North Carolina, and it was a very pleasant experience for me. On several occasions I dined there with furniture 'Rep's', and had a delightful meal each time. So my choice of restaurants on that fateful night was not surprising.

As we climbed the driveway to the parking lot, I noted that it was getting colder and almost wished that we had eaten at the hotel restaurant instead of venturing out in the cold to go to this one.

Once inside the 'Outback', we joined a group of people already in the lounging area, patiently waiting for an available table. My first thought was to leave and go back to the hotel, but the thought quickly passed, and we settled in for a fairly long wait. Patience had never been one of my greatest features, and as the time passed my mood became darker, and a little more irritable. All the while, my dear Barb sat quietly and patiently, seemingly enjoying the chatter and bustle of the restaurant.

After a length of time, a hostess asked us if we would like a seat at the bar. "Great", I said, and we followed her to the bar, and took our seats. Immediately we were asked if we would like a drink.
"Ah yes." After we each consumed a gigantic martini, with two olives, we were finally ushered to our table.

Our meal at the 'Outback' was very tasty and was accompanied by another fine bottle of Australian wine. At any other time, I would have declared the meal outstanding, but again, as at our previous meals, I was left with a strange feeling of unrest.

A $10 Taxi Ride
The Difference Between Life and Death

Barb suggested that we take a cab back to the hotel, and at that precise moment a taxi pulled up to the front door. I looked at the cab and agreed that it would be a good idea, but then the couple who had just opened the door, jumped into the back seat of the cab, which quickly drove away.

Again, irritated by the timing of that cab, and the fact that it had disappeared so quickly, I uttered the fateful words, " Let's walk back to the hotel, it will do us good."

When we stepped out of the restaurant, we both noted that the temperature had dropped even more and it was bitterly cold, and perhaps we should have called a cab after all. But, again, I said those fateful words, " Let's hurry, it's only a few blocks to the hotel."

At the bottom of the drive there was a crosswalk leading across the street. As we approached it, I thought that perhaps we should cross there and walk back on the other side, but then again, reasoning, "What would be the point," and so we continued walking toward the hotel on the same side of the street as before.

At the exact point on the sidewalk where I had considered climbing the snow bank on our way to the restaurant, I stopped and said, "Why don't we put up the hoods on our jackets?" The jacket that I wore was over ten years old, and I had worn it countless times before, but had never even thought of putting the hood up, because I always considered hoods to be completely useless, and quite frankly not at all 'macho'.

While packing clothes for the trip, I compared two jackets that seemed most appropriate. One, a quilt-lined leather jacket would have been fine, but for some reason I chose the other, which was made from a heavy quilted material, and which had a hood.
Strangely, the hooded jacket was the least desirable of the two. It was bulky and somewhat worn. Actually, if I am to be truthful, it was soiled and a little shoddy, but, reasoning that it would be cold in Toronto, I decided that it was the one to take.

When Barb and I stopped opposite the snow bank leading up to the restaurant, and I suggested raising the hoods on our jackets, I had no idea that this simple action would have such unbelievable consequences for us. Putting up the hoods on the jackets probably took no more than two minutes, but that short time was enough to make all the difference between life and death.

Removing my hat only took a few seconds, I then unzipped the hood and pulled it from its pouch at the neck of the jacket. By that time Barb had her hood in place and she then turned to help me with mine. She quickly tied the cord, cinching it about my neck, patted my face, and smiled up at me. In that split second I realized just how deeply I loved my Barbara.

For over a quarter of a century, ever since she had been involved in a very bad accident that almost cost her life, I had done everything possible to show her how much she meant to me, and how very precious our time together was, and just how committed I was to making every moment we had together count. When I lifted my eyes from that beautiful face, I took her hand and we then turned toward our hotel.

Suddenly I became aware of two beams of light coming toward us. The lights appeared to be separated as they might be on an aircraft. I thought that it was an airplane, and that it was flying very low, just above the ground. My first impulse was to throw Barb into the snow bank beside us, but I began to reason with myself that the plane would probably fly overhead, and that we would look pretty foolish. Those thoughts flashing through my mind likely lasted only a second or two but they are still as clear and as fresh to me now, as though they only happened yesterday.

Suddenly I felt a great fear. I was aware of no sound or pain, only a mystical sensation of watching a black velvet curtain covered with pinpoints of bright light slowly descending over me, and then total blackness. Gradually light returned, and I sensed that I was lying in the snow, my head was freezing, I couldn't move anything but my right arm. I lifted it in the air and began calling for help, I had no idea what had happened, only the realization that something terrible had occurred.

"What is it Lord, we've only come to a gift show, what is it?"

A man ran over to where I lay, took one look at me, and said, "Oh my God! I'll call 911." As he moved away I turned my head in his direction and suddenly became aware of my Barbara lying a little way off; she was very still. " Oh God! She's dead." Once again, everything returned to darkness.

My next moment of awareness occurred as I was being placed in an ambulance, I asked the attendants where my wife was. One of them said, "She's okay, we've taken her to another hospital." "She's dead, she's dead," were the only words I uttered before sinking back into that dark, black place.

At some point nurses took me to have a CAT scan. As they placed me on the sliding carriage, I awoke. The nurse told me that I was going into the machine for just a few minutes and asked me if I would be all right.

"Oh yes, I'll be fine," I said, but as I slid into the tubular machine, I was overcome with the frightening thought that I was in a coffin. I tried to remain calm, but when I opened my eyes the grim view of the ceiling, an inch or two from eyes was more than I could handle, and I passed out.

My recollections are not necessarily in chronological order, for everything was surrealistic and muddled. But I do remember police officers standing at the foot of my bed and asking me if I knew my name. Funnily, my mind returned to that day many years before, when a police officer had asked me that same question, and I had confidently informed him that I was Clifford.

This time however, I was not so confident, I knew that I had been seriously injured, but I did not know how or why. I asked the officer what had happened. He was very kind, but his voice faltered as he explained that I been run down by a drunk driver. I asked how fast he was traveling when he hit us.

The question I asked may have seemed a little strange to the policemen, but I was still trying to figure out why I had thought that it was a plane coming toward us, and not a car. After all, we were walking along the side of a main road, and the normal thing would have been to recognize it as an approaching car. This thought puzzled me for a long time, and it was only some months later that my son Michael informed me that the drunk was driving a pick-up truck at a very high speed, and had driven over an arched bridge that covered a railway line, and at the moment that I first saw him, he was likely airborne.

When the officer asked me if I knew who I was, I informed him that my name was Clifford Clarke, and I lived in Mill Bay, British Columbia, and my address was 3191 Mutter Road, my telephone number was 743-4083 and finally, they should inform my daughter Marlene Willock at 743-7993, who lived across the road from me.

Each time that I regained consciousness my thoughts were worse than any nightmare. All I could think about was that this terrible thing had happened because we had not taken a taxi back to the hotel, and the horrible rationalization that, if we had taken a measly ten dollar taxi ride, my beloved Barbara would still be alive.

Lying on that bed in the intensive care unit at Sunny Brook Hospital in Toronto, listening to the various machines whirring and thumping and keeping me alive, was beyond anything that I had ever imagined. The feeling of intense pain in my legs, the vice that seemed to grip my entire body and the grief of knowing that my Barbara was gone, was more than I could bear. I was constantly asking for my Barbara, and not understanding why no one would answer my questions. During those hours, I repeatedly tore the tubes from my mouth and nose, and finally my right arm, the only moving part of my body, was strapped to the bed.

When I awoke and discovered that my right arm was no longer movable, I experienced total despair. My legs seemed to be chained to a post in the centre of the bed, the pain throughout my body was excruciating, in spite of heavy sedation. It seemed that there were tubes protruding from every part of my body. The ceiling was swaying in time to the noise of the machines. The walls appeared to be made of chocolate and covered with grotesque faces, slowly oozing down toward me. I had no doubt that Hell would have been a picnic compared to this.

At one point when I opened my eyes, I saw my children standing at the foot of the bed. They were smiling at me as though part of a dream. I thought that I had died and was in heaven looking down on them. But they started speaking to me, asking me how I felt, telling me that everything was going to be all right. The joy of seeing my beautiful children standing so close to me lifted my spirits beyond any pain and grief. I could find no words to express my love for them, and once more I slipped away to that dark place.

During my semi-conscious moments I remember hearing the words that I was going to be paralyzed for the rest of my life, never able to walk again. But the possibility of not walking again seemed insignificant compared to the overwhelming grief I felt knowing that I would never see my Barbara again. The accident happened around 8:00 p.m. Toronto time, approximately 5:00 p.m. Mill Bay time

My Family is Informed

At 11:00 p.m., a policeman knocked on Marlene's door. She and her husband Bernie were in their night dress and ready to retire. The constable asked her if her parents were traveling in Toronto, "Yes" she answered. "I'm terribly sorry," he said, "But there has been an accident, your mother did not make it and your father is not expected to live the night."

The shock of hearing this news must have been unimaginable for Marlene and Bernie but, knowing that every moment was important, Bernie quickly phoned Leck Bekesza, a close friend and pastor of their own church. Leck came over to the house and spent the rest of the night ministering to the family. Bernie then phoned my other children, his own mother and dad, my brothers and sisters, and all the other people that he felt needed to know. He arranged for his mother Josie, to pick up Marilyn and Michael and to drive them up to Mill Bay, and then phoned a travel agent he knew, and asked them to arrange for a flight to Toronto for Marlene, Marilyn, and Michael.

When Marilyn received the phone call, she was just finishing some painting in her condo in Victoria, and was still up. Bernie told her that there had been an accident and that she should sit down. He then gave the phone to Marlene.

The devastating news left her in a profound shock. Her partner was in Vancouver on a business course and she was alone in the condo. Her mind was numb, she felt completely helpless, she could not think of what she should do next, except that she had to phone her partner and let him know that she was leaving for Toronto right away.

After reaching him in Vancouver and giving him the news, he gently walked her step by step through all the things that she must do before her ride arrived. He continued guiding and counseling her until Bernie's mother Josie arrived. They then drove over to Michaels home and picked him up.

At 5:00 a.m. my children were driven to the Victoria airport where they boarded a plane for Vancouver. Once there, they continued their long, painful journey to Toronto. The Toronto police faxed the plane and informed them that they would be meeting the plane. When they landed two officers in plainclothes escorted them through the airport and then drove them to the hotel where they had made arrangements for them to stay, and remained with them until Barb's sister and her husband took over for them.

At 1:30 a.m. Tamarindo time in Costa Rica, Bernie phoned Maureen. She and her family were living in Costa Rica at that time, and had recently accepted an offer on their property there. Bernie informed her that there had been an accident but then faltered and, unable to continue, turned the phone over to Marlene.

During the early morning hours, Maureen managed to contact the owner of the local airline that serviced the sleepy village of Tamarindo, only to find that the plane was fully booked. Knowing that she had to get to San Jose immediately, she went to the open field that served as the Tamarindo Airport, at 7:00 a.m. hoping to persuade some passenger to give up a seat for her. Unfortunately, no one would give up a seat. Desperate, she approached a small plane parked at the edge of the field, and asked the pilot if he would fly her to the San Jose airport, so she could catch a flight to Houston, Texas and then on to Toronto.

The pilot said, "Hop in." He then taxied to the other end of the rough field, and with no more fanfare, lifted off for San Jose.

Bernie had arranged for the flight out of San Jose at 2:00 p.m., and had also arranged for a connecting flight from Houston to Toronto. Maureen was in such a state, that she did not think to bring anything other than the clothes on her back. The fact that she was flying into a very cold part of the world did not enter her mind at all.

During the flight to Houston Maureen sat stunned, unable to think clearly. There would be a maximum of forty five minutes to make her connecting flight once in the Houston Airport and she had no idea what to do once she arrived there. In a near panic, she related the details of the accident to a flight attendant, who radioed ahead asking for assistance. When the plane landed in Houston her mind was in a fog, she was completely lost, she had no idea where she was, where she was going or how she was going to get there.

Standing in the centre of that enormous airport must have been the most frightening experience of her life, but suddenly she became aware of a woman coming toward her and calling her name.

"Are you Maureen Bundy?" the woman asked.

"Yes!" said Maureen, and without another word the lady took Maureen by the hand and literally ran with her in tow, through the crowds, and past the immigration cues, and to her connecting flight to Toronto.

Incredibly, Maureen's passport had expired but in the rush and excitement no one had noticed that very important detail, including Maureen herself. I can only believe that this was just one of the countless blessings that the Lord had laid out for my family and me during this long and difficult journey.

That particular flight was very rough, as it encountered a lot of turbulence along the way. However Maureen took little notice of the shaking and bouncing of the craft, not really caring whether the plane crashed or not; for her, nothing mattered anymore. When the aircraft arrived in Toronto at 11:00

p.m. Monday, her three siblings were there to meet her.

"Where is your coat?" they asked, "It is minus forty degrees here, you'll freeze."

When Maureen stepped out into that frigid air that night, she almost passed out with the shock. When she left Tamarindo the temperature had been almost forty degrees Celsius, and there in Toronto it was minus forty degrees.

Barb's Sister and Brother-in-Law Arrive

My brother-in-law Art, and Barb's sister Marion arrived from Montreal shortly after receiving the sad news, and had made contact with Marlene, Marilyn and Michael at the airport. During their stay in Toronto, the two acted as both guide and chauffeur for the group. Though suffering greatly from the loss of her sister, Marion and her husband Art had offered their support and strength for the family, and also arranged for suitable clothing for Maureen through her daughter-in-law, who happened to be Maureen's size.

When the family first saw me, they did not recognize me. Evidently my injuries had disfigured my normally pleasant facial features, and created somewhat of a monster in the process. My back was broken in three places, causing spinal cord damage that resulted in my paralysis. My legs were fractured in several places and required extensive surgery to save them. A steel rod was inserted in my left leg and the right leg had been built up with enough metal to resemble the Eiffel Tower. This intricate maze of ironwork subsequently became infected, eventually requiring further surgery.

My left arm had been fractured and required a steel reinforcing tube to stabilize it. Although not recognized at the time, my left rotor cuff had been badly torn, rendering my left arm completely useless. A long gash above my eye was not a pretty sight. My nose was broken, and the tubes that had been inserted into it, must have caused a great deal of discomfort, which probably explained why I kept removing

Brother-in-law Art and Barb's sister Marion

them against the doctors orders.

The numerous tubes that had been inserted down my throat and into my stomach in order to drain the flow of blood that resulted from my internal injuries probably frightened my children more than anything else.

There was a large container standing behind my bed, which held the 'coffee grounds' that were being removed from my stomach. The very name suggests that the contents of the container were not all that bad but, coffee grounds or not, they were not a pleasant sight.

My nephew Robert happened to be passing through Toronto that day, and came to visit me, but was unable to approach my bed due to the sight of the many tubes and machinery that surrounded the bed. His brother Barry was also there. He came right up to me and held my hand. I became so excited that the monitors attached to my body went berserk, setting of all sorts of alarms, which brought the nurses running.

All the faces of my loved ones seemed to float back and forth and in and out of my consciousness during those early days in Sunny Brook Hospital. There were so many operations being performed on me that first week, that my children lost track of them.

Senseless tragedy halted happiness

My wife Barbara and I were visiting Toronto on Jan. 25, 1998, to attend a gift show. In the evening we dined at a restaurant near the airport.

After dining, we decided to walk the two blocks back to our hotel. We stopped to adjust the hoods on our jackets. We stood there for the two or three minutes it took to arrange the hoods, then my wife playfully touched my face and smiled up at me.

It was the last time I was to see that lovely face.

As we started to walk hand-in-hand toward our hotel, a vehicle driven by a drunken driver suddenly veered on to the sidewalk and struck us. My wife was severely injured and died moments later.

Letter Of The Day

PHOTO SUPPLIED BY CLIFFORD CLARKE

LIVES SHATTERED: Clifford and Barbara Clarke were happily married for 47 years when a tragic accident stole her life and left him in a wheelchair.

My injuries included two fractured legs, a fractured back with spinal cord injuries that left me a paraplegic.

My left arm was shattered with muscles of the rotor cuff torn off. My head was badly lacerated and my nose broken.

For the past year, I have struggled through physical pain and mental anguish trying to make sense of this senseless tragedy that robbed me of my wife and left me in a wheelchair.

Each day I think of my wife and all the wonderful things that we did during our 47 years of marriage and all the things we were going to do in the coming years.

We had so many plans, so many walks, so many quiet moments to look forward to.

Now my world of happiness has come to a halt.

Each moment of each day, I think of my lost love and try to make sense of this sad trick of fate.

As I struggle through my everyday chores, I remember the joy of walking and of running.

At 64, I took great pride in my physical strength and endurance and my ability to handle all things.

Great joy enveloped me each time I looked upon my wife and partner, each time we held hands while walking, each time we dined or shared a glass of wine.

When I close my eyes at night, I think of my love and pray that she is in the arms of our Lord.

Each morning when I awake I reach out to the side of the bed that now lies empty and ask why has she been taken away; what did she ever do to deserve this; what did I ever do to deserve this?

My only hope is to one day see my love again when it is my time to see the Lord.

The great tragedy is that one inconsiderate person refused his wife's pleading not to drive and to take a taxi home.

Though I live a long way from Toronto, each day I relive that moment of hell and wonder if the person or persons responsible for this act ever think of the lives that have been destroyed or of the dreams that have been extinguished.

CLIFFORD C. CLARKE
Mill Bay, B.C.

Toronto Star
January 26, 1999

Pastor Bob Holmes Visits Me

During those first few days I suffered greatly from hallucinations and nightmares. Bob Holmes, formerly a pastor of the Central Baptist Church in Victoria, was living and pastoring in Toronto and was asked to visit me and minister to me.

The first question I asked him was, "Where was God when this happened? I had always believed in the Lord, I always said my prayers each night before going to sleep. For many years I asked God to watch over and bless Barb and me, to allow me to take care of her, to allow us a long and happy life together, to allow me to make up for all the many years that I had neglected her. How could God have abandoned me like this?"

Pastor Holmes told me that sometimes it was very difficult to understand the ways of God, and why things like this happened, even to those who believed in Him and His son Jesus Christ. But somehow, if we remained faithful, if we allowed His love and Spirit to enter our hearts, God would heal those wounds, and set us free.

Though I tried to understand or at least to accept my situation, bitterness crept into my heart, filling it with such pain and grief there was no room left for God.

Pastor Bob was a wonderful person of Faith, though practically crippled him self, and forced to walk with two canes. He visited me often, doing his best to ease my pain and grief, and somehow, ignoring his own pain, he made me feel much better for those visits.

Several days passed before the doctors had completed all the operations that had to be performed on me, and the next step was to get food into me. One morning I was aware of a nurse trying to feed me porridge, telling me that I needed to get something into my stomach. My four children were still with me, spending every moment possible at my bedside. Even though having to witness my suffering, they were quite confident that I would make it.

The nurse was doing her best to get me to swallow a spoonful of porridge, " Now Mr. Clarke, be a good fellow and take this spoonful, it is very good for you."

Having no appetite for anything, much less food, I looked at her standing there, holding a spoon full of something close to my mouth. My thoughts turned to an advertisement that I had seen many times on television. A boy was encouraging his dour Scot father, to try a new kind of porridge instead of his regular fare. He swallowed a spoonful, looked at his son and growled.

The words that he uttered, came to me, and I said in my best Scottish brogue, " It's not Oatmeal!"

Everyone present laughed, and one of my children said, " Dad's back." After spending several days in the care unit, I was taken to a private room so that my children could tend to me more easily. For some reason I thought that they had placed me in a bed in the parking lot. I was sure that I could hear the cars driving back and forth, and I swear that I was close to a concrete pillar that supported the structure.

That pillar was a constant source of interest to me, and I was sure that it was corroded around the base, and was badly in need of repair. Being a former carpenter and contractor probably accounted for this interest that I had in the condition of the pillar. For some time, I occupied myself devising ways to repair the base of the support; always aware that if I could not repair it, there was a good possibility that the whole structure would collapse.

On one occasion when Pastor Bob Holmes visited me, I spent most of our time together, describing the fractures in the base of the pillar, and the problems that I had encountered, trying to repair it.

Bob was very helpful in helping me to solve the problem of the concrete support, but then he was also a tower of strength when I informed him that I had just purchased an entire monastery that was filled with antiques including, oak, Jacobean furniture, and numerous hand carved pews.

One day, after experiencing a vivid dream, or perhaps better described as surviving a nightmare, I was certain that I had purchased a four storied building and I was trying to stock it with furniture in time for the next day's half price sale.

Bob Holmes happened to drop by to see me that particular day and, as a he had on several other visits, managed to set my mind at ease regarding the sale, and was also able to convince me that the sale and the four storied furniture store was likely just a bad dream after all. Gradually, as the days passed, I became more lucid, and eventually I was able to hold a fairly sensible conversation with Bob and others, without drifting off to never-land.

Marilyn and Maureen Leave for Home

Marilyn and Maureen were only able to stay in Toronto for ten days or so. Maureen had to return to Costa Rico to complete the sale of their home, and Marilyn had to get back to Victoria to organize my affairs and tend to her own.

Michael and Marlene stayed for the three weeks that I was in Sunny Brook Hospital, caring for me and watching over me as a mother hen watches over her chicks. During those days there were many tests and procedures that had to be carried out to ensure that I was doing okay.

One day I was taken down to a little room that seemed to me to be in the hospital's boiler room. Someone was going to look into my stomach to see how everything was healing. My feelings about having more invasive procedures, such as forcing what seemed to be a large camera down my throat did not sit well with me, and evidently I informed the doctor just how I felt about his camera and what he should do with it.

The doctor may not have been in the best of spirits when I had that discussion with him, for he informed me that if I didn't want to have my stomach checked , then I could go back to my room. He assured me, however, that the procedure would not hurt me, and that it was necessary for my health to go along with him in this instance.

Opening my mouth, he proceeded to squirt some foul tasting concoction down my throat. This completed, he then tried to slide what seemed to be a monstrous object down my throat. My subconscious mind did everything possible to stop this process; evidently it had not recovered from the previous two week's continual barrage and frontal assaults, and was doing its best to thwart the doctor. Finally, the procedure completed, the doctor informed me that I had two large ulcers in my stomach, and that they would have to be treated.

Throughout the course of this medieval form of torture, I had the feeling that the doctor and nurses had not been informed of the extent of broken bones that I had incurred, and were not aware that every movement of my body produced varying degrees of excruciating pain. Of course, in all fairness to the hospital staff, one should also remember that I had not fully recovered my faculties at that point and everything done to me seemed to be surreal, and part of an unhappy dream.

Marlene Exerts her Authority

When I informed my guardian angel Marlene that I felt like a bag of potatoes that was being carelessly tossed about, she took matters into her own hands and called the head nurse and her staff in for a round-table discussion. She evidently informed the group that I was her only father, and no one was going to roughhouse me in any way, shape or form.

Thereafter, the nurses attended me with the same love and attention that I had received from my dear mother, those many years ago. Although, it may also have been the fact that each day I was becoming more and more aware of the kindness and gentleness that everyone lavished on me.

On at least one occasion, I informed my doctor that I truly appreciated the care and attention that everyone so willingly gave me and how I was more than impressed that they had been able to take a bag of old, broken bones, such as I was, and put me together again. He graciously admitted that it was his job.

One morning, that same doctor, accompanied by a nurse, ran a series of tests on me to ascertain just how much feeling or movement I had in my lower body. The paralysis reached from above my belly button, right down to my toes. The doctor poked and prodded me with both the sharp point and the dull end of a safety pin. I did my best to feel which end of the pin he was using, hoping to tell him that I had some sensation. Though I concentrated with all my being, I was unable to feel or move any part of my lower body. When he was finished with his needlework, he looked at the nurse and shook his head. That gesture irritated me to no end, and I vowed to myself that he was wrong and I was going to prove it

Preparing for Barb's Funeral

As the days passed, the subject of a funeral for Barb was raised. I was adamant that there would be no funeral unless I was there beside her. Unfortunately, as it was pointed out, I was in no condition to travel, or even sit up in a wheelchair, owing to my broken back and legs etc.

With my usual flair, I informed the nurses that I had to be able to sit up in a wheelchair for at least five hours, and furthermore, they had one week to accomplish the task. Immediately, the nurses began my wheelchair training, and so began one of the most difficult stages of my rehabilitation.

A metal jacket had been molded to fit my body and was strapped in place. The contraption was probably the most uncomfortable piece of equipment that I had ever been forced to wear. When strapped into the device, I was able to sit up for a few minutes, however, at the end of that short period, I would collapse and have to be returned to my bed.

Getting in and out of bed was incredibly difficult. First the metal vest, which I referred to as the 'Iron Maiden', was strapped around my chest. This process took a considerable amount of time, as at least three attendants were necessary to turn or lift me. All the effort was accompanied by much grunting and groaning, most of which came from yours truly. Finally a lifting device, equipped with a plastic sling, was used to accomplish the feat.

The sling was placed under my rump, and two flaps were placed under my legs, and then the contraption would then lift me up and swing me outward, leaving me hovering above the wheelchair. The weight on my numb legs was agonizing, and caused me to make a few acerbic comments to the assembled crew.

Slowly I was lowered until I settled onto the chair seat. Once more or less comfortably seated, Marlene or Mike would push the wheelchair about the room and then out the door, and down the hallway. On the first trip down the hall, I held out for about seven minutes and then I made it known that it was time to be put back into my bed.

Surprisingly, the nurses and attendants who helped me with this exercise were extremely patient with me, and encouraged me and helped strengthen my resolve, and never complained about the time and effort that they expended for me. My kids, Marlene and Michael spent every minute with me, helping me with all my daily routine, and in their in-between-time, went about the hospital offering comfort to others.

There was a wonderful lady in charge of my case, and making the necessary arrangements to secure transportation back to Victoria for me when the time came for me to leave Sunny Brook. The first thing that she had to decide was who would be paying for my flight back home.

My children had not given much thought to immediate financial matters, other than talking with a firm of lawyers in downtown Toronto about handling my case, and money to pay for such things as my airfare home was the last thing that anyone had even thought about.

The lady, however, was well aware of the potential costs involved, and after consulting with the kids, phoned my automobile insurance company, ICBC, in Victoria, and informed them that I was one of their clients, and that I had been involved in a terrible accident in Toronto.

She told them that I needed to be flown back home by private jet, as it would be all but impossible to get me onto a commercial flight. The cost of the flight would be in the neighbourhood of $25,000. Without a moment's hesitation, the gentleman in charge of the department that handled out of province claims gave her the okay to send me home, regardless of costs.

Throughout all my dealings with ICBC, from that time right up to the present, I have been treated with the utmost respect and fairness, and have always found a sympathetic and caring reception whenever dealing with the company.

After three or four days of painful trips in the wheelchair, the final one lasting twenty minutes, I was informed that my flight back to Victoria had been booked with a company operating out of California, and I would be leaving the next day. Finally, after three weeks in Toronto, I was going home.

In the back of my mind was a thought that, once I escaped Sunny Brook I was in the clear, and all I had to do was get well, and after that I'd be back on my feet in no time. But first, I had to take care of Barb's funeral

My Trip in a Lear Jet

As I was wheeled across the tarmac toward the Lear Jet waiting to take me home, my thoughts were racing, I could smell fresh air and it was wonderful. The jet itself was very small. The inside seemed less than six feet in circumference, and probably no longer than fifteen feet. The stretcher that I had to lie on, in the jet was barely fifteen inches wide and I was securely strapped in, but I did not mind in the slightest, I was on my way.

There were back-to-back seats for the paramedic and the nurse who would be looking after me during the trip. Across the back there was a single seat suitable for only one passenger. For this reason, my son Michael had decided to fly home by Air Canada the previous day, and let Marlene fly back with me in the Lear jet.

When I was strapped into place, the paramedic and the nurse began attaching all sorts of electronic gadgets to me, and then connecting them to a monitor. My first impulse was to tell them that they would not need that paraphernalia, as I would be just fine. But, figuring that they probably knew best, I kept my thoughts to myself.

The pilot, co-pilot, nurse and paramedic, had flown from California to Florida that very morning, in order to drop off a patient there. They then flew to Toronto to pick me up for the flight to Victoria. They informed me that after dropping me off they would continue their flight back to California, and hopefully get back home in time for a little sleep.

The Lear Jet took off with a roar, climbing to an altitude above thirty thousand feet in just a few minutes. The sensation was exhilarating and I was literally on cloud nine the whole time in the air during that leg of the journey.

The first leg of the journey took us to Fargo, North Dakota, where the plane was refueled. During our stop there, I had to go through customs, but as it would have been very difficult to get me off the plane, the customs officer came out to me. This was indeed a blessing, as it was sub zero temperature outside.

After a thirty or forty minute pit stop in Fargo, we again took to the skies but on this part of the trip we flew even higher and reached an incredible forty thousand feet. It was almost like going on a space voyage in a cigar tube but, to tell the truth, I never really wanted to go to space, or even come close, unless it was my time to go and the Lord was calling me.

At some point, while streaking through the earth's atmosphere above the forty thousand foot mark, my mind suddenly took a nosedive, and I began to slip into a coma like state. The sensation was quite frightening; it felt like I was walking among sand dunes on the hottest desert imaginable. My tongue was parched, the heat was oppressive and in desperation I took refuge in a metal box in the middle of a vast expanse of sand and sun. As soon as I entered the box, the door closed, and I was certain that the next step would be straight into Hell.

At the moment I slipped into the coma, the equipment that I was attached to evidently started chattering wildly, which brought Marlene and the two attendants to their feet. Immediately the couple began restorative procedures that scared the very devil out of Marlene, but managed to bring me back from wherever I was. Upon awakening I realized just how fortunate I had been having those two Angels on board, and how shocking it must have been for Marlene to see me losing consciousness.

The rest of the trip to Victoria seemed to take forever, but at long last the wheels of the jet touched down on the runway of the Victoria International Airport. Transferring me from the plane to an ambulance took quite some time, as I was not nearly a cheerful or as helpful as I had been when we left Toronto. The paramedic, the nurse, as well as the pilots, accompanied me to the hospital, for I was their responsibility until I was officially handed over to the hospital staff.

Driving to the Victoria General Hospital from the airport was agony. I did not know what to expect, where the hospital staff would place me once I was there, or even if they had a place for me. Fortunately my daughter Marilyn was a nurse at the Vic General, and had managed to pull enough strings to get me admitted and into a private room no less.

Before leaving Toronto, Marlene asked me if some of the family could meet me when we arrived at the hospital, and I readily agreed. When the ambulance arrived at the hospital I was unloaded and then wheeled in through the main entrance, accompanied by the two pilots, the paramedic and the nurse.

As we entered the lobby, I noticed that there was a crowd of people lined up against the wall. After a few moments I began to recognize faces, and suddenly, I realized that all those people were there to see me, and overcome, I began to cry. In what seemed to be slow motion, I was wheeled down the row of smiling, crying faces, and each and every one of those friends, and family members, reached out and hugged me as I went by.

The poor attendants were doing their best to get me into admitting and out of their hands, so they could continue their journey back to California. But bless their hearts, they patiently allowed each and every one to hug and kiss me, and by the time we reached the end of the line they too were crying. When the four jet people finally bid me goodbye, they hugged and kissed me as though they were leaving a close friend behind. I felt the same toward them. Everything was a blur from that point on. I was immediately taken to my private room, where the head nurse asked me if I wished to see the people who were still waiting outside my door. My reply was, "Absolutely!"

For the next two or three hours a continual parade of loving friends and family visited me in my room. My heart was bursting with love for each and every one of them, and I did not want the time to end, but finally the head nurse put her foot down, and said, "I am very sorry Mr. Clarke, but this has got to stop. You must rest."

My reply to the nurse was just as emphatic, I said, "The love of all these people is what is keeping me alive, without them I would be lost, please be patient with me."

My daughter Marilyn knew most of the nursing staff on the floor where my room was, and persuaded everyone to humour me a little. Marilyn's string pulling efforts were a perfect example of, 'It's not who you are, but who you know' philosophy, and is likely the main reason that I got away with so much during the three or four days I was there at the 'General'.

Final Days Adjusting to the Wheel Chair

While I was staying in the Victoria General I managed to take a few trips in a wheelchair. These excursions were not at all enjoyable, but were absolutely necessary for me to strengthen my back and condition myself so that I could remain in an upright position for at least five hours.

Trying to fit wheelchair therapy into my day was difficult, as there was a constant stream of visitors through my room from morning until night. Many of those visitors were old friends that I had not seen for many years, and we shed many a tear during those visits. Many of those wonderful people were relatives of Barb's, including her beloved brother Wally, which made it doubly difficult for me, as I had to console them as much as they consoled me.

Several doctors and specialists, encouraged by Marilyn, visited me and kindly helped to ease my pain and concerns. Strangely, I had not contacted my own doctor in Shawnigan Lake, and for some reason I completely overlooked him, until he came to see me while I was in the GF Strong Unit in Vancouver.

Time never fully registered with me in the early days after the accident, and I never really knew just how long I was in any one hospital, but after a relatively short time at the Vic General, I was transferred to the Gorge Road Hospital for rehabilitation therapy in preparation for my next stop, the GF Strong Spinal Cord Injury Centre in Vancouver. There again, I was not sure if the therapists were aware of the extent of my injuries, for it seemed to me that I was given some exercises that were very difficult to perform. In retrospect however, I realize that everyone must have been aware of my plight, and everyone cheerfully did his or her best to help get me into condition for the wheelchair endurance test, which was yet to come.

My bed was in a ward with three other men. The constant stream of visitors continued unabated during my short stay in the Gorge hospital, and once again nurses began to wonder where all these people were coming from but I was treated like visiting royalty by all the staff, particularly the head nurse. She and I got along especially well, and she spent far more time with me than she was probably supposed to. Of course she knew what lay ahead for me, and her heart was filled with compassion. To this day I am not sure how long I spent in the Gorge Road Hospital, although I suspect that it was at least a week.

The Funeral

Barb's funeral had been set for February 27, 1998, one month and two days after her death. Both Marlene and Bernie were members of the Central Baptist Church while they lived in Victoria, and so arranged for the funeral to take place there.

The service was to include a eulogy from Marilyn, Maureen and Michael, and Marlene would sing two songs, 'You'll Never Walk Alone', and 'Wind Beneath My Wings'. Knowing how difficult it would be to control her emotions, I suggested that she pre- record the songs on a tape, and we would have them played for her.

Two days before the funeral, a tape recorder was set up in the nurse's lounge on the main floor of the hospital. That particular room was the only space available in the building, but it was suitable and we were able to accomplish the task. Taping those two songs proved to be very difficult for everyone in the room, and many tears flowed that day, from all of us.

Finally the day of the funeral arrived. A group of nurses was assigned to me with the express purpose of getting me up and ready. A suit, shirt, tie etc. were brought to me, and then the crew set to work cleaning me up, and dressing me. Once all the protective under garments were in place, the metal breastplate was strapped around my chest, which more or less helped me to sit upright. Dressing me in a shirt, tie and suit, as well as shoes was a formidable task, but the team succeeded and finally, I was ready for the ordeal ahead.

A special van, fully equipped to handle wheelchairs, was waiting at the front door for me, and I was loaded on by way of a platform hoist, and then the wheelchair was securely buckled to the floor of the vehicle. That van had been loaned to us for the full day at no charge. The owner of the rental company had heard about the accident, and wished to help out in any way he could.

The Central Baptist Church on Pandora Avenue was almost filled when I arrived that day. The church itself was adorned with baskets of flowers and looked absolutely beautiful. A feeling of love and warmth seemed to surround me as I was wheeled down the aisle to the front pews. When the service began, the church's Pastor spoke about the mysteries of life and how we are sometimes faced with unbelievable trials that defy explanation. But if we would trust our Lord, our pain and suffering would someday be taken away or at least understood.

Listening to those eloquent words spoken by that fine man did help to ease my pain, and I fully realized that the key to my healing rested in not my own hands, but in the hands of our Lord and Savior. Yet, somehow, there was a void in my innermost soul; I felt that I had been let down, even abandoned by God.

Evidently, feeling let down and abandoned in this type of situation is not unusual. In my case I always felt that God was with me. I prayed each night for good health and the ability to watch over my wife, and asked that we be allowed many more years of happiness. So when this terrible thing happened to Barb and me, I did feel cheated.

My children Marilyn, Michael and Maureen, spoke straight from their hearts, about their mother, and the love they felt for her, and I was so proud that they were able to convey their loss so clearly and so eloquently. When Marlene's voice filled the church with her songs, "You'll Never Walk Alone," and "Wind Beneath My Wings", my Spirit was lifted up, as though by God's Hands, and I gave thanks for the gift of my precious children.

An old friend of the family, Stanley Martin, a singer with a magnificent voice, had offered to sing the Lord's Prayer at the service. As his incredible voice filled the church, I thanked God for this wonderful man.

Following the hearse that carried Barb to the cemetery was the most difficult part of the day for me. The hustle and bustle of life along the streets continued as though nothing unusual had happened. Cars were full of happy, laughing couples going about their lives; children were chasing one another along busy streets. Everything appeared quite normal, yet for me, my life was as good as over. We were taking the lady that had been part of my life for almost fifty years to a cemetery; this was to be the final farewell.

Many of my relatives had been interred in the Royal Oak Burial Park over the years, and I was quite familiar with the surroundings, and had attended many services there. But this time it was entirely different. This was not just a relative, this was my Barbara, and there was no relief or closure for me. As she was lowered into that cold grave, I wanted to be with her, I did not care that

I still breathed, that I still had life. My place was with her. The finality of the words spoken at the graveside left me completely drained and all I wanted at that moment was my bed. The trip back to the Gorge Hospital remains a blur, but as I was being wheeled back to my ward, I glanced at a clock on the wall, and noted that I had been away exactly five hours.

The GF Strong Rehab Centre

A day or so later, I was informed that there was a bed available for me at the GF Strong Spinal Cord Centre in Vancouver, and I was to be moved there on March 2, 1998. Though it meant being away from my family for several months, I was quite anxious to go the GF Strong unit, for I was under the impression that I could overcome the paralysis once all my bones had healed. Little did I know just how devastating spinal cord injury could be, and just how permanent the resulting damage to my spinal cord would be.

In the back of my mind, I imagined that the GF Strong was a hospital and a place where people with the will would be fixed up and back walking in no time. I assumed that the GF Strong unit was a place where I would be healed, a place where I would learn to walk again even if it meant a few more operations to get things working right.

Actually the function of that hospital is to teach injured people how to cope with their injuries, so that they can carry on as normal a life as possible. And in that regard the GF Strong Unit is an incredible place. There were so many people there, young and old who had suffered crippling injuries and could not have survived without the encouragement and assistance of the highly trained staff at that remarkable place.

As soon as patients were admitted, they received a warm welcome by a member of the staff. In my case it was the head nurse on my floor. As I later discovered, her role was to act as my chief nurse, mentor and Guardian Angel. Any question or request that needed to be answered or attended to would be directed to her, and if she was unable to answer the question or fill the need, she would find someone who could.

In the first few days of my stay there, I kept the dear lady hopping, not necessarily on frivolous requests, but on very important matters. For instance, I needed a TV, a fax line, and telephone, and a bed by the window, so that I could see what was happening in the outside world, a desk to store the many books given me by dear friends, get–well cards, and all sorts of miscellany collected over the previous weeks, plus a lap top computer that my son-in-law, Bernie felt I needed to keep up with the world. Even though I had a computer at the store, I had no idea how to use it. Actually, I didn't even know how to start it up, so the laptop lay where it was for several weeks.

My assigned quarters held two beds. Separating my room from an identical one next door were two bathrooms, one equipped with a toilet and a sink, the other one a bathtub, although the tub was seldom used as most of the patients required special bathing facilities.

The main bathroom, the one that held the throne, served all four patients, in the two rooms. It was a very busy facility, for there was a constant flow of nurses, cleaning staff and orderlies carrying out their duties, and tending to the two quadriplegics in the next room as well as myself in the other room. At the beginning of my stay I was alone in the room, and that is the reason that it was possible for my head nurse to grant my request for the window bed.

On my 65th birthday, March 6th, coincidentally Marlene's birth date, our entire family came to the GF Strong unit, and helped us celebrate our birthdays. The party was set up in a special room designated for just such an event. A large cake was brought along, as well as balloons, presents and other goodies. My wonderful family did their very best to make it a special day for the both of us, but suffering as we all were from the loss of Barb and my own physical loss, it was a rather somber day.

My recovery from broken bones, was remarkably swift, but the spinal injury was painfully slow. It took me three months before I could sit up without help, and even then I needed an automatic bed to get me up in the mornings. Any movement required the assistance of at least one nurse, and I was totally reliant on the help of others for absolutely everything I did.

My life had always been one of complete independence. There wasn't anything that I couldn't do or handle by myself, or at least that is what I believed. When I set my mind to a task I found a way to complete it, come hell or high water. Finding myself in the position where I was unable to do even the simplest task without help caused me more frustration and disappointment then anything else that had ever happened to me in my life.

Here was the great Cliff Clarke, practically bed-ridden, unable to do anything for himself, needing help to wash himself, requiring assistance to go to the washroom, having to be placed in bed for the night, his legs propped up by pillows so as to avoid bed-sores, not able to turn over by himself. Life began to look hopeless.

Lying on that bed, night after night, thinking of my Barbara, crying out with grief, is something I can never forget. Some nights a passing nurse would come and sit by my bed and hold my hand. I would lay awake for hours praying for Barbara to come to me. She never did.

A friend of mine by the name of Roisin, who was living in Ireland, heard about the accident from her daughter while I was in Toronto, and immediately sent flowers and words of comfort.

This friend had a great knowledge of the Spiritual world, and had the mystical gift of clairvoyance. She had a dream a day or so after the accident. In this dream she saw Barb sitting alone, crying. When she asked her if she was all right, Barb said she was looking for Clifford but could not find him. When my friend told me about her dream, I was beside myself with grief. The thought of my Barbara being alone was almost more than I could bear. Each night, my dreams consisted of unending searches for my love.

Those dreams continue to this day, and in them I am continually searching for Barb, frequently catching a fleeting glimpse of her, often calling out to her, but never receiving an answer from her. My burning desire is to tell her that I love her, to hear her tell me that she loves me. But each and every time I get close to her, I suddenly find myself alone and lost. When I awake the pain is as fresh as it was in those first few hours when I knew that she was gone.

One of my daughter's close childhood friends was involved in a terrible accident some years before my accident. Her injuries left her in constant pain, and often in a wheelchair. She too was unable to sleep at night, due to the pain she suffered, and so she watched television until the early hours of the morning. Many times, around three in the morning I would phone her to talk, and to tell her about my day, and try to console her, trying to make sense of life's tragedies. The sound of her young voice made me realize just how fortunate I was. Here I was an old man, while she was a very young woman with her whole life ahead of her. It made me realize just how fragile life really is, and how important it is to live each day to the fullest.

My Daily Routine

My day usually started at six in the morning. I would raise myself in the automatic bed, and call for some water so that I could wash and prepare myself for breakfast. The night staff spent the hour between six and seven filling in their nighttime reports, and didn't appreciate my ringing the buzzer and asking for a bowl of water. There were one or two of the night staff who informed me in no uncertain terms that they were too busy to be bothered with getting me a bowl of water and I should wait until the seven o'clock shift took over.

There seemed to be a perfectly good reason for asking me to wait until seven. What that reason was exactly has been lost in the sands of time but, logical or not, it didn't stop me from insisting, in my normal charming way, that it be brought to me whether they were busy or not. Somehow this repeated request fell on deaf ears, and so was born the Water Conflict.

Managing to win several nurses over to my side proved to be an exciting victory. I enlisted the aid of two nurses and one Filipino cleaning lady to look after the water supply, but on their days off I was left to the whims of the other two nurses who adamantly refused me any hot water in spite of my pleas. I brought it to the attention of my head nurse, who unfortunately never worked the night shift, and therefore had no sway in the whole episode. One kindly nurse, however, did suggest that I have someone bring me a pot of water before I went to sleep, which could be left on my bed stand.

I explained that my early regime included washing every thing that I could reach, which of course included the place just below my waist, and even though it was almost entirely without feeling, it did react negatively when doused with cold water. The dear nurse offered no more advice and quickly left the room.

Trying to get someone to bring hot water to my bed each morning became an exciting game. The Filipino girl wanted to help, but she was very careful not to get caught by the opposing team, and so her contribution to the water conflict was sporadic at best. The two nurses on my team knew how the opposition felt about the situation and were also very careful not to get caught with their bedpans down. The whole silly game of cat and mouse continued throughout my four-month stay at the hospital and was never resolved. The down side was that during those months of conflict I never dared sleep past six in the morning, lest the opposing team figured that they had won by default.

During the first month of my stay at the GF Rehabilitation hospital I was waited on hand and foot. Each morning, after I had finished my breakfast, a nurse would perform the ritual of the catheter. They carried out this procedure at least four times a day, and it became so commonplace for me, I would think nothing of it. It was understood of course, that eventually I would be on my own. I did not look forward to taking matters into my own hands, and so I delayed the inevitable as long a possible.

Every second day, each patient was wheeled into the throne room for a chance to test out the plumbing. Being an early riser, I was given priority on the throne. This event is probably the main consideration that inspired me to rise early, so I could get into the bathroom as early as possible and hopefully avoid the rush.

The ritual of the catheter could not hold a candle to the throne room event. Each patient was allowed a twenty-minute head start, before the shakers and movers were brought into the scene. The shakers and movers were the nurses who had been blessed with long fingers, and strong stomachs. Not wanting to reveal the depths that this lot went to in their quest to assure a successful outcome, I can only leave the details to the imagination. But it was not unusual, for each patient to have several nurses using their digits in this process.

On one unforgettable occasion I was propped in an upright position, using a pillow to hold my back steady, and left to my own devices. After a short, but uncomfortable time, a nurse whom I did not recognize, without a word tried to work her magic on me. But unsuccessful, she left. A short time later another nurse, likewise unfamiliar to me, tried her best to assist me. But unsuccessful, she too left. Finally, a third nurse, also a total stranger approached, gloved hand at the ready. Having reached the end of my patience, I cried out, "For God's sake, what is your name."

At this point, it behooves me to relate the very short story of my good friend John who, while visiting me one day, asked if it would be okay to use the bathroom. My answer was an unequivocal yes, but he should not be too surprised if two or three nurses inserted their fingers up his bum.

As humorous, or as morbid as it may seem, relating this part of the story has been very difficult for me, due to the unimaginable degradation of the spirit and pride I have suffered due to this injury. Making light of my predicament is not meant to gloss over, or minimize my extremely difficult condition, but only an attempt to shed a little understanding on the plight and seemingly hopelessness of spinal cord victims, and at the same time reveal the humour that may be found in even the most trying situations a human can experience. The Spirit, when God given, can mend or dispel even the deepest grief.

My friend Dean and his lovely wife Marilyn often visited me during the months in the GF Unit. On occasion they would take me out for dinner or for a drive, or merely sit and chat about life in general. Dean had a delightful sense of humour, and would often bring some humorous little object to brighten my day. One day he arrived with a very large bottle, filled with white pills. The label on the outside of the bottle boldly announced that the contents were high potency Viagra tablets, and were accompanied by specific instructions for maximum benefits. After my initial shock and a few ribald comments, we all had a good laugh, and I had Dean place the bottle on the top shelf, just behind my bed.

Surprisingly few of the nurses noticed the bottle or took any notice of it, although one nurse did mutter something that sounded like," For God's sake, don't let my husband see that."

The bottle sat there for the duration of my stay in the centre, and was often a source of fun among my visiting friends, the most common comment being, "What are they for?"

My immediate reply would be, " They are given to all us old timers, it stops us from rolling out of bed at night."

As my departure date approached, I was given a final assessment by a board consisting of physio-therapists, consultant, nurses, attendants and my own Doctor Fish. Arriving early, before Dr. Fish and the others showed up. I brought out my bottle of Viagra, which I had brought along for a little fun, and placed it on Dr. Fish's desk with the label in the position facing his chair.

Shortly after, the remaining members of the board showed up and then proceeded with the assessment hearing. The session was quite informal and in my normal fashion I managed to create a good chuckle here and there, mostly by answering questions with as much humour as possible. At the end of the session, I wheeled over to Dr. Fish's desk and opened the bottle of Viagra and offered him one. Without missing a beat, he declined the offer, and said, " No thanks, they give you a stiff neck."

On my final day at GF Strong, my wonderful head nurse told me a little story. Evidently my bottle of Viagra had the whole hospital in an uproar. There was much discussion among the nurses as to the best way of handling this ticklish situation. They finally decided that the head of the pharmacy department would quietly analyze the contents of the bottle before further action was taken.

After the pharmacist had applied his analytical skills to the contents of the bottle, he announced his findings to the nursing staff. " The pills won't hurt him, they are peppermints."

A Long Painful Journey

As soon as my bones had sufficiently healed I was introduced to daily physiotherapy. In the beginning, the physiotherapists took great care to avoid further injury to the joints and muscles in my legs and back and, as a result, progress was slow and often painful. Even the simplest movement caused multiple spasms and discomfort.

Each patient was assigned a physiotherapist for a one-hour session five times a week. Most of the therapy was done on large padded platforms or benches. During those sessions I was taught to transfer from my wheelchair to the bench by sliding along a transfer board. Once on the bench I was given several types of exercises designed to strengthen my limbs and muscles. Gradually I was able to manage small movements on my own, and even though progress was very slow, each small movement was a major victory for me.

Sitting in an upright position was a challenge for me, owing to the back injuries I had suffered. But little by little, after much coaching and pampering, I managed to raise myself into the vertical position, even managing to perch on the edge of the bench for short periods, although the fear of toppling off the bench was ever-present.

Moving my legs seemed impossible at first, but after months of work and encouragement, I managed to move them ever so slightly. This of course seemed a great accomplishment for me, and so I continued, convinced that it was only a matter of time before I would have complete success.

Every therapy session was exciting for me, and I made sure that I was always early and ready to go for my programs, so that there would be no wasted time. On Saturdays, Sundays, and holidays, when the exercise rooms were closed, I would make use of a bench just outside the therapy room, doing as many exercises as I could manage by myself.

My left arm continued to be a problem, as it was impossible to lift because of the torn rotor-cuff muscles but strangely I was able to lift myself straight up from the chair by extending the arms. After two years of special exercises, I was able to lift my arm up to shoulder height, and even flick a light switch. But there was absolutely no strength in the arm for the first five years; however, it can now perform many functions satisfactorily.

Patients were encouraged to play basketball and other games in the gymnasium most days of the week, and I joined them on several occasions. It was absolutely amazing how the young people sped about the floor while chasing the ball. Somehow they managed to get their wheelchairs going at an incredible rate of speed, but I found it difficult to keep up with them, and even more difficult to catch or hang on to the ball with only one arm. Although, on one or two occasions I did get hold of the ball in my right arm and managed to hurl it through the hoop much to the delight of the other players.

Each day, many patients including myself would practice wheeling our chairs up and down ramps in the hospital, and on the sidewalks surrounding the facility. Often a group would go on a jaunt around the block or even further. These excursions were great fun, but I was usually the last over the finish line, except when accompanied by the kindly supervisors, who patiently stayed by my side.

.....What Goes on Behind Closed Doors

The Gf Strong unit was an intriguing warren of small offices and rooms, each one inhabited by a specialist, seated at a computer and seemingly very busy doing something. One day, I was informed that I would have to visit one of those little cubbyholes to answer a series of questions. Evidently someone noticed that I was often very forgetful and if I had not written it down, I would sometimes miss special appointments or forget simple everyday tasks.

I took the elevator to the correct floor, and then wheeled down a long corridor, anxiously searching for the door to the room where I would be interrogated. After much searching, I located the numbered room. Tentatively I entered, not knowing what to expect. To my surprise, a charming young woman welcomed me, and then invited me into an area where the testing was to take place.

After a period of questions and answers, the lady placed a stack of pictures before me with objects and faces on them. I did recognize most of the objects, but I had no idea whose face it was in the photographs I was looking at, not that it mattered anyway because it was not a test about whom I knew, but whom I remembered seeing. For an hour we sat looking at people and objects, all the while trying to correctly identify the faces and objects I had looked at. This was much harder than I had anticipated, for I became very confused at the parade of images that were shown me. Although some of them were correctly identified, many were merely a blur as they passed through my hands.

A series of tests continued one after the other, for a full four hours without a break. I was beginning to feel like 'Little Bo Peep who lost her sheep', being interviewed by the Spanish Inquisition. Finally the interrogation ended, the young woman thanked me for my time, and I quickly returned to the relative safety of my own quarters in the saner part of the facility.

Several days later I was called back to that little room, tucked away at the end of a long hall, and informed that the head injuries I suffered in my accident had caused damage to my short term memory, reducing it by approximately thirty five percent. This information was not a complete surprise to me, for I had suspected that something was not quite right in the gray area above my eyebrows, and I found it very difficult to remember even the simplest detail for any length of time unless it was written down in my daily reminder book. There were many occasions when a friend or relative would visit me, but I would not be able to remember who it was, or what we talked about. This of course caused me some concern and quite often embarrassment. Once I was diagnosed with a short-term memory loss, I vowed that once I returned home I would exercise my memory along with my body each and everyday.

When I first entered the GF Strong Unit, I asked the head doctor just how long I would have to spend in rehabilitation? Dr Fish, a wonderful human being, told me that I would stay just as long as I needed to be there.

My reply was, "You have until June 25th 1998 to get me ready, and I trust you'll make it."

Evidently word spread to the hospital staff that they were all on a strict timetable regarding my rehabilitation, and that they should pull out all stops for the duration of my stay. It was however, never completely clear to me whether they were working hard to help me, or actually doing their best to get rid of me. Whatever the intent, they all performed wonderfully, and kept me right on schedule.

Keeping Busy during the Week

Weekdays in the GF were better than the weekends, for there were many activities to keep us busy and involved. When the weekend arrived all the physiotherapists went their own ways, probably very happy to be away from the grind for a few days. Some of the patients went home to their families for a day or two, while the rest of the inmates did their best to keep busy whatever way possible. Fortunately, I had many weekend visitors to help while away the time. My children particularly helped me keep my sanity.

Daughter Marlene was at my side as often as possible, usually staying overnight at a facility for families of patients, that was set up in an unused ward in the Children's Hospital a block away, or she quite often stayed at the Easter Seal Hotel, a block from the GF Strong Unit. While Marlene was with me everything was fine, but when it came time for her to leave for the night, my spirits fell. Imagining her walking alone, crossing several parking lots to get to the Children's Hospital or to the Easter Seal building, was very unsettling for me, even though she always phoned to let me know that she had arrived safely.

Many friends visited me while I was at the rehabilitation centre, and their company helped me cope with the keen sense of loss I continually experienced. Many of those dear people would gather around and pray for me, asking the Lord to help me, to watch over me, to take my pain away. There is no doubt in my mind that the prayers were answered, and that God was listening, that He had not abandoned me.

Each night I would say my prayers, as I had always done, and continued to do right up to the night of the accident. Though most nights I did not feel very close to the Lord, it was as though my heart had shriveled and was incapable of feeling any joy as it had in the past years while Barb was alive. My prayers seemed to be shallow and hollow, merely mutterings of self-pity and disappointment. As hard as I tried, I could not overcome the sense of aloneness one feels when God is not a part of their lives.

In every prayer I asked God to open my heart, to take away the grief and the pain that had hardened it, but my prayers seemed to disappear into the darkness of my room, as though they were never spoken. Night after night the pain in my heart seemed to increase and lying alone in the darkened room was complete hell for me. I could not move, I could not reach my Barbara. The dark hours seemed to stretch into an endless tunnel of despair.

Another Patient Moved into my Room

Having a room to myself seemed a good thing at first, because spending time alone allowed me to grieve without having someone close-by. But gradually I began to realize that having company in the room might not be a bad thing after all.

One day, after several weeks alone in the room, my nurse informed me that there would be a young man moving in with me that day. He was a quadriplegic named Tom. He was about thirty-five years of age, had a wife and children, and had been logging for several years, and was very experienced as a faller. A year before moving into my room at the GF Strong Unit, he had an accident that paralyzed him.

At the end of a long day, tired and anxious to go home, he made a tragic mistake, a mistake that has claimed the lives of many professional loggers before him. He decided to fall one more tree before calling it quits for the day. Unfortunately the tree got hung up in another tree, and did not fall all the way to the ground. The wise thing would have been to call for a bulldozer working close by and have it pull the tree free.

Sometimes, crucial decisions that are quickly made involve our pride. In the case of Tom, he did not wish to look foolish in front of the other fallers, so, he tried to cut the tree free himself. The top of the tree was rotten, and when he cut into it, the top snapped off and fell to the ground, striking him on the head. In that instant, Tom, a healthy young man with a long life ahead of him, was rendered a quadriplegic. His spinal cord was severely damaged at the upper section of his spine, affecting every part of his body from the shoulders down.

On the day that Tom checked into the hospital, he had driven from his home near Revelstoke, alone in his specially equipped van. After he had been admitted, he was wheeled into the room where I lay, and placed on the bed next to mine. He was obviously tired from his strenuous journey, and very quiet. We did not talk that night, and other than a simple nod and hello, we said very little to each other.

The following day I thoroughly grilled him, finding out as much as possible about him, his age, his marital status, his injury level, where he came from, why had he come to the hospital now, almost a year after his accident, how long he would be with us, and a whole lot of other useful information.

His story was very moving. He had a wife and two teenage children, and had recently moved from his dream home, which he had built, into another specially equipped home, built to accommodate his special needs. The new residence was nice, but it was not the home he had constructed out of love for his wife and family. The new building was certainly wheel chair accessible with ramps to the front and rear entrances. He could comfortably access the kitchen cupboards, get into the shower by himself, and do many other simple every day tasks, but it was not the home he had dreamed of and built.

Adjusting to Spinal Cord Injury

There are so many adjustments that a person has to contend with when faced with spinal cord injury. Probably the most difficult is the realization that he or she is no longer in control of his or her own life and is reliant on others for basic needs.

Though most spinal injured people learn to look after themselves, and some even excel in sports and outdoor activities, most don't. But no matter how self sufficient one becomes, there is the overwhelming reality that we cannot do the things we used to do: walk up or down a flight of stairs, reach an item on a shelf, jump in or out of bed, travel without encountering incredible difficulties, dress oneself while standing up, and countless other basic tasks carried out by able-bodied folk. The grim reality is; life is not, and can never be, the same as it was before and no matter how hard we try to disguise it, each and every disabled person prays for deliverance.

Tom stayed at GF Strong for several weeks for re-assessment. He had been having problems with his movement and stability, and was there for some special therapy. We became very close over the weeks. He spoke of all the changes in his life since he became paralyzed, and confided his innermost thoughts.

There was an underlying sense of despair throughout our talks, and I was very concerned about his well-being and mental state. He felt that his life was not worthwhile, that his family was drifting away from him, that he was unable to participate with his family in the many activities they had always enjoyed. He felt that the only peace he was able to attain came while driving the many logging roads in the mountains above his home. There he would seek solace, often stopping on the gravel roads, opening the car door and enjoying the sun's warmth, sometimes for hours on end.

Despite his pain and the loss of much of his normal movement, Tom did the best he could to overcome the many obstacles that he faced as a quadriplegic. Even the simplest activities were often beyond his capabilities. Watching him struggle to get out of bed, watching him shave, listening to his labored breathing at night, brought tears to my own eyes. Strangely, I was no better off than he was; yet I felt his pain and his frustration. I felt the terrible loss that he had experienced, particularly the fear that his wife had become weary of the situation she found herself in, and was becoming ever more distant in her relationship with him.

It is a sad fact that many couples are unable to cope with the problems they face when one or the other of them becomes disabled. Even though there are many partners that manage to hang in there and are able to cope with the situation, there are many who tragically feel that they must opt out of the relationship, usually leaving behind a devastated and shattered partner.

In my case I had already lost my partner and, though I suffered from the pain and grief, I still had my wonderful children and friends to support and love me. My situation was quite different than my young friend, for I knew that my loved ones would never forsake, or leave me, and I was determined to carry on no matter the odds.

At that stage in my wild adventure, I still wasn't convinced that I would never walk again. The whole premise that I would be confined to a chair for the rest of my life was just not a feasible or even reasonable option. There was no way that this accident was going to rob me of both my wife and my legs. I would show the world just what I was made of. Hard work and a strong mind would surely overcome any injury that I had sustained.

Tom. on the other hand, had retreated into a fantasy world, a place where he was whole again, a place where he was secure, surrounded by a family that loved him, a place that unfortunately was not accessible to his family. After he left the GF Strong Unit, he often phoned me to keep me informed with the latest developments in his life. Sadly things did not go all that well for my friend, an operation that promised him some freedom from the bladder and bowel problems that he suffered from was not successful, and his life became even more difficult. Gradually his phone calls ceased, and my calls to him were not returned. In my prayers I asked God to watch over him, to give him some hope for the future. I pray that God heard this request, and that Tom is living in His Light.

Life in the GF Strong Spinal Cord Unit continued its normal course. I would wake up at 6:00 each morning and try to persuade some nurse or passerby to get me a bowl of hot water. On good days, one would come to my rescue; on a bad day I would have to wait till seven-thirty.

Showering was Scary

Twice a week, whether we needed it or not, an orderly would wheel us down the hall in a heavy, stainless steel wheelchair to a specially designed washroom, and assist us with a shower. This was always an interesting experience for me, as I still had great difficulty sitting up without adequate support. By that time I no longer wore the metal straight-jacket which had been assigned to me while in hospital in Toronto. It had become far too cumbersome and uncomfortable, especially after I gained back some of my lost weight. Without the jacket, sitting up for any length of time was a challenge. The first time that I had a shower I nearly toppled out of my chair. Fortunately the orderly was close by and managed to avoid a messy situation.

Trying to hang onto a slippery bar of soap, and also keep upright while doing your best to reach those out-of-the-way places, would make an incredibly funny movie, especially when only one arm is functioning properly.

The orderlies were great fellows. They had wonderful senses of humour and managed to keep us in good spirits by telling funny stories of past predicaments. These stories kept our minds off our own problems and made life a little more bearable. Getting back into bed after having a hot shower was very refreshing and helped relieve the boredom, an ever present reality of hospital life.

Learning about the Birds and the Bees

A normal weekday, filled with various programs including therapy, exercise and sex education passed by fairly quickly. One day, I was informed that I had been scheduled to have a sex lesson, which supposedly, would help me cope with my injury. The lesson would take place in one of the offices on the third floor of the hospital.

I wasn't sure why I had been chosen for this type of therapy, and I let the person that arranged the session know that I wasn't too keen on learning about the birds and bees at this stage of my life. Actually, considering my injury, there was as much chance of me reaching a successful conclusion as there would have been if they had taught me to sky dive. But, what the heck, I would do it, if only in the interest of science. Perhaps I might even be able to teach the instructor a thing or two.

Wheeling about the hospital hallways was most interesting, I often wondered just what went on behind those mysterious little doorways and one by one the little mysteries were revealed to me. The sex shop, or rather, the therapy centre, as it was officially known, was under the management of an attractive woman in her late forties. She quickly put me at ease and then proceeded with the interview.

It immediately became apparent that I was not going to able to teach this lady anything that she didn't already know. As the session progressed, she brought out a number of little gadgets and an unusual assortment of paraphernalia, all tools of her trade so to speak, and one by one explained their use and where they fitted into the scheme of things.

Ever patient, the dear lady listened to the many reasons I offered for not wanting or needing that particular type of therapy. She explained that my reluctance to involve myself in this form of therapy was very normal, and even though I did not care one way or the other about sex at this time, there could be a time when I might find it quite beneficial.

For two hours she discussed the various ways and methods spinal cord patients could live a very productive and sexually satisfying life. She recounted the many case histories of patients who were able to father children even when completely paralyzed. The amazing stories of people, both male and female, who managed to overcome even the most disabling injury was inspirational. I marveled at the power of the human Spirit and it's ability to deal with even catastrophic injuries.

The Man from Antigua

There was a young man from Antigua who moved into my room the day that Tom left for home. He had been involved in a motorcycle accident and suffered a spinal cord injury, which left him a quadriplegic. Before the accident he was in excellent physical health. He used to run several miles every day, work out in a gym, and play numerous sports.

At the time of the accident, Antigua had no rehabilitation facilities for such injuries, and so he was sent to Jamaica for therapy. Sadly, the hospital where he ended up had no useful program either, and for several months he received virtually no help at all.

After languishing for many months he lost the ability to perform even the simplest tasks. He could not transfer alone, he could not feed himself, nor use the washroom without assistance. It was impossible to dress himself. In all, he was completely reliant on other humans to tend to his daily needs. However, in the GF Strong Unit, all these simple tasks were taught, so that anyone with even modest limb movement could look after themselves.

Fortunately for this young man, an exceptional young woman from Vancouver, B.C., while living in Antigua, recognized that he needed professional help, and arranged for an assessment at the GF Strong Unit. The poor man was in such terrible shape, not only suffering neglect, but also suffering from severe bedsores, that he was admitted to the hospital and immediately enrolled in a program to tend to his sores, and to teach him basic day-to-day self-help.

This remarkable young lady raised funds to pay the costs involved in this venture, using all her own savings as well. The funds helped pay for the trip to Vancouver, and a short six-week program for her friend, and the plane tickets back to Antigua.

The change in this young man was remarkable. By the time they left for home, he was able to feed himself, and to carry out many of the tasks that were impossible for him a few short weeks earlier.

We continued corresponding, and several years later, the couple visited me on my farm in Mill Bay. She continued helping him and he continued improving, not only physically but also mentally, managing to regain the humour and cheerful outlook that he had before the accident.

It would seem that there are angels in everyone's life, even though they are not always recognized. Certainly there have been many angels that have helped me along the way, and I thank God for every one of them

Each day I became more aware of the power of my inner Spirit and how it influenced my life. Even though my body had been severely damaged in the accident, I believed that if I looked deeply into my inner self I would find a way to overcome my paralysis.

Throughout my entire life the act of overcoming adversity was an integral part of my existence and I was fully conditioned to surmounting most problems. As I had many times before I confronted this my paralysis head-on.

There was a very limited schedule of therapy assigned to the patients of the GF Strong. For me, the most important time was the single hour of each day that I would spend with my personal therapist, working on general body movement. This hour was so important to me, because it provided the only scheduled time that I could learn to move certain parts of my body. After spending months working on my legs, they gradually responded with a little movement, although the muscles controlling them often went into spasms, making it extremely difficult to make much progress.

My darling therapist was always encouraging, constantly assuring me that I could do it as long as I kept working. During our therapy sessions there was little time left to work on my left arm, so she started coming in early before her shift began so that she could work on that arm. Though progress was very slow, she always encouraged me to exercise the arm regularly.
Every day, right up to the present, I faithfully exercise my arm, and I have been rewarded with movement that I once thought impossible.

For the first months following the accident I would lie on my bed in the same position throughout the whole night. I had both feet resting on a pillow so that my heels wouldn't develop bedsores, pillows under my side to ease the stress on my back, and a bladder bag which was attached to my water works by way of a long tube, and left dangling over the side of the bed. Several times a night the nurses would stop by to see if I was okay, sometimes turning me on my side for an hour or so. Remembering how uncomfortable and miserable I was during those long painful nights, always reminds me of the great blessings that I have received and continue to receive.

Rolling over in Bed

The one great desire that I entertained during those tortuous months was the ability to turn over in bed. Whenever I had the opportunity, I would visit a different therapy room from my usual one. It consisted of several large rooms with many patients and therapists hard at work, and had many interesting pieces of equipment in it.

One of the most appealing items for me was a double bed, which sat in a far corner of the room. Each time I visited the room I would transfer to the bed, and then do my best to turn over. As simple as that particular movement appeared, to me it was a seemingly impossible task.

Week after week I would visit the room and lie on the bed. I am sure that most of the folk who observed me hard at work lying flat on my back probably thought that I was merely resting. However I was working as hard as I could to turn over and funny or not I was dead serious.

No one in particular paid much attention to me while I laboured on the bed, although occasionally some therapist would glance my way. But as they already had their hands full with their own patients, it was only a cursory glance at best. Finally, the day came that I was able to fully roll over on the bed. At that moment I let out a whoop of joy, and instantly every eye in the room was upon me.

Two therapists came running over and asked me if I was all right. I was so excited, all I could say was, "I rolled over!"

My next accomplishment came very quickly. After mastering the roll over trick, I managed to raise myself up onto my knees, and though very shaky, crawled forward a short ways before collapsing on the bench. At my next session with my own therapist, I showed off my new trick, raising myself onto my knees and crawling along the bench on all fours.

She was very pleased with my progress and said, "You'll be walking in no time."

The very next day she fitted me with a set of leg braces designed to keep the legs straight so that one could walk, albeit it very tentatively, between metal exercise bars at the other end of the exercise room.

The experience of standing on my own while holding onto the metal bars, was exhilarating, and I believed that it was only a matter of time before I would be up and running. Each day I was taught new exercises and movements, and I applied myself as never before in my efforts to get back on my feet and get my legs moving, even it was only for a few minutes at a time.

Departure Date

My departure date, which I had set for June 24, was quickly approaching and I was spending every minute possible exercising, stretching and learning to look after myself, so that I would be ready when the day arrived.

Whenever I had visitors, I would guide them around the hospital in my wheelchair, showing them the various rooms that I worked in and the equipment used for my rehabilitation. In my enthusiasm, I did not notice the look of sadness that would often come over my friends and loved ones when I rattled on about my progress and how I would soon be out of this place and home again. I am sure that most of them realized that I was probably destined to spend the rest of my life in a chair, but strangely that thought never fully occurred to me. As far as I was concerned, it was only a matter of time before I would manage to overcome the spinal cord damage and get back on my feet.

There was a steady stream of loved ones visiting me while I was in the G F Strong Unit, and I looked forward to their visits with all my heart. Many of my visitors had a strong faith in the Lord, and would spend hours speaking of his love and mercy, and how he alone could heal my hurts. They would pray for me, often with tears streaming down their faces, and I would join in the prayers, tears also flowing down my own cheeks.

At night, alone in my bed I would cry out to God, asking for his help, but somehow my heart would not fully open to him. It seemed to be shriveled and empty. An overwhelming sense of grief was always with me.

During the daytime I could manage the pain by keeping busy, but when alone at night or whenever I allowed myself to open the place in my heart where my Barbara lay, the agony would sweep over me, and the never ending, excruciating pain, would rob me of my desire to live. While I did not fully blame God for this terrible tragedy, the unrelenting pain, caused bitterness to creep into my heart, and left me with a huge knot in the place where God would normally dwell.

A month prior to leaving the hospital, I was given driving lessons so that I could better retain my freedom, and a Ford Van was ordered for me that was eventually delivered in January of 1999.

As the time of my departure drew near, a panel of my doctors, therapists, nurses, and other interested parties gathered to assess my progress and to decide whether I should be allowed to leave the centre and move back into my own home. Most of the hospital staff believed that I was ready for the move, but there were some reservations on the part of a few, that perhaps I needed more time to learn to deal with my emotions as well as my physical limitations.

They decided that I should spend several days untended in a special room, maintained for just that purpose. There I would tend to my own requirements without the assistance of the staff. Of course I could still go to the cafeteria and therapy rooms as I saw fit, and still had the freedom to roam the hospital at will.

The first night was frightening. There was no one I could call on, unless I became desperate, but I knew that this was just what the doubting Thomases would be looking for, and so I fought the urge to abort the mission, and forced myself to act as if nothing whatever was troubling me. It was probably the first time during my whole stay at GF Strong that anyone heard me whistling.

Finally June 24, 1998 arrived. Some of the staff held a going away celebration for me, and I gave them flowers and little gifts in appreciation for all the wonderful care they had given me during my stay. In spite of the joy that I felt, there was a tear or two shed that day.

Arriving home was a mixed pleasure. It was wonderful to see the homestead again, just as I had left it months before, and a joy to see all my family waiting to welcome me home, but it was strangely quiet, there was a sense of emptiness about the house. That feeling of emptiness and the accompanying loneliness never fully left me, and to this day I still experience moments of complete disbelief that Barb is no longer here.

My injuries still required full time attention, so several live-in caregivers were enlisted to watch over me, each one taking a shift to ensure my wellbeing. I was even equipped with an alarm to summon help if a care worker was not immediately available. All I had to do was press a button and a phone message was sent out to a call centre in, of all places, Toronto, indicating that I needed help. Immediately I would receive a call from the centre asking me if I was all right. If I didn't answer the call right away, they would notify 911 and an ambulance would quickly be dispatched to my home. Fortunately the ambulance was never called, for I always managed to answer the call myself and assure the operator that I was okay.

Actually I did set the alarm off a number of times quite by accident. The alarm gadget was attached to a string and worn around the neck, and was easily set off with a minimum amount of pressure. Sometimes I would inadvertently press the button while rolling over in bed, or while getting dressed, or often by accidentally dropping it on the floor and running over it with my wheelchair. After many calls from the alarm centre, I decided that I could get along without it and turned it in for a cell phone. That way I could always call someone if I was in trouble.

Getting around the house wasn't too difficult because I had many alterations done to it while I was in hospital, and most of the doorways were wide enough for my chair.

An elevator was installed in the main house, which allowed me complete freedom indoors, and several ramps were installed outdoors so that I could have access to all the buildings on the property. The gravel driveway was paved with asphalt. All in all, everything was done to make me as comfortable as possible.

Planning Barb's Garden

During my stay at the GF centre, I was constantly thinking of doing something for a memorial to my Barbara, and trying to decide just what it could be, to make it a permanent record of my love.

One day, while sitting on the porch gazing at the view and the pasture area between the house and the storage barn, I came up with the idea of building a garden just for Barb, with a large pond and a beautiful gazebo right in the middle of it.

Taking paper and pen, I began sketching different ideas for the garden, including a large pond, a gazebo, and a spacious patio at the side of the pond. The patio would be large enough to hold a fairly large group of people in case we ever wished to hold a special outdoor gathering.

Once I had committed the plan to paper, I enlisted the help of many talented people to put it together. The pond was designed and installed by a creative company called Shibusa Ponds. My son-in-law Colin Bundy built the extensive rock walls. My dear brother Frank created the magnificent gazebo and arched bridge. The landscaping was done by Cantri Designer gardens, and my dear son Michael painted all the woodwork.

I designed the stone bridge leading to the gazebo so I would be able to wheel up it myself. But when my dear friend Joe Medlyn saw it, he immediately informed me that it was merely a sloped bridge and it would not suit the project at all. It would have to be arched. My instant reaction was that I would not be able to get up on the gazebo without help. Joe said that it didn't matter. It had to be arched. Joe won out, and so I designed an arched bridge which proved to be absolutely perfect for the site.

A few months later, after spending a wonderful evening out with Joe, he phoned and told me that he had terminal cancer. His wife Vivian was away in Cape Breton and not expected back for a few days. When she arrived home Joe met her at the door and told her that he was dying. Fifteen days later he was gone.

The day before he died I visited him in hospital. By that time he was very weak and barely able to speak, but he somehow managed to tell me that he had been working on a stained glass window for the gazebo as a memorial for Barb. With a shaking hand he sketched the outline of the window for me, but said that he would not be able to complete it. I assured Joe that I would finish it, and it would be installed in the gazebo just as he had planned.

When the window was completed it formed a wonderful backdrop, just as Joe would have wished. On a pillar at the top of the arched bridge, I installed a plaque that tells the story of how the bridge was inspired by my good friend Joe Medlyn.

Many visitors to Barb's Garden comment on the serenity and the sense of peace that comes over them when they enter the garden. I explain that there has been such an outpouring of love from friends, loved ones, and even complete strangers that it seems that the garden has been touched by the hand of God.

When I decided to build the garden as a memorial, the word seemed to spread very quickly and many friends and acquaintances began offering their

Barb's Garden under Construction

help as well as items for the garden itself.

Nadina, an acquaintance from my theatre days, wrote me a very wonderful and moving letter, asking me if I would care to have a special carving that her husband had just finished. It was a Celtic carving, depicting the 'Cross of Infinity' carved into a solid piece of granite. Her husband Martin Schaddelee, an internationally renowned carver, had recently finished the work as his own interpretation of the connection between Heaven and Earth. The Ring of Infinity was symbolic of the love that we often hold in our hearts, a love that does not die but is forever captive in our heart and soul. Martin and Nadina had read about my accident and the loss of Barb, and understood the meaning of eternal love. They felt the pain that I was experiencing, and wished to express their love by giving me a very precious gift of love, the 'Cross of Infinity'. Nadina also filmed and narrated a fine documentary recording the progress of the project.

As work progressed on the memorial garden, many people became actively involved in the project, often giving their time and energy freely. One day, a lady came into my store and asked if I would like to purchase a bronze statue for the garden. It was an original bronze piece titled, 'The Mermaids Purse', and created by a Salt Spring artist by the name of David Helliwell. The bronze was an absolutely incredible piece of art, and I immediately said, "yes" as I felt that it would be a great addition to the garden. My hope was that David Helliwell would personally dedicate it to Barb's Garden when the garden was completed. The lady contacted David and he agreed, saying that he would be delighted to join us at the dedication ceremony.

Barb's Garden was completed over a period of six months and the dedication ceremony took place on Mother's Day, May 1999. Many of the guests brought plants and shrubs for the garden. These gifts were gratefully accepted and now form a wonderful backdrop for weddings and special occasions that take place in the garden each summer.

Leck Bekesza, the pastor from Cobble Hill Baptist Church, a very close friend of my daughter Marlene and husband Bernie, dedicated the garden on that beautiful Mother's Day. He noted that, by God's Grace, I was able to share my love for Barbara with whomever entered the garden. It had been inspired by the love of one human being for another.

Martin Schaddelee and David Helliwell, with unusual compassion, offered their love and humanity to the garden and declared their pleasure of sharing the joy that this memorial would bring to others.

Over-seeing the construction of the garden that long painful winter had provided me with some relief from the overwhelming grief of reality. Barb was gone, I was unable to walk, the pain of paralysis was ever present, life as I had known it had ended.

Memorial Window

Designing Murals for Toad Hall

When I met David, I was very impressed with his manner and charming personality, and we quickly became the best of friends. Shortly after meeting, I commissioned him to paint two murals for me. They were to depict certain characters taken from 'Wind in the Willows' by Kenneth Graham. The main characters of 'Wind in the Willows' were Mr. Toad, Ratty, Mole and Mr. Badger. [picture of murals in Toad Hall]

Mr. Toad was a very interesting character that I played in several productions many years ago when I was performing in theatre. My association with 'Toady' was one of the joys of my life, and I always held a special place for him in my memory.

David sketched several ideas he had developed as possibilities for the murals. One of the ideas saw Toad adopting a new personality as 'Robin Toad', and Badger as 'Little John' of 'Surewood Forest'. Ratty and his companion Mole remained their own inimitable selves, always trying to keep Toady in check, but seldom having much success and, as usual, they failed to discourage Toad from running around the country in the characterization of 'Robin Toad.

He painted the murals on two walls of my former warehouse, that now form a part of my little theatre, 'Toad Hall'. This little theatre was designed as a place for me to pursue my love of story telling, and to showcase some of my own stage productions.

Care-Workers

As I grew stronger, my dependence on care-workers gradually diminished until I no longer needed night attendants, so I set about finding a suitable care worker to assist me. After a long search I met Parida Wood, a delightful woman who was originally from Thailand. When I first interviewed her, it became apparent that she loved gardening, and as I needed someone to look after the garden she seemed the perfect fit so I hired her straight away.

At first I thought that I would have to hire another person to look after the many household chores, but Parida assured me that she could handle everything, and I did not have to find another helper. As soon as she started working for me I realized what a gem I had found. There was absolutely nothing that she could not handle, be it cooking, gardening, plumbing, helping me with my daily exercise, or a multitude of other chores associated with the Pine Lodge Farm.

Parida was employed five days a week, but on the weekends lady friends would often visit me, sometimes staying for three or four days. This was an ideal situation because not only would I have companionship, but my friends would also help me with my exercise and some of the day-to-day chores as well. These visits from very wonderful friends were just a few of the great blessings that I received during those grief filled days, and to this day I feel blessed for having known them.

Once Barb's Garden was completed word began to spread and we had many visitors dropping by to see our memorial. In the early stages the garden plants, while very lovely, were still in their infancy, and so the overall effect was not as impressive as it was to become when nature finally took charge and full growth filled in all the empty places in the garden.

The First Wedding in Barb's Garden

People suggested that the garden would be a great place to hold weddings and other outdoor activities, and so I began to entertain the idea of holding special events there. When an acquaintance asked to hold her daughter's wedding there, I readily agreed. Although I had nothing in the way of equipment to host those types of functions, I quickly set about getting whatever I would need to launch this new enterprise.

The first purchases I made were two white tents, enough tables and chairs to accommodate the wedding, and a few other necessary items. When trying to decide the amount I would charge, I considered that the garden was not built as a commercial venture. I didn't really want to turn it into a money making project anyway, so I set a very low price, much to the delight of the bridal family. Word quickly spread that Barb's Garden was available for special events and we soon hosted an anniversary, a birthday party, and more weddings.

It rapidly became evident that I would need far more equipment than I already had, if I was to continue hosting weddings and parties, and I continued to add to my inventory, eventually acquiring everything from sound equipment to a kitchen and appliances, and several new tents. We also added to the facilities in the bathroom of the old school house on the property, happily ending the waiting time for the commode. 'Toad Hall' doubled as a dance hall, and added greatly to the success of our events.

As the costs of the operation steadily rose I came to realize that, like it or not, I needed to make a profit on the garden activities or I would not be able to continue hosting them, or even maintain the garden. Thus began the steadily increasing charges for any event

Toad Hall

Transforming my barn, or stable as it was formally called, into a theatre was a major achievement by my brother Frank. The stalls where I previously kept my horses became a storage area for tables and chairs and other odd pieces of equipment. The main room became the theatre, and featured a small stage, designed only as a storytelling space.

In the beginning my focus was on music and storytelling, and we hosted many wonderful programs, featuring well-known tellers and singers, including my daughter Marlene, an accomplished singer and actress.

Over the years we developed a faithful following of patrons, both young and old, usually selling out each performance well in advance. We tried to improve and vary each event, in order to keep the customers entertained and coming back for more.

My own stories were usually well received, and so I was encouraged to learn many different stories. My greatest interest lay in the realm of whimsy and humour and I found a wealth of material in stories from old books.

Each story has many different characters, and I try to bring each one of those characters to life, as though I were acting in a play on a stage. The great thing about storytelling is that you can spend as much time learning the part or character, as you like. Taking words off a page and bringing them to life is both challenging and personally gratifying.

My Association with Chemainus Theatre

Through a very dear friend, Sister Mary Michael, I had the pleasure of meeting Ken Hill, who built the Chemainus Theatre as an outlet for Christian theatrical productions. He continued his support of the struggling company of actors and directors throughout its infancy, helping it to become one of the leading professional theatre groups in the country.

Knowing that I was an avid supporter of theatre, Ken invited me to join the Board of Directors, and put my name forward as a potential candidate. I was accepted for the board, and very honored for the opportunity to work with the group. Being accepted by the Chemainus Theatre was just one more of the countless blessings that I have received over the years since the devastating loss of Barb and my own crippling injuries.

For a long time after the accident that ended my life as I knew it I was severely depressed. The grief was almost unbearable; it seemed to eat away at me like a cancer. I often thought of ending the pain by taking my own life.

At night, lying alone by myself in the dark was the worst part of my ordeal. Life was pointless. Barb was gone and I could no longer walk. I was not sure that the Lord had not abandoned me, and the constant pain was a reminder that this was not just a bad dream, that I would not awake and find it just a hideous nightmare.

During the day I kept very busy. Friends dropped by to help me cope with my demons. I was never alone and there was always someone to give me strength, to encourage me to continue with my work. But when the night came I slipped back into that world of grief and pain, sometimes sitting in the middle of my magnificent living room, remembering the years of happiness and joy that I had experienced in this home. Often I cried out with the pain that accompanied those memories.

Each night I would crawl into my bed as early as possible, watch television until I was tired, and then fall into a restive sleep. My dreams were never enjoyable or peaceful; they were always filled with fruitless journeys, where I was constantly searching for Barbara. Sometimes I would see her and try to talk with her, but it was always in vain. She never answered me. She remained a lonely, shadowy figure, inaccessible to me, a form that would suddenly disappear into the darkness without a word, leaving me with overwhelming sadness.

Each night I would pray for deliverance from the world of pain. I begged the Lord to come into my heart, to take the pain away, but my prayers remained unanswered, seemingly rejected. My heart was empty; where there was once incredible joy and contentment there was merely emptiness and a sense of loss and abandonment.

Three years after the accident the physical pain associated with my injuries, though constant, was manageable but the intensity of the pain in my heart never diminished. Every waking minute there was some reminder of my past life, the way things had been. My only escape from the nightmare that had hold of me was the continuing challenge of completing the work on the garden and buildings, and my theatre. The only way I could block the ache in my heart was to work as hard as possible, to keep busy with my friends, and to work until I was exhausted.

The Spirit of God and his Son Jesus Christ

At exactly three o'clock one morning I awoke and was aware of a glowing light that filled the room. I thought that I had not switched it off before I fell asleep. But it wasn't the overhead light; rather the room was illuminated as if by some mysterious power source. I began to feel the presence of something supernatural. At first I thought it was my imagination, but as I looked around the room I gradually realized that it was the Spirit of the Lord that was there in the room with me.

Every night since the accident I had prayed for God to enter my heart and to fill it with the love of Jesus, to lift my burden and now He was there.

As I lay there, hardly breathing, I felt the Spirit of Jesus sweep over me, filling my heart with the joy that was once there, and immediately my burden of grief was lifted from me and I was free. From that moment I knew that God had not abandoned me, that He was merely waiting for the time when I would truly allow Him into my heart. I began to realize just how many blessings had been bestowed upon me. The feelings of self-pity and anger were gone. I was not a victim, but a victor.

The change in me was very visible. I began to look at my journey as an exciting new adventure, and I saw all the friendships and projects that had come my way as great blessings. Barb's Garden and the theatre would allow me an outlet for both my Spiritual and emotional needs, and bring many more wonderful and gifted people into my world. With the renewed energy that only comes from God, I set about making my remaining time on earth, a commitment to Jesus.

Of course old habits are hard to break, and I continually have to stop what I am doing and say I'm sorry for my bad behaviour, particularly the use of bad words that often pop out when I'm aggravated, especially while I am driving. Some days are much harder than other days to be a good Christian and often someone close to me, usually one of my daughters, who has witnessed one of my typical outbursts will ask me if that is the way a good Christian should behave. After using all the excuses I can think of, I quite often fall back on the answer that I am praying daily for God to make me as perfect a human as I am capable of being.

Trying to Explain the Spirit of Christ

One of the most difficult things for a novice Christian to do is spread the word about God and Jesus Christ. Over my lifetime I always admitted that I was a Christian, but at the same time I found it extremely difficult to pass on or explain my belief in God, or why I felt as I did about the whole concept of Christianity. Probably the main reason for my difficulty communicating with others, stemmed from my lack of Biblical knowledge or understanding. I seldom ever read the Bible, and therefore was usually at a complete loss when engaged in conversation with an atheist or a non-believer.

Whenever I was asked why I believed in God, or how I knew that the bible was the truth, I would be unable to answer their questions. Many people would tell me that they were good people, and that they lived an honest life, never hurt anyone. They loved their wives and children and did their best to bring them up the same way. Many of these people had experienced the false teachings of some evangelists and preachers on television, and noticed just how corrupt they were in spite of their earnest and often eloquent words. Consequently and understandably they had become gun shy of any Bible talk, firmly convinced that all preachers were tarred with the same brush.

When I became a practicing Christian, I opened my heart and my ears to God's word and became aware that the greatest requisite of a believer is faith. Without faith it would be somewhat of a stretch to accept all the knowledge and wisdom of the Bible as the truth. But with faith, one can look beyond the confines of one's own learning, and accept it as the real word of God.

Strangely, the more faith we have, the more we understand. For myself, one of the most significant parables that Jesus uttered, was the 'Parable of the seed.' This wonderful passage opened my eyes to the possibility that one does not have to be fluent in the wisdom of the Bible to be able to spread God's word. Rather, all one has to do is cast the words of the Lord and they will become the seed which grows in fertile minds.

This parable has helped me to realize the importance of even the smallest seed or thought that passes from one human to another. The power of 'The Word' is amazing in its simplicity and, like the tiniest mustard seed when planted in fertile ground, it will often germinate and flourish.

Prior to my accident, I was very comfortable with my life. I was reasonably successful in business, happily married with a fine family, possessed excellent health, and enjoyed many ventures and hobbies that I managed to fit into my busy schedule. In a word, I really didn't need too much religion to complete my happiness, although I was always very careful not to burn any bridges as I traveled my path.

Looking back on my life, I slowly became aware that even though I had not given much of my time to the Lord, He had heard my prayers and was always with me. Throughout the years, whatever venture I was involved in, I would pray for His help and He would usually see me through it, bringing me some success. There were times when the outcome wasn't as successful as I would have liked, and it seemed that perhaps He had not heard my pleas, but I now know that the projects that failed were doomed from the start, if only I had listened.

Whenever I set my eyes on a goal I would work as hard as possible until the goal was accomplished. If there were barriers or hurdles in the way my strength and perseverance would help me overcome the obstacle. My credo was, ' Don't complain, and don't explain.' What I did not understand was that I was not doing it on my own, but rather doing it in spite of myself.

Many people that I met over the years were successful because of their strength and determination. They would not allow themselves to fail; if they fell down they would jump up and work even harder to overcome whatever problem confronted them. In short, they were self-made men and women. Success usually means wealth. But too often I noticed that this hard won wealth did not necessarily bring them happiness. I observed that many people living in great mansions were very lonely or ill, or just plain unhappy.

Since the Lord lifted me from my world of grief, I have been blessed by the introduction of many wonderful people into my life. What is abundantly clear to me is the quality and richness that they enjoy when their spirit is committed to God. Many of these people have wealth, but have learned that their wealth, no matter how hard-earned, does not belong to them but has merely been put in their care to be used as God directs them. Their stories have inspired me spiritually, and encouraged me to re-evaluate my own values. After a lifetime of acquiring things, I now realize that those special objects that were collected were placed under my care for a short time only, to be enjoyed not as a possession, but as a gift.

While planning Barb's Garden, my desire was to create something that would not only commemorate my love for her, but would be a beautiful place that could be enjoyed by others. I was unwittingly setting out on my preordained path, which inevitably led me to a place of awareness where I began to understand the event that had taken place that freezing winter day in Toronto.

Humans tend to blame God for their misfortunes, and I was no different. What we don't realize is that God is there to help us when we are in need, not to watch over us and protect us from whatever may happen. In His great wisdom, however, He knows that some misfortune helps to strengthen us, and he does not interfere unless we call upon him for help.

In my case, I know that I have been spared from the consequences of bad decisions many times over, and can only attest that it was much more than plain good luck. If I had listened carefully, I would have recognized the source of the protective shield that surrounded me.

Many of my Christian friends make no important decisions without first consulting the Lord, unlike myself who spent a lifetime making my own, frequently wrong decisions. Today, I often pray for direction, for help or guidance and I am amazed at how my prayers are answered.

It seems that some prayers go unanswered. I have prayed non-stop for relief from my pain. I have asked God to touch my spinal cord and heal it, to strengthen my legs so that they will be able to hold my weight. But even though there has been very little improvement, I am constantly aware of all the other wonderful blessings that He has given me.

The Spirit Working in Me

When first injured, I was unable to feel anything in my lower body. I had no control over normal bodily functions. I was plagued by bladder infections that required heavy doses of drugs. My right leg became extremely infected and was in danger of amputation and was only saved by the use of powerful antibiotics. Internal injuries caused ulcers to develop, which in turn caused bleeding problems in my esophagus and a severe drop in my hemoglobin count. My right arm, badly damaged in the accident, was all but useless; life in general was not too comfortable.

Now, after years of rigorous daily exercise, I have managed to regain the use of my left arm and I am no longer plagued with infections. Most of my other medical problems are under control, I have movement in my legs and almost normal feeling in my lower body. While I realize that a lot of the improvement has come about by my own hard work, I also know that through my prayers, God has given me the strength to triumph over my physical disabilities.

While far from being cured, I am thankful that my health and endurance has steadily improved, allowing many activities not normally possible for others in similar situations. Each day presents many challenges, but also brings about solutions that are only conceivable as the work of the Spirit.

The Spirit in Barb's Garden

Barb's Garden has been the setting for countless weddings, and we have been privileged to meet wonderful people from all walks of life, many who share a love of Christ. So many weddings have been favored by small miracles that we accept the fact that the garden is truly blessed. Whenever a bride or her mom shows concern about impending bad weather we say that they must not worry, for the garden is blessed and weather will do nothing to take away from the joy of the day, and it is always so. From the first celebrations in the garden, we witnessed happenings that can only be explained as the presence of a Holy Spirit.

The first Easter after the garden's completion we held a sunrise ceremony in the garden gazebo, with twenty members of our Baptist Church. Everyone arrived shortly before sunrise. It was bitterly cold, the entire sky was a black-gray colour, and a constant drizzle of rain fell upon the assembly. The group formed a circle in the gazebo, and the pastor began playing familiar hymns on his guitar, followed by prayers.

The pastor spoke of the garden and why it was such a special place. He spoke of Barb and how we all loved her, and how she was there in spirit. As he spoke, I caught some movement out of the corner of my eye. Looking to the east, I watched as a small wedge of blue slowly appeared in the gray sky and a beam of bright light shone through the haze directly onto the gazebo. It brought back the memory of that shaft of light that had sliced through an identical sky, and through the dining table then through Barb many months before.

As the light approached, a sense of loss swept over me; was this another omen, another warning, I wasn't sure, but slowly I became aware of a feeling that this light was not of the same origin as the former. This light was a confirmation that Barb's presence was here in the garden. As I became aware of the significance of the light the tears began, and through the mist I observed tears coursing down the cheeks of others in the group.

During many weddings and concerts remarkable things happened, which could only be explained as workings of the Spirit. One lovely summer day, a bride and groom were standing on the bridge leading to the gazebo. The bride had recently lost her mother in an airplane crash and had asked her father to join them on the bridge while they said their vows. As the minister led them through the ceremony, an airplane suddenly appeared and swooped down toward the gazebo, seemingly hovering for a moment and then quickly rising and disappearing from sight.

When the airplane approached them, the bride and her father raised their eyes toward the sound, and slowly every eye followed theirs, silently watching until it disappeared from sight. The bride smiled and said, "It's mom".

There was not a dry eye throughout the rest of the ceremony.

There have been many wonderful little episodes similar to those that have lifted the spirits of all the people attending the events. Simple little things such as two eagles at play directly above the gazebo during a ceremony. Downpours minutes before the bride walked down the long pathway from the lodge, and then bright sunshine throughout the rest of the ceremony.

A young bride who was so ill on the morning of the wedding that she had to lie down right up to the time that the formalities were to begin. She did not think that she would be able to carry it off but the pastor and the guests prayed for her and then, with the aid of her bridesmaids, she began the walk down to the gazebo, slowly regaining her strength and managing to overcome her illness long enough to see the fulfillment of her many months of planning.

Toad Hall Blessed

Our little theatre Toad Hall has also been blessed since it was constructed. From the first story telling performance that we produced there has been terrific support from many friends and acquaintances, and most of the events were quickly sold out. The hall has been a wonderful showcase for many performers, storytellers and singers as well as actors and actresses. Initially the storytelling was limited to one performance, but as time passed we increased the number of shows. In 2004 we produced our first play, ‘The Best Christmas Pageant Ever’ and it was a hit.

In 2005 I rewrote, ‘A Christmas Carol’, by Charles Dickens, and performed Ebenezer Scrooge. Re-writing was necessary as the original play, written years before, would not fit our little stage, nor would it have been suitable for me to play Scrooge. My greatest concern was that the audience might not accept Scrooge in a wheelchair, but they did, and it turned out to be an even greater success than we imagined.

The play required a cast of over thirty actors. Our little stage would not accommodate that many characters, so Marlene and I had seventeen actors take all the roles. Marlene not only helped direct the play, she also took the role of the washerwoman. Because of the limitations of the stage we used the entire theatre for the production, with much of the action taking place along the outer walls of the room.

We scheduled six performances, hoping to be able to attract enough of an audience to pay the expenses. The costumes were rented from a local costume studio; the lighting was installed and operated by Don Miller who was also an actor and took part in our show the following year.

When the Victoria Operatic Society produced ‘The Stingiest Man in Town’ in the 70’s, I was chosen to play the part of Scrooge, and enjoyed the role immensely. It was always in my mind to repeat the role. Little did I know that the next time would be from a wheelchair.

The play, as I wrote it, included a new role, that of a narrator who depicted Charles Dickens as if he were writing the story himself. While preparing the script, I had a certain actor in mind for the narrator. The role demanded a very strong character actor with an exceptional voice, and I was blessed when the very talented professional, David Holmes, accepted the part.

Finding seventeen actors was a challenge, as many of the experienced thespians in the valley were involved with other theatre groups, and had already accepted roles in other Christmas shows. Facing a serious shortage of actors was a worry, but we enlisted the aid of Marlene my co-director, and my two Filipina care-workers, Maritess and Divina, as actors, costume assistants and general factotums.

Maritess, though never appearing on stage before, was handed no less than three roles to perform, as well as the job of stage-manager. Divina was appointed as costume mistress and coffee maker, along with numerous other chores. Directing Maritess proved easier than I first thought. During the day I was able to coach her with lines and stage movement, while she tended to her ongoing household chores. At night in the theatre, she was able to carry out the stage-manager responsibilities, while at the same time performing her three roles, no mean feat for a novice.

Well-known actor-entertainer Ian Rothnie took two roles in the production, as did actors Terry Halonen, Pat Wheatley, Derek Coughlin, Cliff Bratten, Ian Monohan, Jacquie Welsh, Miriam Coughlin, Mary Gibbs, Jennifer Monohan, Tom Browne, Rachel Bekesza, Abby Bekesza, and Levi Bekesza. Musical accompaniment was supplied by Keith Clarke, sound effects by Judy Bronson, sound and art design by Frank and Gail Neumann, costumes supplied by Yvonne Brilliant, and lighting by Don Miller and Ian Rothnie. Terry Halonen was excellent in his two roles and was slated for a role in our next production, but tragically died a short time after our production was finished.

As directors, Marlene and I wanted to bring out the true message of the story. While the original story did not mention the Spirit of God, we felt that the play definitely did have that undercurrent, and we wished to make it an integral part of our play.

Once our production began rehearsals there were many details to tend to. Firstly, our little theatre had only basic stage lighting, so we had Don bring in his own lighting board and lights. Two or three scenes needed a hazy, mystical setting, so we ordered a fog machine from an American supplier to create the special effect. We also ordered several microphones, and a new mixer from the same supplier.

Normally microphones are not required in a small theatre, but several effects required them, particularly when Tiny Tim sang 'Good King Wenceslas' from off stage, and when Scrooge as a child spoke to his sister in his former schoolroom. Other scenes benefited from the use of the microphones as well.

Several set pieces had to be specially constructed. One was a four-poster bed where Scrooge first encounters the ghost of Christmas Past. The bed was half sized and had no mattress so that the 'wheelchair Scrooge' could appear to be in bed. The black curtains were also necessary to hide Scrooge while the stage manager helped him on with his nightshirt.

Christmas 2005

In Scrooge's counting house were two desks, one for Bob Cratchit the other for Scrooge. Bob's desk had to be scaled to size, to fit the stage, and Scrooge's desk needed to be the right width and height to accommodate the wheelchair.

The main door to this office was used in all the scenes where a door was required. The door had to be unobtrusively opened and closed to allow the three ghosts to come and go not appearing to have opened it themselves.

The narrator's desk was an authentic beautiful Georgian drop-front, which could have easily graced Charles Dickens's original office. We rigged fishing line from it to a wall at the end of the room. A weight was attached to the line at the wall and the other end was fastened to a fishing reel and attached to the narrator's desk which was set in an alcove at the back of the stage. Whenever the door was to be opened by one of the ghosts David, the narrator, would release the reel allowing the weight at the end of the line to pull the door open, and then reel it in like a fish when it had to be closed, all the while being careful not to let the cat out of the bag.

We had several concerns. Would the audience accept Scrooge in a wheelchair? Would they accept our adaptation of this great classic? Would we be able to bring out the true spirit of the tale? Could we pull it off without elaborate sets, and costumes? And finally would we be able to sell enough tickets to pay the bills?

With all the stress of the production, I developed the worst case of laryngitis that I ever experienced. The fear of being unable to perform this very difficult and demanding role caused me even more stress than usual. The laryngitis continued for weeks, barely improving as the time of the production approached. Each night I prayed as I never prayed before. "Please God, let my voice return in time for the performances. Please God let the audience accept the production as I've written it. Let them accept my wheelchair, the costumes, the sets, the cast, and the unorthodox staging. Oh God help me out of this mess I'm in and finally, please supply us with enough patrons to pay for it."

The production slowly took shape and we began to think that we might just pull it off. My laryngitis continued however, and my spirits were definitely sagging. But, in the past God had always heard my prayers and helped me out of worse jams than this one. So I turned it, in its entirety, over to God. " Oh Lord, this is beyond my control, I am powerless to alter the outcome. Thy Will Be Done."

When the Spirit of the Lord fills one's heart, a wonderful transformation takes place. Though still suffering laryngitis and concerns regarding the play, my own Spirit soared. There was no doubt in my mind that He would watch over the production and give us success.

For one month I spent every possible moment contacting the people on my list of theatre patrons. From the first storytelling event after the accident, I had kept a record of everyone who had attended our shows. By the time we produced 'A Christmas Carol', there were several hundred names in the book.

Contacting all those people took a great deal of time, but it was a necessary exercise if we were to have any success at all. I only phoned them once. I would describe the show and suggest they phone me back if they were interested. I did not want to bother them by repeated phone calls. The response initially was not too exciting but as the month passed by I began getting many calls. Some people ordered ten or more tickets, and before long we had sold out most shows.

On the evening of our dress rehearsal, my voice came back from wherever it had been, and my fears evaporated. The entire cast was superb, costumes were effective, the lighting and sound was even better than I had hoped, and everything worked, as it should.

On opening day it snowed. Most tickets had been bought and paid for so it was not a total disaster, although it did keep half the audience away.

There is no doubt that snow can be one of the worst things that can happen to any public event. But the audience that made it to the show loved it, and consequently the next day the phone started to ring and we quickly sold out our last performance on Sunday. The following day the snow melted, and the remainder of the shows played to full houses

My Prayers Answered

Many, many people phoned or emailed, telling us how much they enjoyed the show. The audience loved the cast, mentioning how professional they were; they loved the special effects and particularly the Spiritual strength of the play. Letters arrived telling us that Scrooge had given one of the best performances they had ever seen. Five minutes after appearing on stage, the wheelchair was completely forgotten, and his transformation from the miserly old man to the bright, lovable Scrooge that we all love, brought tears to their eyes.

The comments that we received were overwhelming, and every member of the cast and crew including my daughters Marilyn, Maureen and Marlene were extremely proud of the production, When the review appeared in the weekly newspaper, I knew that God had indeed watched over our show and had answered my every prayer.

The newspaper heading read; PINE LODGE CAROL, A VALLEY BLESSING. All the right ingredients in place to make this an exquisite version of the Dickens' classic. The reviewer went on to describe it as a heartwarmingly effective version of Dickens's 'A Christmas Carol'.

The audience was treated to sound, lighting and fog effects that evoked timeless messages about ignorance and greed. Clarke was superb as Scrooge, creatively using his wheelchair to lend the role authenticity; one barely notices the chair, as the repentant miser is haunted by Christmas Eve spirits. Toad Hall's acoustics and clear diction allowed Dickens' tale to unfold, ably assisted by David Holmes as the Victorian wordsmith.

The newspaper reviewer praised all the members of the cast for a job well done, summoning up the article by pointing out the wonderful message of hope written more than a century ago. Giving hope to the homeless, the orphans and the needy, and the power of the spirit; and as Tiny Tim once said, "GOD BLESS US EVERYONE"

Our show ended on a high note, Not only did we cover all the costs of production, we also made a modest profit which we divided between a fund for needy people, and the local food bank.

When the show ended, David Holmes said, "Well, what are we going to do next year?"

Without missing a beat, I said, " Lets do a play about the birth of Christ."

Within a short time David and I began writing a musical play, named 'What Child is this.'

As I worked on the script, David wrote the lyrics. It was incredible, for even though we were working in our separate homes, our script and lyrics were amazingly similar, and often the lyrics echoed the sentiments of the play word for word. David's daughter Sarah, a professional composer living and working in England, began preparing the score for the play. As quickly as David finished a number, Sarah would set it to music.

There are many musical numbers in the production and each one is very important to the plot, and required a great deal of time to complete. Throughout February, March and April, we three impresarios worked hard to complete the play, even though we ran into many interruptions. My wedding season started early in April and continued full steam through September and into October. Sarah was sent to China to initiate a music program for use in schools there, and David had his plate full with equally important work.

In preparation for the new play, we had extra lighting and sound equipment installed in Toad hall. We enlisted the aid of Ian Rothnie to build the flats for the sets, and a talented artist was hired to paint the elaborate, biblical sets.

There was very little work done on the play throughout the summer months, as we were all preoccupied with our own commitments. Sarah, however, did spend the summer in Victoria and managed to find some time to work on the score for the play. Unfortunately, due to other demands, she was unable to complete the last solo or the finale.

Our weddings finally ended in early October. It was the most successful season to date and we received many wonderful letters of thanks, but we were all exhausted. The thought of preparing our play for an early December run was daunting to say the least.

Lord, What Should We Do?

Most of the casting was complete, except for the two boy-sopranos, and one or two other characters. Finding boys capable of carrying these very important roles was more difficult than we had anticipated, but we kept up the search, all the while hoping that the score would be completed on time.

As the point of no return approached, when we would have to make the crucial decision to go ahead, or abort the whole thing, I began to get cold feet. So, I put it in the hands of the Lord, asking Him to give me a sign, one way or the other, of whether we should continue with the play or not. The answer was soon forthcoming.

At the next rehearsal, one of the 'Three Wise Men' informed us that he would not be able to do the role. The following day the artist who was going to begin painting the set within the next day or so, phoned me and broke the unhappy news that she and her assistant would not have the necessary time to devote to painting the complex set after all.

This was a surprise to me, because many months before we had gone over the set in great detail and agreed that, though it was a challenge, it would also be a terrific accomplishment for any artist. While the artist was giving me the reasons for not having the time to do it, it became clear that the real issue was that the amount of money she would be paid probably wouldn't cover the time it would take her to complete the set.

Actually, the possibility that it would take longer than she had originally estimated was mentioned at a meeting that we had the week before. When the question of 'what if', came up, I fear I blew it. Her question was, "If it takes longer than we thought to paint this set, who will pay for the extra time?" My answer should have been, "We can work that out when we get there."

Unfortunately my answer though sincere, may have seemed frivolous to her. When she asked who would pay for it, I answered, perhaps too quickly, " Then, you will be working for Christ."

This was definitely the wrong answer for her, for she was most emphatic in her response, and said in no uncertain terms that the 'Lord's Work' would not be adequate compensation. The notice of resignation from the artist was immediately followed by a call from David. He asked if I thought it wise to continue in the face of these setbacks. Having already reached the conclusion that it was not in the cards for that year, I relayed the message from the artist,and confided that it probably was not in our best interest to continue, and perhaps we should postpone it until the following year.

At the next rehearsal, we informed the remainder of the cast of our decision to postpone the show until the following year. Everyone was quite disappointed that there would be no Christmas show, and suggested that we pool our talents and put on a Christmas concert instead.

Over the years I have produced many concerts which have been successful, but somehow I wasn't too keen on doing one that year. However, in spite of my reluctance to work on a concert, I invited the group to throw out any ideas that they might have on the type of material we could use for the program. There was a lot of enthusiasm and some very good suggestions from the company, so we decided to go ahead and produce a Christmas concert instead of our play. Each member would sing in the chorus and also perform one or two solos. The cast provided first class entertainment, and it looked as if the show would be successful.

My contribution was to be a story about The Fourth Wiseman, a very moving and inspirational tale about a Persian Nobleman called Artaban. He was to accompany the three Wisemen across a vast desert as they followed the Great Star toward the birthplace of the Messiah, in the distant lands of Judah.

The Wise Men, Artaban, Melchior, Baltazar and Gaspar, were to gather at a meeting place on the Euphrates River as soon as the star appeared. The meeting place was several days' travel from the mountains of Persia where they lived, and each man was to find his own way there.

Artaban, late in starting the journey to meet the other Wiseman, stopped along the way to minister to a dying man, and so narrowly missed the caravan that carried his companions across the desert toward the birthplace of the Messiah.

The Fourth Wise Man was forced to sell one of his three precious jewels that were intended for the Messiah, and procure his own caravan and provisions for the journey. Owing to other acts of mercy along the way, Artaban was never able to catch up with the other travelers, and spent the remainder of his life searching for Christ, the Messiah.

Learning the story of the weary traveler, though very difficult and time-consuming, proved to be one of the best and most rewarding stories that I ever committed to memory. There is a powerful Spiritual value to the story that is absolutely profound, and which leaves both the audience and the teller visibly moved.

Several church leaders that attended our concert told me that the story of joy and sacrifice was one of the most powerful and inspirational messages they had ever heard. One of the ministers invited me to his church to retell the story the following week.

There were over two hundred in the sanctuary having an early Christmas dinner and the atmosphere was very festive. Normally I do not like telling stories to dinner groups because, once dinner is done, folks like to move about and chat, which makes it very difficult for a teller to hold their attention. But on this occasion there was a minimum of movement or chatter, and everyone settled down very quickly to listen to my story.

As soon as I was introduced, the lights in the sanctuary were lowered and I began the tale of this extraordinary traveler. There was hardly a sound or a movement throughout the story and at the end of it, there was a complete silence, as if the audience was mesmerized.

In the weeks leading up to the Christmas concert, I once again asked the Lord to help me with the production, to grant the cast and myself the energy and strength to see it through. There were the normal problems and set backs while preparing the show, but I had complete faith that He would watch over us.

Three young schoolgirls who had originally been cast in our play, 'What Child is This' were part of our company. They had many commitments at school and found it difficult to make all the rehearsals. Several of the cast where unable to attend more than one rehearsal each week, or had scheduled other activities for some of those nights, all of which added to my concern. Fortunately Marlene was able to fill in for those who were absent and also helped with the direction of the musical numbers, while Maritess handled the stage lighting and sound.

Fe, a new Filipina care-worker, had joined me when Divina moved on to another position further up-Island. She was very shy but loved singing. I overheard her singing one afternoon, and realized that she had a good voice and invited her to join the chorus. She quickly learned all the music, attended every rehearsal, and proved to be a wonderful addition. The young ladies also managed to do well with their solos and also did well as a trio. Don, the lighting man had a successful turn on stage in 'The Twelve Days of Turkey', and Larry performed the bouncy number, "Have a Holly Jolly Christmas.'

Our intention when planning shows had always been to provide good entertainment along with a strong message of love and hope. We did attain it in 'The Best Christmas Pageant Ever', in 2004, and 'A Christmas Carol' in 2005, and we earnestly wished to continue the spiritual message with our 2006 Christmas concert.

The first half of our concert consisted of happy traditional Christmas music, with some funny bits of business thrown in for good measure, plus a delightful reading of Dylan Thomas's "A Child's Christmas in Wales' by David Holmes. Marlene finished the set with 'Have Yourselves a Very Merry Christmas', and 'I'm Dreaming of a White Christmas.' In the second half we introduced the real message of Christmas. Jabin Kim, a beautiful Korean girl, sang, 'Oh Holy Night' and Hark the Herald Angels Sing', David presented a moving, 'Mary's Boy Child' assisted by the three young ladies, followed by 'Mary's Lullaby', a number from 'What Child is This', featuring Jennifer and Terry.

At the end of my story, 'The Fourth Wiseman', Ian sang 'I Wander as I Wander'. This particular song was perfectly suited, adding greatly to the Spiritual message of the Tale. Artaban, at last finds Christ the Messiah, only to discover that He was to be crucified that very day. Unwittingly he stumbles on a young girl being dragged through the streets of Jerusalem by soldiers intending to sell her into slavery. The girl breaks free of the soldiers and begs him to help her. Artaban, by this time old and feeble after a lifetime of searching for the King of the Jews, pays the girls ransom with the last jewel that he had kept for the King. The soldiers, believing that Artaban is a beggar and a thief, seize him and drag him off to Golgotha, the place of crucifixion. There he finally comes face to face with His King, and unknowingly gives Christ a gift greater than the finest of his jewels.

While Ian sang the beautiful, 'I Wander as I Wander', several of the cast lit candles that were passed among the audience. Lights were slowly dimmed, and the theatre was bathed in candlelight.

Our music director and organist, Keith Clarke, began the carols, 'Oh Come All Ye Faithful, 'Away in a Manger', and finally, 'Silent Night'. The audience sang along with the chorus members, fully enjoying the true Spirit of Christmas.

The weekly review in the newspaper was headlined "PINE LODGE OFFERS FINE PRESENT. Holiday show a heartfelt treat. Cliff Clarke's transcendent 'Fourth Wiseman', lit up Pine Lodge Farm's Toad Hall the way the North Star illuminated Bethlehem so long ago. Clarke told the story of selfless determination given its final reward by the Son of God. Clarke's story followed a delightful evening of carols, yuletide tales and music. Part party, part church service, 'A Christmas at Pine Lodge Farm', was a perfect follow up to last year's production of 'A Christmas Carol' starring Clarke as Scrooge.

From childhood, my life was always driven by the desire to succeed at any cost. There wasn't anything that I could not do or achieve; after all I was the great Cliff Clarke. I was strong, healthy and determined. If anyone wished to help me, great! If not, too bad! What I did not know or understand was that God had a purpose for me. All those narrow escapes, all the near failures, even the modest successes, were not by my strength alone, for God had always been there with me, only I didn't know it.

Recognizing the Blessing in my Life

Nine years have slipped away since the accident that altered my life. Since then I have come to understand so much more than I thought possible about life and it's intricacies. My belief in God has become absolute. There is not a doubt in my mind that He is always with us, everyday, at all times. He is like the air we breathe. His Spirit surrounds us, and He is there, waiting for our call for assistance. He is there when we stumble; He is there when we succeed. But the degree of success depends on our faith; it depends on just how much trust we place in Him. Since the Holy Spirit replaced the grief in my heart, I have come to realize how important it is to have God as a full partner, rather than just an entity standing by in case of emergency.

Blessings are sometimes difficult to recognize. Often we look upon good things that happen to us as merely a lucky break, a spot of good fortune, or even a reward for a job well done. Ever since the day of my accident, I have been overwhelmed by the support and love I have received from my family, and many friends and strangers. In my past life I never experienced that kind of love except from my wife and my family, nor did I expect it. After all, when one is a hard driving, self-indulgent individual, the only appreciation he truly receives is the money he deposits in the bank.

Though money was never the driving factor in my life, it did play a very important role. It allowed me to look after my family, have a home and generally enjoy some worldly pleasures. More important was the satisfaction of achieving some success in spite of my limited education and the fact that I was married at the age of eighteen, and soon after that, a father of four.

Associating with Christians and observing them has become a wonderful vocation for me. Every morning at six o'clock I switch on The Vision channel, and enjoy all the stories of faith and love offered daily by people of faith. Their ministries cover the world, drilling wells in Africa, building houses in impoverished countries, feeding starving children, and helping poor people set up little businesses in areas of abject poverty. So many incredible people were doing the work of the Lord with little reward, other than the satisfaction of helping others less fortunate than themselves. The enormous amount of money spent on saving others in far off lands is absolutely astonishing. People throughout the world are sharing whatever they have with those in need. This is The Spirit of Christ at work. He never had wealth, yet He gave of himself completely, feeding the poor, healing the sick, and finally offering Himself as atonement for our sins.

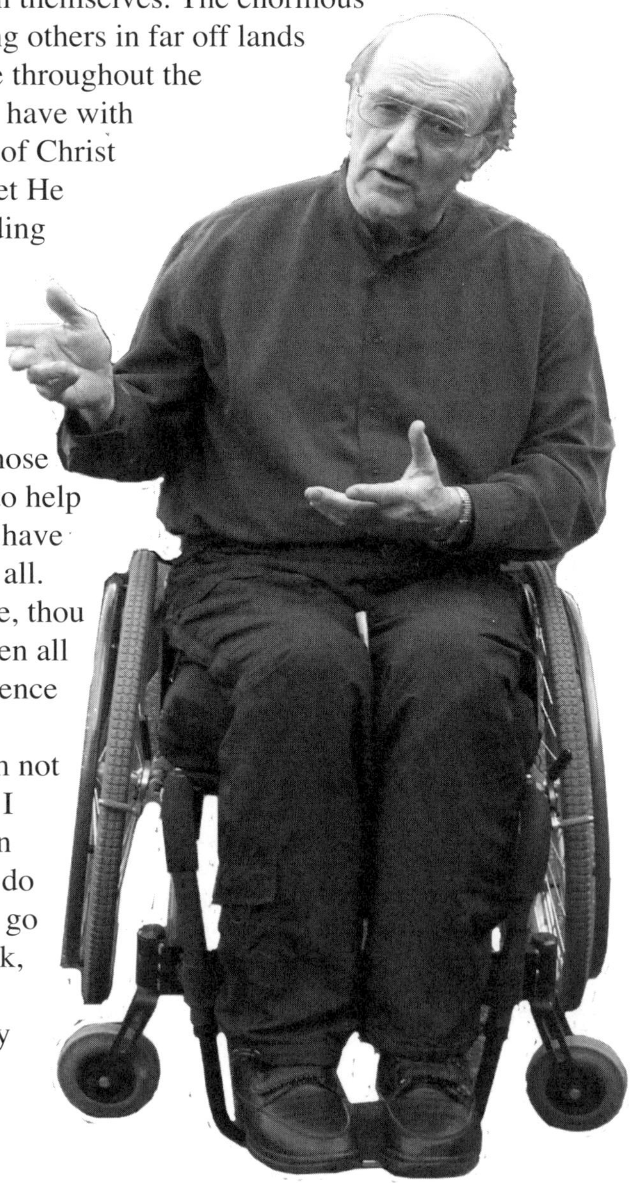

Knowing people who give of themselves has been an enormous blessing for me. All those friends that gave of themselves to help me through a very difficult time have been the greatest of blessings of all. The Lord said that what you give, thou shalt receive, and if this is so, then all those blessed friends will experience love tenfold.

Whenever I feel that I am not doing enough to serve the Lord, I reflect on the times that Christian friends have reassured me that I do and, even though I am unable to go afield to practice the Lord's Work, my farm with all its frequent events allows me the opportunity to serve Him in many different ways.

Sisters, Marie and Nell Called Home

Between 2004 and 2006, my dear sisters Marie and Nell passed away. When I visited Marie in hospice, I asked her if she had given her life to Christ, and she said that she had, and that she was not afraid of death but was looking forward to seeing her husband again.

Nell always believed in God and lived her life accordingly. Her life was devoted to helping others less fortunate than herself. On her last morning she ran errands for several of the residents in her retirement home, and then lay down and quietly passed on.

Time passes very quickly, but as we grow older it seems to go even faster. Before we know it most of our friends begin to look old, our children start to catch up to us in age, and our mirror becomes brutally frank. For the non-believer it can be devastating.

In the face of the believer however, one can see the radiating Spirit of Christ shining through in all its glory. There is a depth of beauty that overflows straight from the heart, over-riding the lines and blemishes that time has left in its path. The expectation of eternal life erases all fear of the aging process, and one views the advent of old age as a new adventure.

When I was young I wanted to live forever. There were so many great

Children and Grandchildren

GR.Son Robert Clarke • Mike Clarke • Marlene Willock • Curtis Rasmussen • Melody Horsefall
Kevin Rasmussen • Maureen Clarke(Bundy) • Benjamin Willock • Marilyn Clarke
Jessica Bundy • Jennifer Willock • Christian Horsefall

things to do in life, I wanted as long as possible to try to get them all done. But when tragedy struck, all those seemingly important things suddenly became unimportant. All the money in the world could not begin to pay for our loss; nothing could replace that which was taken away.

Reliving the hours when Barb and I were together, never fails to bring sadness for all the lost opportunities when I could have told her that I loved her, that I appreciated the years of sacrifice she had made while supporting me. The joy I felt when arriving home after a long hard day, seeing her standing at the window, waiting for me. The times when I was down or discouraged, and how I was lifted up by the thought that she was there for me, ready to help me, ready to hold and comfort me. Though I can't see her, I know that she is near. In my prayers I ask the Lord to care for her, to let her be waiting when I pass from this life into the next.

Walking the Long Tunnel

One night while lying in the darkness of my room, I began to think of the long tunnel that we supposedly walk down when passing from this life. I wondered what it would be like at the other end. Would the bright light be there, would it shine upon our loved ones who have gone on before us?

In the midst of this dream-like state, I was suddenly struck with a terrifying thought; what if the light goes out before we reach the end of the tunnel, what happens to our spirit, what if there is no spirit. What if there is no after-life.

"Oh God", I prayed, "please let there be Eternal Life, let my Barbara be waiting for me".

For several days this thought weighed heavily upon me. "Oh Lord please fill my heart with your Spirit, let me rid myself of this negative thought".

Several days later, there was an article in the Time-Colonist, written by two doctors in England. They had recently completed an involved study on Life After Death. They had been present when patients actually died on the operating table but had been brought back to life. They witnessed many miraculous recoveries, and over a period of time spoke with all the people who had experienced death.

A reasonably high percentage of those patients told of seeing loved ones who had already passed away, or had the experience of walking down the long tunnel toward the bright light. The doctors were able to calculate the precise moment of death, and also the exact minute they were brought back to life, and with precise calculations were able to conclude that there was indeed a spirit or soul that lived after death. They also confirmed that the soul or spirit was still very much alive even when one was suffering from dementia or even brain damage and in a comatose state.

As I read this article I was once again aware of a great weight being lifted from my shoulders and a wonderful sensation of warmth flooding my heart, as if the Lord in answer to my prayers had directed me to that article in the paper and calmed my fears.

The doctor's report reminded me of a conversation that I had with Jack Inkpen, an old friend who was my best man when I was married. He attended the dedication of Barb's Garden and was telling me of the day he died from a heart attack as he lay on the operating table.

He recalled walking down the long tunnel toward the light. His feeling was one of peace as if he was on a very natural journey, but suddenly he heard a voice calling "Jack! Jack!" He didn't know that the voice was calling his name and he kept walking toward the light, but the voice became more insistent and he began to realize that it was actually calling his name. He turned around and began walking back toward the voice. The next moment he was awake. The doctor, who had been calling, later told him that he had died on the table and that they were trying to call him back.

Whenever I have any doubts or lapses of belief in Heaven and the hereafter, I ask Jesus to renew my spirit, to help me out of that dreadful pit, for that state of unbelief is not a happy place to be. It is a place that robs one of the simple joys of living.

If I allow my mind to wonder back to the days before the accident, I remember the wonderfully simple act of walking, the joy of running and jumping. Each morning precisely at seven, I would jump out of bed, do ten minutes of stretching exercises on my bedroom floor, perform my morning ablutions, put the coffee on, and then go outside to tend to my early morning farm chores. Nothing was done at a walk, for I enjoyed running whenever I could, from the house to the chicken coop, then down to the cattle barn, and finally up to the front gate to pick up the morning paper. By the time I had fed the cattle, released the chickens and picked up the newspaper, the coffee had finished brewing, and I was ready to enjoy whatever had been prepared for breakfast that morning. Barb would join me and together we would plan our day and, if my memory serves me well, those were among the happiest moments of our life.

My Wheelchair Friends

Many people who have suffered an accident and are unable to walk, and confined to a wheelchair, spend much time watching others walking, wondering if those same people realize just how fortunate they are. They are thinking, "Walking looks so easy, why can't I do it?" and observing how they move so effortlessly across a parking lot or get into their vehicles and remembering the days when they could do the very same thing themselves. That simple act of remembering can be very devastating to the wheelchair person, for it brings back the pain and frustration of their own loss.

Each month, I join several of my wheelchair friends at one of our homes for coffee, and it is always a happy occasion. The talk usually centers on events and accomplishments of other wheelchair persons that we know. Seldom does anyone mention or complain about his or her own situation. Usually everyone is very up beat, and quite often involved in some venture or project of his or her own.

These projects vary from rebuilding antique motorcycles, organizing sailing lessons, sponsoring golf competitions, manufacturing carrying trays and baskets which can be attached to any wheelchair, raising money for charity, framing pictures, creating graphics for numerous clients, including the advertising, posters and programs for my own shows.

Whenever I have the pleasure of attending one of these coffee gatherings, I am always aware of the resilience of my wheelchair bound companions, and aware of the indomitable spirit that lifts these people above their affliction. I marvel at the unfathomable wisdom and love that God bestows on each one, allowing them to rise above their own limitations and continue a life of productivity and achievement.

In almost every instance of disability, I have observed that there is a person, be it a husband or wife or caregiver, dedicated to the task of watching over and tending to their special needs. Unfailingly, the attention given is unconditional.

Cliff and friends in the Vesuvius Pub, Salt Spring Island 2001

What have I learned from this devastating event that changed my life? I have often asked myself that very question and, though the answer was somewhat vague in the beginning, it slowly dawned on me that I had learned a great deal about myself. I have come to appreciate life far more than ever before. I discovered that I loved my family and friends more than I ever thought possible, and there is also a deep awareness of the pain and suffering of others. In the darkness of my own pain and grief, I was touched by the radiance and uplifting power of God. The painful burden that had engulfed me was lifted from my heart and replaced with the love of Christ.

What would I give if I were allowed to go back to the way things were? Many times I have said that I would gladly give everything that I possess to have Barb back again, to walk again, to have my life as it was. But then I realize that it is a loaded question and probably not beneficial to my wellbeing. What has happened can never be reversed. The unthinkable happened, but life goes on. The old saying 'Count your blessings' has never been more relevant for me than it is today.

What would it be like to have missed the opportunity to meet so many wonderful people that have come into my life? Would I be willing to give up the joy that came into my heart that early morning when God spoke to me? Could life ever be the same as it was before?

If I were allowed to go back, knowing what I now know, it would be so simple. I would tell Barb about all the things that I had learned while she was away. She would hear of my newfound knowledge of what love truly means; the supreme joy of loving Christ; the satisfaction of helping someone in need; the comfort of knowing that The Father who loves you, is willing to help you if you will only call on Him.

There would be the unbelievable joy of knowing and living the near perfect life, acknowledging all the blessings we have received, knowing the pitfalls in advance so that we could avoid them instead of stumbling around in the dark. But most of all, understanding just how precious our love was for one another.

Unfortunately that can never be. If one could go back, all the newly gained knowledge would be erased from our memory and life would continue on as it had before, we would be blissfully unaware of the wonderful potential for that perfect life.

The Devil wants us to be discontented with our existence; he wants us to go about with a burden of grief and doubt weighing us down. He doesn't want us to know Christ's love. He would be so happy to think that he had won out and that our lives were wasted or ineffective.

From the beginning of my disability I consciously made the decision that I wasn't going to allow this calamity to change me, at least inwardly. Outwardly, apart from the obvious loss of mobility, I would continue on as I had in the past and accept the event as a new and challenging part of my life. Even though the paralysis appeared irreversible, I was going to do my best to overcome it, to regain as much movement as possible, to prove to myself that with perseverance and hard work, nothing was impossible.

Creating a beautiful Memorial Garden for Barb was such a joy, and from the time of its inception a stream of concerned and caring people coursed through my life, offering an endless source of inspiration and encouragement. Establishing our little theatre 'Toad Hall' created even more opportunities for expressing ourselves and also reaffirming our faith in the Spirit of love and compassion. Each production is chosen with this thought in mind, 'The Spirit of man is indeed indomitable, and capable of incredible strength and determination'. If one will draw upon the inner Spirit, the Spirit of God, there is absolutely nothing that cannot be achieved.

So what would I give to reverse my situation, to be able to go back to the way things were, to have my life back intact? Firstly, there would have to be a clear and irreducible agreement that I would be allowed to retain my newly gained knowledge that I would be free to continue to follow the way of the Lord, and that every blessed person that has entered my life would still be there for me, and I for them. For I have put my trust in the Lord; whatever path He has chosen for me is the path I will and must take. My answer to the question is simple, "I would gladly give my soul."

THE END